Contemporary Issues in Financial Institutions and Markets

This book brings together academic work on contemporary issues in financial institutions and markets. The general theme is designed to allow for a wide range of topics, covering the diverse nature of academic enquiry in banking and finance. The contributions thus address a broad spectrum of contemporary issues including bank diversification and securitization activities; bank regulatory reforms and competition; the performance of mutual funds and alternative asset classes; role of liquidity in price discovery for credit derivatives; and the existence of the compass rose pattern within option contracts market.

This book was originally published as a special issue of *The European Journal of Finance*.

John O.S. Wilson is Professor of Banking and Finance, and Director of Research, in the School of Management at the University of St Andrews, UK.

Barbara Casu is Reader in Banking, and Director of the Centre for Banking Research, at Cass Business School, City University London, UK.

David G. McMillan is Professor of Finance in the Accounting and Finance Division at Stirling Management School, at the University of Stirling, UK.

Contemporary Issues in Financial Institutions and Markets

Volume I

Edited by
John O.S. Wilson, Barbara Casu and David G. McMillan

Routledge
Taylor & Francis Group
LONDON AND NEW YORK

First published in paperback 2024

First published 2013
by Routledge
4 Park Square, Milton Park, Abingdon, Oxon, OX14 4RN

and by Routledge
605 Third Avenue, New York, NY 10158

Routledge is an imprint of the Taylor & Francis Group, an informa business

This book is a reproduction of *The European Journal of Finance*, volume 17, issues 9-10. The Publisher requests to those authors who may be citing this book to state, also, the bibliographical details of the special issue on which the book was based.

Publisher's Note
The publisher has gone to great lengths to ensure the quality of this reprint but points out that some imperfections in the original copies may be apparent.

British Library Cataloguing in Publication Data
A catalogue record for this book is available from the British Library

ISBN: 978-0-415-64513-3 (hbk)
ISBN: 978-1-03-293006-0 (pbk)
ISBN: 978-1-315-87288-9 (ebk)

DOI: 10.4324/9781315872889

Typeset in Times New Roman
by Taylor & Francis Books

Contents

Citation Information

The chapters in this book were originally published in *The European Journal of Finance*, volume 17, issues 9-10 (October-November 2011). When citing this material, please use the original page numbering for each article, as follows:

Chapter 1
Introduction: Contemporary issues in financial institutions and markets
John O.S. Wilson, David G. McMillan and Barbara Casu
The European Journal of Finance, volume 17, issues 9-10 (October-November 2011)
pp. 765-768

Chapter 2
Does securitization reduce credit risk taking? Empirical evidence from US bank holding companies
Barbara Casu, Andrew Clare, Anna Sarkisyan and Stephen Thomas
The European Journal of Finance, volume 17, issues 9-10 (October-November 2011)
pp. 769-788

Chapter 3
Bancassurance efficiency gains: evidence from the Italian banking and insurance industries
Franco Fiordelisi and Ornella Ricci
The European Journal of Finance, volume 17, issues 9-10 (October-November 2011)
pp. 789-810

Chapter 4
Financial deepening and bank productivity in Latin America
Georgios E. Chortareas, Jesús G. Garza-García and Claudia Girardone
The European Journal of Finance, volume 17, issues 9-10 (October-November 2011)
pp. 811-827

Chapter 5
Islamic mutual funds' financial performance and international investment style: evidence from 20 countries
Andreas G.F. Hoepner, Hussain G. Rammal and Michael Rezec
The European Journal of Finance, volume 17, issues 9-10 (October-November 2011)
pp. 829-850

Chapter 6

The effect of liquidity on the price discovery process in credit derivatives markets in times of financial distress
Sergio Mayordomo, Juan Ignacio Peña and Juan Romo
The European Journal of Finance, volume 17, issues 9-10 (October-November 2011) pp. 851-881

Chapter 7

Return reversals and the compass rose: insights from high frequency options data
Thanos Verousis and Owain ap Gwilym
The European Journal of Finance, volume 17, issues 9-10 (October-November 2011) pp. 883-896

About the Editors

John O. S. Wilson is Professor of Banking & Finance and Director for the Centre for Responsible Banking & Finance at the University of St Andrews, UK. His research focuses on the areas of Industrial Organization, Banking (in Europe, Japan and the United States) and Credit Unions. The results of this research have been published in many international peer reviewed journals including: *European Financial Management, International Journal of Industrial Organization, Journal of Banking & Finance, Journal of Financial Services Research,* and the *Journal of Money, Credit and Banking* He is the author/co-author of books, a monograph, chapters and articles. His books include *European Banking: Efficiency, Technology and Growth; Industrial Organisation: An Analysis of Competitive Markets; Economics of Business Strategy;* and *Industrial Organization: Competition Strategy and Policy* (now in its fourth edition with translations in Italian and Greek). John edited *A Routledge Major Works in Banking*. He also co-edited the *Oxford Handbook of Banking* (with Allen Berger and Phil Molyneux).

He is Chair of the British Accounting and Finance Association Financial Markets and Institutions Special Interest Group. John served as Treasurer and General Secretary of the British Accounting and Finance Association in 2009 and 2010, and 2010 and 2011 respectively

John serves as Associate Editor to the *British Accounting Review, European Journal of Finance* and the *Journal of Money Credit and Banking*. He also serves on the editorial board of a number of journals including the *Journal of Business Finance and Accounting* and the *Journal of Financial Economic Policy*. In the period June 2011 to April 2012, John served as a full member of a Commission on Credit Unions established by the Irish Government.

Barbara Casu is Reader in Banking at Cass Business School, City University London, UK, where she is also the Director of the Centre for Banking Research. Barbara's teaching experience is mainly in the banking area, both at the undergraduate, postgraduate and MBA level. Drawing on teaching experience, she has co-authored (with C. Girardone and P. Molyneux) the book Introduction to Banking (FT Pearson Education).

Barbara has published over 30 papers in international peer reviewed Journals. Her research interests focus on the areas of empirical banking, and include studies on securitisation, bank efficiency and productivity change; the implication of the Single

European Market for financial services on bank structure, competition and performance; bank privatisation and M&As; and bank stock performance. Her research has been presented at international conferences and published in leading journals, including the *Review of Economics and Statistics*, the *Journal of Banking and Finance* and the *Journal of Business, Finance and Accounting*.

Barbara is Associate Editor for the European Journal of Finance, as well as acting as a referee for a number of leading banking and economics journals. In addition, Barbara is Associate Senior Fellow at the Centre for European Policy Studies in Brussels (Financial Institutions and Prudential Policy Unit).

David G. McMillan is Professor of Finance at the University of Stirling, UK, having previously held a similar position at the University of St Andrews, UK. He has also held positions at the Universities of Aberdeen and Durham.

His research interests include forecasting asset returns with a particular emphasis on employing non-linear techniques such as threshold and smooth-transition modelling and asset return volatility, including its application to risk management. His research also includes examining the linkages between asset prices and macroeconomic variables and examining the behaviour of financial and investor ratios, both in terms of prediction and understanding their implications for valuation. He has published widely on these topics in both internationally respected peer-reviewed academic journals as well as practitioner based journals.

Introduction

Contemporary issues in financial institutions and markets

John O.S. Wilson,[a] Barbara Casu[b] and David G. McMillan[c]

[a]*University of St Andrews, UK;* [b]*City University London, UK;* [c]*University of Stirling, UK*

On 9 December 2009, the 1st Annual Conference for Emerging Scholars in Banking and Finance took place at Cass Business School, City University, London. The conference was jointly organized by the Centre for Banking Research at Cass Business School and The British Accounting and Finance Association's Financial Markets and Institutions Special Interest Group. The aim of the conference was to bring together emerging scholars working on contemporary issues in financial institutions and markets. The general theme of the conference was designed to allow for a wide range of submissions covering the diverse nature of academic enquiry in banking and finance. The conference also hosted a keynote speech entitled *The Financial Crisis, Systemic Risk and Macro-prudential Supervision*, delivered by Philipp Hartmann (European Central Bank), as well as a panel discussion on *New Directions for Research in Financial Markets and Institutions*.

Over 40 papers were submitted to the conference; after a refereeing process, nine papers were selected for presentation. The rest of this editorial provides a brief overview of the six papers ultimately selected for this special issue of the *European Journal of Finance*. The themes addressed cover a broad spectrum of contemporary issues in banking and financial markets, including: bank diversification and securitization activities; bank regulatory reforms and competition; the performance of mutual funds and alternative asset classes; role of liquidity in price discovery for credit derivatives; and the existence of the compass rose pattern within an option contracts market.

One of the major recent features of modern banking business is the growth in structured credit products (Berger, Molyneux, and Wilson 2010). Banks have actively created off-balance sheet vehicles that packaged various market and credit risks by pooling assets (such as bonds, loans, or mortgage-backed securities) and then divided the resulting cash flows into various tranches (according to their risks proxied by a credit rating issued by external agencies) that were then sold to investors. Banks were also attracted to the securitization business as it allowed them to reduce their regulatory capital charges by transferring credit risk to other parties. The view (until the onset of the financial crisis at least) was that the new structured credit products were beneficial as they allowed greater risks to be shared across a broader spectrum of investors, or to put this another way, banks no longer had to be the major holders of credit risk (Keys et al. 2010). The paper '*Does securitization reduce credit risk taking? Empirical evidence from US bank holding companies*' by Barbara Casu, Andrew Clare, Anna Sarkisyan, and Stephen Thomas examines the link between changes in credit risk taking (proxied by a change in risk-weighted assets to total assets ratio) and Bank Holding Companies securitization activities between 2001 and 2007. The analysis starts from 2001 because of new US reporting requirements that provide more detailed information on bank securitization activity. The authors note that securitizing banks are larger, less liquid, less deposit-dependent, and more profitable than their non-securitizing counterparts. The model regresses the (change in) credit risk measure against securitization (securitized assets/total assets) and a variety of other covariates. The main finding is that securitization leads to a reduction in credit risk taking. In furthering the analysis by the type of underlying assets, the authors find that the negative relationship between outstanding securitization and risk taking is primarily driven by securitizations of mortgages, home equity lines of credit, and other consumer loans. Securitizations of all other types of assets, on the other hand, seem to have no significant impact on bank credit risk taking. Consequently, the authors contend that the net impact of securitization on the risk-taking behavior is ambiguous.

In recent years, many of the largest banks and insurers in many countries have transformed themselves, typically via mergers and acquisitions, into multi-product financial service conglomerates with offerings including: retail banking, asset management, brokerage, insurance, investment banking, and wealth management (Genetay and Molyneux 1998; Herring and Carmassi 2010). One of the main reasons driving the conglomeration process in European banking is the perceived ability of diversified financial institutions to reap both cost and revenue synergies through the joint provision of several different financial products. In the paper entitled '*Bancassurance efficiency gains: evidence from the Italian banking and insurance industries*', Franco Fiordelisi and Ornella Ricci assess the cost and profit efficiency gains of *bancassurance* in Italy over the period 2005–2006. The authors find little evidence of *bancassurance* gains in the banking industry, but substantial gains in the insurance industry. A further investigation into the insurance industry highlights the competitive viability of *bancassurance* as a distribution channel. In terms of profitability, the authors suggest that the mix of products offered should be continuously revised to adapt to customer needs. Consequently, ownership links are not necessarily the best strategy to achieve gains in profit and cost efficiency. Instead, more flexible forms of cooperation, such as cross-selling agreements and non-equity strategic alliances, provide more appropriate strategies.

Regulatory reforms aimed at increasing competition and financial development occurred in most banking systems in the 1980s and 1990s. The aims of such reforms were to create an expansion of credit (via the mobilization of savings into investment projects), thus increasing the marginal productivity of capital through the intermediation function of banks operating state-of-the-art risk management systems. Ultimately, financial development is expected to feed through to macroeconomic growth (Levine 1997; Beck, Levine, and Loayza 2000). The paper '*Financial deepening and bank productivity in Latin America*' by Georgios Chortareas, Jesús Garza-García, and Claudia Girardone considers the link between financial deepening and bank productivity change as well as the direction of the causality. The authors focus on two main questions, namely whether financial deepening affects banking productivity in Latin America and whether channels of reverse causality exist between the two variables. The authors utilize the Malmquist index to measure banking productivity. Subsequently, they use a panel data framework that applies the generalized methods of moments to test their main hypotheses. The authors find strong evidence of causality from financial deepening to bank productivity and weak evidence of reverse causality. Their results suggest that, in addition to the macroeconomic benefits, policies aiming to enhance financial development can generate a virtuous circle between financial deepening and financial institutions' productivity.

Islamic financial services are an important contemporary issue in modern day financial systems (McKenzie 2009). In the paper entitled '*Islamic mutual funds' financial performance and international investment style: evidence from 20 countries*', Andreas Hoepner, Hussain Rammal, and Michael Rezec utilize a large dataset of Islamic funds to assess the performance of 265 Islamic equity funds from 20 countries over a 20-year sample period. Specifically, the authors examine whether the financial performance of Islamic equity mutual funds differs from the respective equity market benchmarks. Based on a standard Carhart model (Carhart 1997), the authors find that more than half of the equal weighted national Islamic equity fund portfolios significantly underperform their national equity market benchmarks. To control for regional and global factors, the authors also develop a three-level Carhart model and find that around 40% of the national Islamic equity fund portfolios significantly underperform international equity benchmarks, while a quarter of them significantly outperforms.

The role of liquidity in price discovery for credit derivatives has taken increased importance over the recent past, following the work of Garbade and Silber (1983), who examined spot and futures markets and built a model of price discovery to allow for agent participation in more than one market. The paper '*The effect of liquidity on the price discovery process in credit derivatives markets in times of financial distress*' by Sergio Mayordomo, Juan Ignacio Peña, and Juan Romo extends this work and develops a model appropriate for the credit derivatives market, while utilizing the econometric framework associated with the work of Gonzalo and Granger (1995). Employing a permanent–transitory decomposition, the paper calculates price discovery metrics for the credit default swaps (CDSs), asset swap packages (ASPs), and bond markets. The paper shows that in the pre-crisis period, the CDS market was more efficient, while during the crisis, the ASP was relatively more efficient. The paper claims the results show that liquidity affects the price discovery process. Finally, the authors also argue that the ASP spread is superior for assessing credit risk.

Evidence of a graphical pattern in phase plots of stock market returns dates back to Crack and Ledoit (1996), who argued in favor of a compass rose pattern when the data are truncated for extreme observations. Since then, the pattern has been found in other markets such as the foreign exchange market. However, its usefulness to market participants remains unclear. The paper '*Return reversals and the compass rose: insights from high frequency options data*' by Thanos Verousis and Owain ap Gwilym tests for the existence of the compass rose pattern within the option contracts market for 28 firms during a high frequency sample period that covers the year 2005. This paper reports such evidence for many, though not all, of the contracts depending on the frequency of observation. The paper also reports evidence of a returns reversal pattern and estimates a model to explain its existence. The paper argues that such a pattern could be exploited in trading.

This special issue of selected papers from the 1st Emerging Scholars in Banking and Finance Conference provides the reader with new insights and valuable contributions to the theoretical and empirical research on financial institutions and markets.

Acknowledgements

The Guest Editors would like to thank the Editor, Professor Chris Adcock, for commissioning this special issue and for providing advice and guidance throughout the process. Thanks also go to Pat Anderson at the *European Journal of Finance* for administrative assistance. We would also like to give special thanks to Philipp Hartmann for providing an excellent keynote presentation. Thanks to Phil Molyneux, Jerry Coakley, Andrew Clare, and Stephen Thomas for their contributions to the panel discussion. We are also indebted to Francesca Arnaboldi, Mascia Bedendo, Olivier De Jonghe, Alessandra Ferrari, Neil Kellard, and M. Iqbal Asaria for acting as discussants. We acknowledge the financial support of Cass Business School, the British Accounting Association (BAA), St Andrews University, the University of Ulster, the Institute of Chartered Accountants of Scotland (ICAS), the Association of Chartered Certified Accountants (ACCA), and Pearson Education. Conference organization was overseen by a scientific committee comprising, in addition to the Guest Editors of this special issue, Claudia Girardone, Philip Hamill, Shelagh Heffernan, and Phil Molyneux. It remains for us to thank all of the presenters, discussants, panellists, and participants at the 1st Conference for Emerging Scholars in Banking and Finance. The usual disclaimer applies.

References

Beck, T., R. Levine, and N. Loayza. 2000. Finance and the sources of growth. *Journal of Financial Economics* 58, nos. 1–2: 261–310.

Berger, A.N., P. Molyneux, and J.O.S. Wilson. 2010. Banking: An overview. In *Oxford handbook of banking*, ed. A. Berger, P. Molyneux, and J.O.S. Wilson, 1–36. Oxford: Oxford University Press.

Carhart, M.M. 1997. On persistence in mutual fund performance. *Journal of Finance* 52, no. 1: 57–82.

Crack, T.F., and O. Ledoit. 1996. Robust structure without predictability: The 'compass rose' pattern of the stock market. *Journal of Finance* LI, no. 2: 751–62.

Garbade, K.D., and W.L. Silver. 1983. Price movements and price discovery in commodity markets. *Review of Economics and Statistics* 65, no. 2: 289–97.

Genetay, N., and P. Molyneux. 1998. *Bancassurance*. London: Palgrave MacMillan.

Gonzalo, J., and C.W.J. Granger. 1995. Estimation of common long-memory components in cointegrated systems. *Journal of Business and Economics Statistics* 13, no. 1: 27–35.

Herring, R., and J. Carmassi. 2010. The corporate structure of international financial conglomerates: Complexity and implications for safety and soundness. In *Oxford handbook of banking*, ed. A. Berger, P. Molyneux, and J.O.S. Wilson, 195–232. Oxford: Oxford University Press.

Keys, B., T. Mukherjee, A. Seru, and V. Vig. 2010. Did securitisation lead to lax screening? Evidence from subprime loans. *Quarterly Journal of Economics* 125, no. 1: 327–62.

Levine, R. 1997. Financial development and economic growth: Views and agenda. *Journal of Economic Literature* XXXV, no. 2: 688–726.

McKenzie, D. 2009. *Islamic finance 2009*. London: International Financial Services London.

Does securitization reduce credit risk taking? Empirical evidence from US bank holding companies

Barbara Casu[a], Andrew Clare[a], Anna Sarkisyan and Stephen Thomas[a]

[a] *Cass Business School, City University London, UK;* [b] *Essex Business School, University of Essex, UK*

This study investigates the impact of securitization on the credit risk-taking behavior of banks. Using US Bank Holding Company data from 2001 to 2007, we find that banks with a greater balance of outstanding securitized assets choose asset portfolios of lower credit risks. Examining securitizations by the type of underlying assets, we find that the negative relationship between outstanding securitization and risk taking is primarily driven by securitizations of mortgages, home equity lines of credit, and other consumer loans. Securitizations of all other types of assets, on the other hand, seem to have no significant impact on bank credit risk-taking behavior. We attribute these results to the recourse commonly provided in securitization transactions, as it might alter the risk-taking appetite of the issuing banks across asset classes. Therefore, we conclude that the net impact of securitization on the risk-taking behavior of issuing banks, and consequently on the soundness of the banking system, is ambiguous and will depend on the transactions structure. In particular, it will depend on the relative magnitude of credit support provided by banks. This leads us to suggest that banks have typically viewed securitization as a financing rather than a risk management mechanism.

1. Introduction

Securitization has been a key bank funding, risk management, and performance improvement tool over the last two decades. However, the financial crisis of 2007–2009 has shown that securitizing, as well as holding securitization-related products, might create significant financial problems for banks and consequently lead to widespread problems in the banking sector. It is therefore a crucial contemporary issue in financial institutions and markets research to foster the understanding of banks' securitization activities, their inherent benefits and risks, and the resulting financial system implications.

In the two decades leading up to the recent financial crisis, banks have been operating in increasingly competitive markets and as such have been forced to take on more risks and to seek out higher margin activities. Securitization has facilitated this quest for higher margin business, by allowing banks to convert illiquid loans into marketable securities and therefore release capital for other investment opportunities. The increasing volume of securitization activity in the run up to the financial crisis raised the concerns of researchers as well as those of analysts, investors, and regulators over the potential for an increase in systemic risk.[1]

In general, previous empirical studies of the impact of securitization on the issuing banks have suggested a positive link between securitization and bank risk.[2] By allowing banks to convert illiquid assets into liquid funds, it has been argued that securitization may well increase the expansion of credit and cause banks to hold riskier assets. The existing literature on the former issue shows that securitization reduces the influence of a bank's financial condition on credit supply (Loutskina and Strahan 2006). However, little evidence has been collected on how securitization affects banks' willingness to increase the proportion of risky assets in their portfolios.

Since securitization provides banks with an additional source of loan financing and liquidity, it might motivate them to shift their portfolios toward higher risk/return assets (Cebenoyan and Strahan 2004; Purnanandam 2009). However, issuing banks typically retain first-loss contractual interests and/or provide implicit recourse in securitizations. These arrangements mean that the risks inherent in the securitized assets have not been transferred to investors and are, in effect, still held by the issuing bank, but off-balance sheet (Calomiris and Mason 2004; Higgins and Mason 2004; Niu and Richardson 2006; Federal Deposit Insurance Corporation 2007; Chen, Liu, and Ryan 2008; Vermilyea, Webb, and Kish 2008).

Therefore, outstanding securitization exposes the issuing bank to the credit risk associated with the transferred assets. Assuming that the risk exposure arising from the securitized pool is understood by the bank, we hypothesize that this should have an impact on its risk-taking behavior. In particular, greater outstanding securitization, and therefore greater credit risk exposure arising from the pool, should make banks more risk-averse and motivate them to shift their portfolios toward assets of lower credit risk.

This study aims to contribute to the existing literature by assessing the impact of securitization on the credit risk-taking behavior of US bank holding companies (BHCs). We first examine whether the aggregate outstanding securitization affects banks' risk-taking behavior. Second, we test whether the effect differs across securitizations of different asset classes using new data on banks' securitization activities mandated by changes to regulatory forms in 2001, whereby banks report securitization by type of underlying assets.

Our results show that bank credit risk-taking behavior is negatively associated with securitization, suggesting that banks with a greater balance of securitized assets outstanding choose asset portfolios of lower risk. Examining securitizations by type of underlying assets reveals that the negative relationship between outstanding securitization and risk taking is primarily driven by securitizations of mortgages, home equity lines of credit, and other consumer loans. Securitizations of all other types of assets, on the other hand, seem to have no significant impact on bank credit risk-taking behavior. We explain these results with reference to the 'recourse hypothesis', that is, the credit risk retained by the issuing banks in connection to the securitized assets through the recourse explicitly and/or implicitly provided in securitization transactions.

The remainder of this paper is organized as follows: Section 2 provides a brief review of relevant literature; Section 3 describes data and provides brief descriptive statistics of the sample; the empirical specification is presented in Section 4; Section 5 reports results of the analysis; and finally, Section 6 discusses the findings and concludes the paper.

2. Literature review

Securitization occurs when a bank transforms its illiquid assets, traditionally held until maturity, into marketable securities. In a typical securitization transaction, the originating bank transfers a pool of financial assets with fixed or nearly fixed cash flows to a special purpose vehicle (SPV), a legal entity that in turn finances the purchase through the issuance of securities backed by the pool. The transfer of assets must qualify as a 'true sale', where the transferor (i.e. the originating bank) surrenders control over the financial assets and can therefore remove the assets from its balance sheet.

To reduce credit risk for investors, thereby increasing the credit rating of the asset-backed securities, and to mitigate adverse selection problems arising from issuers having superior information about the credit quality of underlying assets than do the investors, the SPV obtains credit enhancements. These enhancements typically come from the originating bank and can include both contractual and non-contractual arrangements. Examples of contractual arrangements, or explicit recourse, include retaining interests in the transferred assets such as credit-enhancing interest-only strips and subordinated securities and providing standby letters of credit to the securitization structures. Non-contractual arrangements, or the so-called implicit recourse, include: (i) selling assets to the SPV at a discount from the price specified in the securitization documents; (ii) purchasing assets from the SPV at an amount greater than fair value; (iii) exchanging performing assets for non-performing assets in the SPV; and (iv) funding credit enhancements beyond contractual requirements.[3] The provision of implicit recourse violates the 'true sale' condition; however, it allows issuers to maintain their reputations for consistent credit quality over repeated sales.

Early theoretical work suggests that securitization provides a means of reducing bank risk (Greenbaum and Thakor 1987; Pavel and Phillis 1987; Hess and Smith 1988). Later research investigated the effect that securitization had on bank risk from several perspectives and has reached mixed conclusions. This recent research has focussed on three broad themes: (i) the quality of the assets securitized or retained; (ii) recourse arrangements; and (iii) the impact on overall bank risk.

Cantor and Rouyer (2000) argue that the credit risk position of the issuer improves if the riskiness of the securities sold to investors is higher than that of the issuer prior to the securitization; otherwise, the transaction might intensify the issuer's net exposure to the default risk of its assets. Ambrose, LaCour-Little, and Sanders (2005) find evidence to suggest that, in response to regulatory capital incentives, lenders tend to retain riskier loans in their portfolios while selling safer loans to the secondary market. Contradictory evidence is found by Carey (1998); this study shows that the default rates on the loans kept by the issuer are lower than the default rates on the loans sold to investors. Consistently, Krainer and Laderman (2009) find that the mortgage loans chosen by lenders for private-label securitizations tend to be riskier (i.e. the borrowers associated with the securitized mortgages are more likely to be subprime and tend to have higher loan-to-value ratios) and have higher default rates compared to the loans retained in the banks' own portfolios. Similarly, studies by Dell'Ariccia, Igan, and Laeven (2009), Mian and Sufi (2009), and Keys et al. (2010) find evidence that in the last decade US banks securitized their worst mortgage loans.

The second issue addressed by the literature relates to the recourse commonly provided by the originating bank. In particular, Gorton and Pennacchi (1995) argue that originating banks retain a portion of sold loans on the balance sheet, or offer an implicit guarantee, to reduce moral hazard problems as in these cases there still remains an incentive to screen and monitor the borrowers. Fender and Mitchell (2009a) argue that contractual arrangements differ in their effect on the screening effort due to varying sensitivities to systemic risk factors. They find that, under certain conditions, it would be preferable to have the originator hold a vertical slice of the portfolio rather than to retain a tranched portion of securitized loans. The authors also note that if the choice of the magnitude and the form of retained interests are left to the originator, the retention mechanism chosen may well lead to suboptimal screening effort. Chen, Liu, and Ryan (2008) find that banks' retained interests vary by type of securitization and are relatively low in the case of mortgages, while relatively high for revolving loans such as credit card receivables. Calomiris and Mason (2004) find that in credit card securitizations risk remains with the securitizing banks as a result of implicit recourse. Vermilyea, Webb, and Kish (2008) also find evidence of implicit recourse in credit card securitizations, where banks with poorly performing securitization portfolios claim higher fraud losses.

Finally, a few authors have analyzed the effect of securitization on overall bank risk. Dionne and Harchaoui (2003) find a positive association between securitization and bank credit risk. Franke and Krahnen (2005) and Haensel and Krahnen (2007) find evidence that the issue of collateralized debt obligations increases the systematic risk of the issuing bank. Jiangli and Pritsker (2008), on the other hand, find that mortgage securitization reduces bank insolvency risk and suggest a positive role for securitization. The authors attribute the turmoil in mortgage credit and securitization markets during the recent crisis to excesses in those markets. Affinito and Tagliaferri (2010) find that, once securitized, banks tend to decrease the weight of bad loans to operate with lower capital or to invest the capital into new businesses. Similarly, Cebenoyan and Strahan (2004) find evidence to suggest that securitization reduces bank risk; however, banks use the achieved risk reduction to take on new risks. Purnanandam (2009) also provides evidence to show that banks use the proceeds from securitizations to issue new loans with higher-than-average default risk.

To summarize, most studies of the first strand find that banks securitize their riskier loans while retaining safer ones on their balance sheets. However, the studies of the second strand suggest that the risk remains with the banks through contractual and/or non-contractual arrangements. The third strand provides contradictory evidence: some authors find a positive association between securitization and risk; others find that securitization reduces bank risk, though suggest that banks use the achieved risk reduction to take on new risks. This study attempts to bring these three strands together and answer the following unresolved question: if banks securitize their risky assets but retain exposure to those assets through contractual and/or non-contractual arrangements, does the outstanding securitization, representing this exposure, affect the credit risk-taking behavior of the banks?

3. Data and descriptive statistics

3.1 *Data and sample selection*

To study the effect of securitization on bank credit risk-taking behavior, we use US BHC Data from Y-9C forms, which are filed on a quarterly basis by all BHCs and have been compiled in a data set by the Federal Reserve Bank of Chicago since 1986. We use data for BHCs rather than for commercial banks because risk and capital management are typically administered at the highest level of the financial group. In addition, securitization may involve several subsidiaries of a BHC and affect capital and liquidity planning for the whole group.[4]

The Y-9C reports collate basic financial data from banks on a consolidated basis in the form of a balance sheet, an income statement, and detailed supporting schedules, including a schedule of off-balance-sheet items. Since June 2001, US banks have been required to provide more detailed information on their securitization activities in the regulatory forms. Specifically, Schedule HC-S of the Y-9C form reports the breakdown of securitization into seven categories: 1–4 family residential loans; home equity lines; credit card receivables; auto loans; other consumer loans; commercial and industrial loans; and all other loans, all leases, and all other assets. Securitizations are reported as an outstanding principal balance of the corresponding assets sold and securitized with servicing retained or with recourse or other seller-provided credit enhancements. The incorporation of the new data into FR Y-9C determines the start date of the sample period, which yields 27 quarters from the second quarter of 2001 to the fourth quarter of 2007.

When constructing the data set, we excluded banks with missing information on total assets, total loans, capital, and securitization activities for any quarter of the sample period. When banks go through a merger or acquisition, we maintain the code of the acquiring BHC while the acquired bank is eliminated from the sample.[5] To prevent the possibility of outliers driving the results, we exclude all bank quarters with asset growth over the last quarter exceeding 50% and loan growth exceeding 100%. We also exclude banks in any quarters for which the total loans-to-asset ratio is less than 0.1 or the loan-to-deposit ratio exceeds 10. The final data set contains 42,685 bank quarters for 2190 BHCs.

3.2 *Descriptive statistics*

Before turning to the main analysis, we compare securitizers and non-securitizers along five dimensions: (i) balance sheet structure; (ii) loan portfolio; (iii) regulatory capital; (iv) risk; and (v) operating performance.[6] Given that securitization is a recurring activity, we assign a bank to the group of securitizers if we observe securitization activity in any quarter of the bank's lifetime in the sample. This yields 230 securitizers and 1960 non-securitizers in total for the period from 2001:Q2 to 2007:Q4. We use the quarterly data to calculate time-series averages for each BHC and then compare the averages in cross-sectional tests. The results of these comparisons are presented in Table 1, where we report means and standard deviations for all banks, securitizers, and non-securitizers and the difference in means between the latter two with its statistical significance.

Looking at the first panel of Table 1, the average amount of total assets for the sample BHCs is $5.3 billion. This is the most significant difference between securitizers and non-securitizers; the mean value of total assets for securitizers ($41 billion) is approximately 41 times the mean size of non-securitizers ($1 billion). This finding is consistent with previous research that documents that larger banks are more likely to securitize.[7] Further, securitizers tend to hold less liquid assets (25% versus 27% of total assets), which is consistent with having a better access to external funding and thus needing a smaller liquidity buffer compared to non-securitizers. Originated loans on average constitute 66% of BHC's total assets with no significant difference between securitizers and non-securitizers.

We turn next to the liability side of the balance sheet. Both securitizers and non-securitizers are mainly financed by deposits. However, non-securitizers rely on this source of funding to a larger extent (69% of total assets versus 62%). The capitalization of the sample BHCs constitutes 9% with no distinguishable difference between securitizers and non-securitizers. The proportion of loans to deposits is significantly higher for securitizers (1.12 versus 0.98).

The second panel of Table 1 contains information on bank loan portfolios. The securitizers' loan portfolio is different in terms of both concentration and composition. In particular, it tends to be more diversified, as indicated by the Herfindahl–Hirschman Index (HHI) of 0.56 versus 0.59 for non-securitizers.[8] Further, securitizers tend to hold significantly less real estate loans (67% versus 71%)[9] while keeping more consumer (10% versus 8%) and other loans (7% versus 5%) on the balance sheet.

Looking at the regulatory capital, one can see that the sample BHCs are on average relatively highly capitalized (e.g. 14.8% for the total risk-based capital ratio). Comparing securitizers and non-securitizers, we find that securitizers are less capitalized than non-securitizers on the risk-adjusted basis; however, the difference is not statistically significant. This is consistent with Cebenoyan and Strahan (2004) and Minton, Stulz, and Williamson (2008), who find that banks that are engaged in credit risk management tend to hold less capital.

Table 1. Summary statistics for all sample banks and univariate tests of differences in characteristics between securitizers and non-securitizers.[22]

	All banks			Securitizers			Non-securitizers			Difference in means		
Variable	*N*	Mean	Std. Dev.	*N*	Mean	Std. Dev.	*N*	Mean	Std. Dev.	(abs)	(%)	*p*-values
Balance sheet structure												
Total assets ($ billions)	2190	5.254	52.286	230	40.961	156.486	1960	1.064	5.001	39.897	3749.7	0.000
Liquidity ratio	2190	0.263	0.123	230	0.247	0.111	1960	0.265	0.124	−0.018	−6.8	0.029
Loan ratio	2190	0.664	0.125	230	0.660	0.123	1960	0.665	0.125	−0.005	−0.8	0.577
Deposits/assets ratio	2190	0.681	0.088	230	0.621	0.124	1960	0.688	0.079	−0.067	−9.7	0.000
Loans/deposits ratio	2190	0.999	0.289	230	1.122	0.380	1960	0.984	0.273	0.138	14.0	0.000
Equity/assets ratio	2190	0.091	0.032	230	0.092	0.036	1960	0.091	0.032	0.001	1.1	0.588
Loan portfolio												
Real estate loan ratio	2190	0.708	0.151	230	0.674	0.174	1960	0.712	0.148	−0.038	−5.3	0.002
C&I loan ratio	2190	0.160	0.095	230	0.165	0.086	1960	0.159	0.095	0.006	3.8	0.373
Consumer loan ratio	2190	0.080	0.085	230	0.096	0.115	1960	0.078	0.081	0.018	23.1	0.018
Other loan ratio	2190	0.053	0.081	230	0.065	0.099	1960	0.051	0.079	0.014	27.5	0.042
Loan HHI	2190	0.585	0.150	230	0.560	0.156	1960	0.588	0.150	−0.028	−4.8	0.009
Regulatory capital												
Tier I leverage ratio	2190	9.324	3.822	230	9.274	7.506	1960	9.330	3.120	−0.056	−0.6	0.910
Tier I risk-based capital ratio	2190	13.327	6.636	230	12.743	12.168	1960	13.395	5.644	−0.652	−4.9	0.423
Total risk-based capital ratio	2190	14.836	6.943	230	14.612	12.742	1960	14.862	5.906	−0.250	−1.7	0.769

Risk characteristics												
RWATA ratio	2190	0.712	0.118	230	0.728	0.137	1960	0.710	0.115	0.018	2.5	0.054
Non-performing loan ratio	2190	0.009	0.008	230	0.010	0.007	1960	0.009	0.008	0.001	11.1	0.038
Charge-off ratio	2190	0.003	0.007	230	0.005	0.012	1960	0.003	0.006	0.002	66.7	0.017
Loan loss provision ratio	2190	0.004	0.007	230	0.006	0.014	1960	0.004	0.005	0.002	50.0	0.050
Operating performance												
Return on assets	2190	0.011	0.007	230	0.012	0.013	1960	0.011	0.005	0.001	9.1	0.076
Return on equity	2190	0.124	0.076	230	0.123	0.126	1960	0.124	0.068	−0.001	−0.8	0.970
Revenue HHI	2190	0.697	0.094	230	0.644	0.098	1960	0.703	0.092	−0.059	−8.4	0.000
Interest income/net operating revenue	2190	0.792	0.108	230	0.713	0.154	1960	0.801	0.097	−0.088	−11.0	0.000
Securitization activity												
Securitized assets/loans ratio				230	0.144	0.515						
Securitized assets/assets ratio				230	0.084	0.299						
Credit enhancements/ securitized assets ratio				230	0.068	0.190						
Credit enhancements/assets ratio				230	0.003	0.010						

Note: The table presents descriptive statistics for (i) all BHCs (2190 banks), (ii) securitizers (230 banks), and (iii) non-securitizers (1960 banks). *Mean* and *Std. Dev.* stand for the cross-sectional mean and standard deviation values of the individual bank time-series averages, accordingly. The last three columns report the comparison analysis of bank-specific characteristics between securitizers and non-securitizers. *Difference in means* is calculated as the difference between securitizers' and non-securitizers' means, in absolute (*abs*) and percentage (%) values, with the p-values of t-tests on the equality of means reported in the last column.

Further, we consider four risk characteristics of the banks: (i) risk-weighted assets relative to total assets (RWATA); (ii) non-performing loans;[10] (iii) charge-offs;[11] and (iv) loan loss provisions. For the average BHC in the sample, the non-performing loans and charge-offs constitute 0.9% and 0.3% of total loans, respectively. The loan loss provisions constitute 0.4% relative to total loans. Comparing securitizers and non-securitizers, we find that securitizers are more risky according to all the measures used with the differences being both economically and statistically significant. Similar results are found by Jiangli and Pritsker (2008) and Minton, Stulz, and Williamson (2008) with provision, charge-off, and non-performing loan ratios higher for securitizers.[12]

Finally, we compare performance measures. The results suggest that securitizers have a higher return on assets (ROA) compared to non-securitizers (1.2% versus 1.1%) with the difference being statistically significant.[13] As for the revenue structure, the interest income constitutes the main source of revenue for both securitizers and non-securitizers (over 70%); however, concentration across the sources is lower for securitizers (two-part revenue HHI of 0.64 versus 0.7 for non-securitizers) due to a higher share of non-interest income in their net operating revenue. The latter is consistent with securitizers having an additional source of income in the form of servicing fees and possibly more trading revenue.[14]

Taken together, these comparisons suggest that securitizers improve their profitability through holding riskier and hence more profitable loans in their portfolios and earning a higher share of revenue from non-interest income.

The last panel of Table 1 reports statistics on securitization activities of the banks. The average amount of outstanding securitized assets equals 14.4% of bank's total loans or 8.4% of total assets. The contractual credit enhancements provided by the banks to securitization structures constitute, on average, 6.8% of securitized assets or 0.3% of bank's total assets; these include credit-enhancing interest-only strips, subordinated securities and other residual interests, and standby letters of credit.

Figure 1 shows the volume of outstanding balances of securitization for the sample banks broken down into asset-backed and mortgage-backed securitization for year-ends 2001–2007. It illustrates a general upward trend in total securitization over the 2001–2007 period, with slight

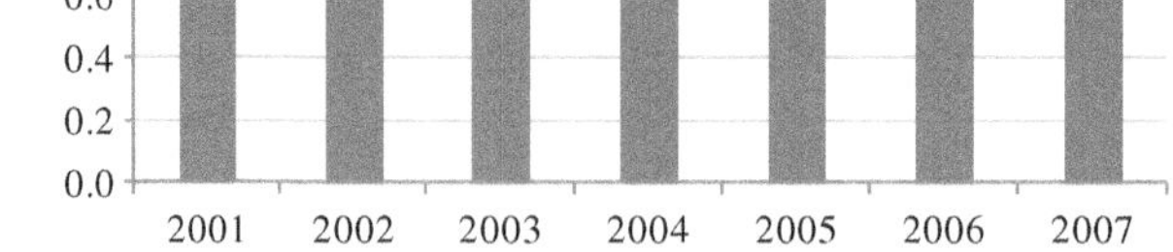

Figure 1. Yearly values of securitized assets.

Note: The figure presents the total balance of outstanding securitization for the sample BHCs for year-ends 2001–2007. The total value of assets securitized is presented as the sum of MBS and ABS values; MBS stands for the value of mortgages securitized, while ABS indicates the value of receivables other than mortgage loans, such as credit card receivables, auto loans, commercial and industrial loans, and home equity lines of credit. The values are in US$ trillions.

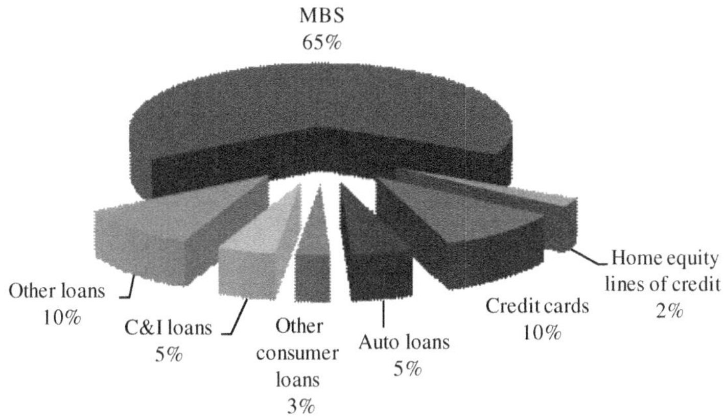

Figure 2. Securitization breakdown by asset type.
Note: The figure illustrates the percentage distribution of securitization by the type of assets securitized derived from the mean values for the sample BHCs. The asset categories are: (i) mortgages (MBS); (ii) home equity lines of credit; (iii) credit cards; (iv) auto loans; (v) other consumer loans; (vi) commercial and industrial (C&I) loans; and (vii) all other loans and leases.

downturns in 2003 and 2007. It is worth noting that the value of securitized mortgages has been fluctuating over the period in general, with the maximum amount of around \$1.37 trillion reached at the year-end 2006. However, the value of asset-backed securitization has been growing steadily throughout the period, with the maximum value of \$614 billion reached at year-end 2007 during the crisis of the US subprime mortgage markets.

Figure 2 presents a detailed breakdown of securitization by asset type. It shows that mortgage-backed securitization makes up the majority (i.e. 65%) of total securitizations. All other loans and leases and credit card receivables, major classes in asset-backed securitization, constitute merely 10% each in total securitization. As for commercial and industrial loans, auto loans, home equity lines of credit, and other consumer loans, their shares are relatively low and amount to 2–5% of total securitization.

4. Empirical specification

We now turn to the empirical analysis to test whether outstanding securitization has an impact on the risk-taking behavior of the issuing bank. Our empirical model includes a number of control variables for bank characteristics and activities, which may influence bank risk-taking propensity or aversion (see, for example, Dionne and Harchaoui 2003; Stiroh 2006; Uzun and Webb 2007). In addition to bank-specific characteristics, we include GDP real growth to control for macroeconomic effects; while time effects are captured by introducing quarter dummies.

The basic regression is:

$$\Delta \mathrm{CrR}_{i,t} = \alpha_i + \beta_1 \mathrm{Sec}_{i,t-1} + \beta_2 \mathrm{Size}_{i,t-1} + \beta_3 \mathrm{Loan}_{i,t-1} + \beta_4 \mathrm{Cap}_{i,t-1} + \beta_5 \mathrm{ROA}_{i,t-1} + \beta_6 \mathrm{ChOff}_{i,t-1} + \varphi' \mathrm{GDPG}_t + \theta' \mathrm{Quarter}_t + \varepsilon_{i,t} \quad (1)$$

where β, φ, and θ reflect the extent to which the relative factor of the model contributes to the change in the dependent variable, and $\varepsilon_{i,t}$ represents the error term for bank i in quarter t. The dependent variable, $\Delta \mathrm{CrR}_{i,t}$, is the change in the credit risk of bank i's portfolio in period t;

Table 2. Definition of model variables.

Variable	Definition	Construction	Expected sign
CrR	Bank credit risk	Risk-weighted assets/total assets	Dependent variable
Sec	Securitization	Outstanding securitized assets/total assets	Negative
Size	Bank size	Ln (total assets)	Positive
Loan	Loan ratio	Loans/total assets	Negative
Cap	Capital ratio	Equity capital/total assets	Negative
ROA	Return on assets	Net income/total assets	Negative
ChOff	Charge-off ratio	Net charge-offs/loans	Negative
GDPG	GDP growth	GDP real growth rate	

Note: This table presents definition, construction, and expected signs on the variables used in this study for the regression of bank credit risk taking. The bank-level balance sheet data are collected from the Federal Reserve's Y-9C reports (See Appendix 1 for details).

$Sec_{i,t-1}$ is the securitization; $Size_{i,t-1}$ is the bank size; $Loan_{i,t-1}$ is the loan ratio; $Cap_{i,t-1}$ is the equity capital ratio; $ROA_{i,t-1}$ is the return on assets; $ChOff_{i,t-1}$ is the charge-off ratio; $GDPG_t$ is the GDP real growth; and $Quarter_t$ the quarter dummies. The timing applied in this model is to ensure that the direction of causality goes from the explanatory variables to the dependent variable (Demsetz and Strahan 1997; Stiroh 2006). The detailed construction of the model variables and their expected signs are presented in Table 2.

Following Avery and Berger (1990), Shrieves and Dahl (1992), Berger and Udell (1994), Berger (1995), and Aggarwal and Jacques (2001), we primarily measure the credit risk of a bank's portfolio (CrR) using a ratio of RWATA.[15] Shrieves and Dahl (1992) suggest that the RWATA ratio captures two principal features of a bank's portfolio risk, i.e. its allocation of assets across risk categories and the quality of its loans. Further, Avery and Berger (1990) show that the relative risk weights used in the framework of the risk-based capital standards correlate with risky behavior and have an adequate informational value in predicting future bank performance problems such as portfolio losses and bank failures.

Kim and Santomero (1988) argue that banks might be prompted to shift to more risky assets by inefficiencies in regulatory capital requirements. According to this argument, bank risk increases due to the low quality of the assets left on the balance sheet while regulatory capital requirements remain unchanged, a process commonly referred to as regulatory capital arbitrage. Our study is different from the previous literature as it covers the period of the development process of Basel II, which supposedly aligns more closely regulatory capital charges on banks' assets, including securitization positions, and the underlying credit risk. As remarked by Randall S. Kroszner, a member of the Board of Governors of Federal Reserve System, on 12 July 2007, there has been 'significant progress in risk measurement and management at many banks in the United States and elsewhere as a result of the Basel II development process' (2007).[16] Therefore, we hope that our results on the effect of securitization on bank risk-taking behavior are less biased by regulatory capital arbitrage than previous empirical work.

Securitization (Sec) is introduced as a bank's outstanding balance of securitized assets scaled by total assets. If the credit risk exposure arising from the securitized pool makes banks more risk-averse and motivates them to shift their portfolios toward assets of lower credit risk, there should be a negative association between banks' outstanding securitization and credit risk taking.

Bank size (Size), measured as the natural logarithm of total assets, is included to capture its possible impact on bank risk taking through a number of channels, including funding and risk management opportunities. For example, Loutskina (2005) notes that only the largest banks in the

USA can have a sufficient quantity and homogeneity of loans to access the securitization market independently of other financial intermediaries.[17] Therefore, given better access to external funds and the credit risk transfer market for large banks, one could expect a positive relation between bank size and its propensity to engage in high risk/return activities.

Additional balance sheet and income statement characteristics of each bank are introduced into the model to control for their possible impact on bank risk taking. From the balance sheet, we include the loan ratio and the capital ratio. The loan ratio (Loan) is measured as loans over total assets and reflects the size of a bank's loan portfolio. Considering loans as a bank's higher risk assets, a bank with a larger loan portfolio is expected to be more risk-averse.

Bank capital (Cap) is measured as the ratio of equity capital to total assets. Considering capital as a 'buffer of uninsured private funds to absorb portfolio losses' (Avery and Berger 1990) yields two views on the nature of the relationship between bank capital and risk taking. On the one hand, diversified owners which do not have a significant fraction of their wealth placed in the bank might tend to advocate more risk taking after collecting funds from bondholders and depositors (Esty 1998; Laeven and Levine 2009).[18] On the other hand, managers with bank-specific human capital and private benefits of control might be expected to behave in a risk-averse rather than value-maximizing way (Demsetz and Lehn 1985). As argued by Saunders, Strock, and Travlos (1990) and Demsetz, Saidenberg, and Strahan (1996), managerial ownership should also be taken into account as managers' incentives to engage in risk taking increase along with their shareholdings. However, Anderson and Fraser (2000) show that for US BHCs, managerial shareholdings and risk taking became inversely related in the early 1990s following additional regulations (i.e. risk-adjusted deposit insurance premium). Therefore, we expect a negative coefficient on the capital ratio variable.

From the income statement, we include ROA and the charge-off ratio (ChOff) to account for the possible impact of the present performance of a bank on its incentive to take on new risks. Particularly, one could argue that poor-performing banks (i.e. ones with a low return on their assets) might pursue risky activities to re-establish profitability. Following this argument, we expect a negative relation between bank profitability and risk. A negative relationship could also be expected between the charge-off ratio and risk taking. The charge-off ratio reflects the asset quality of a loan portfolio. Low quality loans in a preceding quarter (i.e. as evidenced by a high charge-off ratio) should discourage the bank manager from taking on extra risk in the following quarter and motivate investing in low risk/secure return assets.

5. Empirical results and robustness tests

5.1 *Empirical results*

We report our results in Table 3. The regression analysis is based on the sample of securitizers which contains 5067 observations for 230 BHCs; however, the second quarter 2001 observations are lost due to differencing and lagging the model variables, which yields 4837 bank-quarters in the final regression data set. Each regression uses bank fixed effects with standard errors clustered at the BHC level (reported in parentheses). Quarter dummies are incorporated in all of the regressions, but are not reported in the table.

The parameter estimate of most interest in terms of this study is that on securitization. The coefficient on securitization is found to be negative and significant at the 1% level. In other words, a greater outstanding securitization balance is associated with banks choosing to invest in assets with lower credit risk. This evidence supports the proposed hypothesis that securitization should

Table 3. Determinants of bank credit risk taking.

	Model 1	Model 2	Model 3
$Sec_{i,t-1}$	−0.006 (0.001)*	−0.006 (0.001)*	−0.004 (0.001)*
$Size_{i,t-1}$		0.005 (−0.004)	0.006 (0.004)**
$Loan_{i,t-1}$			−0.118 (0.014)*
$Cap_{i,t-1}$			−0.01 (−0.071)
$ROA_{i,t-1}$			−0.027 (−0.075)
$ChOff_{i,t-1}$			−0.153 (0.092)**
$GDPG_t$	0.001 (0.000)*	0.001 (0.000)*	0.000 (0.000)
Constant	−0.001 (−0.002)	−0.072 (−0.056)	−0.015 (−0.051)
Observations	4837	4837	4837
Number of banks	230	230	230
Adjusted R^2	0.02	0.02	0.06

Note: The table presents the results of the regression analysis where the dependent variable is the change in credit risk of bank portfolio measured as a change in the RWATA ratio (ΔRWATA). The independent variables are: (i) securitization ratio; (ii) size; (iii) loan ratio; (iv) equity capital ratio; (v) ROA; (vi) charge-off ratio; and (vii) GDP real growth (see Table 2 for definitions of the variables and the expected signs). Balance sheet measures used are lagged one quarter. The columns represent three specifications of the regression model with Models 1 and 2 using a reduced form of the basic Equation (1). Fixed-effects regressions are run for the full sample of securitizers covering the period from 2001:Q2 to 2007:Q4. Quarter dummies are incorporated in all regressions (not reported). Robust standard errors reported in parentheses are corrected for clustering at the BHC level.
*Significance at 1% level.
**Significance at 10% level.
***Significance at 5% level.

have a negative effect on the risk-taking behavior of the issuing bank as a result of credit exposure arising from the securitized pool.

Further examination of the results reported in Table 3 reveals that most of the control variables included in the model are statistically significant and have the expected signs. Beginning with bank size, the evidence suggests that larger banks tend to pursue higher risk activities. This is consistent with prior empirical studies and could be linked to the size-related diversification effect described by Demsetz and Strahan (1997).[19] The parameter estimate on the loan ratio reflects a significant negative impact of the size of the loan portfolio on bank risk taking. Not surprisingly, a greater amount of loans and therefore higher on-balance-sheet credit risk exposure makes banks more risk-averse. Equity capital has the expected negative effect on bank risk taking; however, it is not statistically significant. The link between bank performance measures and risk taking is negative, as expected, and is statistically significant for the charge-off ratio. This shows that the current performance of a bank influences its risk-taking behavior. In particular, a bank with a lower quality loan portfolio, captured by a higher charge-off ratio, is more risk-averse.

The result of a significant negative effect of securitization on bank credit risk taking discussed above is derived using a broad category of securitization which includes different classes of underlying assets. To examine the impact of securitization in more detail, we decompose the aggregate measure of bank securitization activities into seven categories according to the type of assets securitized, and these are: (i) mortgages; (ii) home equity lines of credit; (iii) credit card receivables; (iv) auto loans; (v) other consumer loans; (vi) commercial and industrial loans; and (vii) all other loans and leases. For this part of the analysis, securitizing banks are classified in the following way: a bank is considered as a mortgage securitizer if we observe outstanding mortgage securitization in any quarter of its lifetime in the sample. The same definition applies to securitizers of other types of assets. We re-estimate Equation (1) using the outstanding amount of securitized assets scaled by total assets for each of the aforementioned loan types. A bank is included in each asset-specific regression only if it is considered as a securitizer for the relevant asset type. The results of the regressions are presented in Table 4.

Examining securitizations by the underlying asset type shows that they differ in their effect on the risk-taking behavior of banks. In particular, the results suggest that securitizations of mortgages, home equity lines of credit, and other consumer loans have a negative and statistically significant effect on bank credit risk taking; among these, credit risk taking is associated most negatively with securitized home equity lines of credit. Similarly, the effect of securitized credit card receivables, commercial and industrial loans, and all other loans and leases is negative, but not statistically significant. In contrast, the parameter estimate for securitizations of auto loans is found to be positive, but insignificant statistically.

5.2 *Robustness tests*

To verify the evidence presented above of a negative relation between outstanding securitization and credit risk taking, we perform a number of robustness tests that either examine subsamples of the data or use alternative data definitions. Table 5 reports these results, in which the first column reports the estimates for the full sample for ease of comparison.

One possible concern is that the results might differ across banks of different sizes. To examine this argument, we split the sample into two subsamples: small banks and large banks. Following Loutskina (2005), we assign a bank-quarter to a group of small banks if its size is in the bottom 75% of the size distribution and to the group of large banks if size is in the top 10% of the size distribution. The subsamples contain 3621 and 486 bank-quarters, accordingly. Beginning with the small banks, the coefficient on securitization changes very little remaining negative and statistically significant. For the large banks, the coefficient remains negative; however, it is four times larger than that for the full sample and not statistically significant.

A second possible concern is that the results might be affected by the onset of the US subprime mortgage crisis. To address this concern, we drop the 2007-year observations and re-estimate the regression for the 4271 observations from the second quarter of 2001 to the fourth quarter of 2006. The results remain qualitatively unchanged.

A third concern is that the RWATA ratio might be inefficient in capturing the true credit risk position of a bank. As suggested by the capital arbitrage hypothesis, banks might shift toward riskier assets within regulatory risk bands. To test this argument, we use a ratio of non-performing assets to total assets (NPATA) as a measure of bank credit risk; this should reflect the true riskiness of a bank's portfolio given its backward-looking aspect.[20] The results remain unchanged indicating a negative relation between securitization and the NPATA ratio and therefore confirm our finding that securitization leads to banks choosing portfolios of lower credit risk.

Finally, we test the 'recourse hypothesis': we suggest that the negative relationship between outstanding securitization and credit risk taking may be the result of the credit risk exposure arising from the securitized assets through recourse. As discussed earlier, recourse can be provided explicitly and/or implicitly. The implicit nature of the latter eliminates the possibility of its identification and, therefore, measuring its magnitude. The explicit recourse is however reported by US banks and therefore can be tested. In particular, we use the ratio of credit enhancements provided by the originating bank to securitization structures (i.e. the sum of credit-enhancing interest-only strips, subordinated securities, and standby letters of credit) scaled by the bank's total assets as a proxy for the credit exposure arising from the securitized assets portfolio. We re-estimate

Table 4. Testing securitization by asset type.

	(1)	(2)	(3)	(4)	(5)	(6)	(7)	(8)
$Sec_{i,t-1}$	−0.004 (0.001)*							
$Mortgages_{i,t-1}$		−0.004 (0.001)*						
Home equity lines of $credit_{i,t-1}$			−0.388 (0.109)*					
Credit card $receivables_{i,t-1}$				−0.062 (0.060)				
Auto $loans_{i,t-1}$					0.018 (0.027)			
Other consumer $loans_{i,t-1}$						−0.205 (0.097)**		
C&I $loans_{i,t-1}$							−0.063 (0.053)	
Other loans and $leases_{i,t-1}$								−0.020 (0.053)
$Size_{i,t-1}$	0.006 (0.004)***	0.009 (0.005)**	0.031 (0.009)*	0.002 (0.006)	0.010 (0.010)	0.028 (0.008)*	0.019 (0.009)**	0.006 (0.006)
$Loan_{i,t-1}$	−0.118 (0.014)*	−0.103 (0.015)*	−0.147 (0.034)*	−0.138 (0.035)*	−0.115 (0.033)*	−0.084 (0.030)*	−0.194 (0.029)*	−0.179 (0.028)*
$Cap_{i,t-1}$	−0.010 (0.071)	−0.098 (0.060)	−0.255 (0.111)**	−0.168 (0.113)	0.077 (0.092)	−0.273 (0.147)***	−0.278 (0.119)**	−0.138 (0.097)
$ROA_{i,t-1}$	−0.027 (0.075)	0.163 (0.158)	−0.231 (0.470)	0.031 (0.161)	−0.079 (0.097)	−0.434 (0.336)	−0.001 (0.443)	−0.048 (0.275)
$ChOff_{i,t-1}$	−0.153 (0.092)***	−0.074 (0.252)	−0.026 (0.432)	−0.228 (0.139)	−0.211 (0.253)	−0.121 (0.332)	−0.349 (0.249)	0.094 (0.326)
$GDPG_t$	0.000 (0.000)	0.000 (0.000)	0.003 (0.001)**	0.001 (0.001)	0.002 (0.001)***	0.002 (0.001)	−0.000 (0.001)	0.001 (0.001)
Constant	−0.015 (0.051)	−0.058 (0.067)	−0.437 (0.137)*	0.075 (0.099)	−0.121 (0.181)	−0.433 (0.126)*	−0.157 (0.139)	0.034 (0.097)
Observations	4837	3605	542	775	722	453	712	1047
Number of banks	230	176	27	37	34	23	32	47
Adjusted R^2	0.056	0.049	0.151	0.084	0.090	0.102	0.101	0.120

Note: The table presents the results of regressions of bank credit risk taking (ΔRWATA) on securitization activities broken down by the type of assets securitized with the first column reporting the basic regression model. Columns 2–8 represent seven specifications of the basic regression model using the following categories of securitized assets: (i) mortgages; (ii) home equity lines of credit; (iii) credit card receivables; (iv) auto loans; (v) other consumer loans; (vi) C&I, or commercial and industrial loans; and (vii) all other loans and leases. The sample covers the period from 2001:Q2 to 2007:Q4; quarter dummies are incorporated in all regressions (not reported). Robust standard errors reported in parentheses are corrected for clustering at the BHC level.

*Significance at 1% level.

**Significance at 5% level.

***Significance at 10% level.

Table 5. Robustness tests for the determinants of bank credit risk taking.

	(1) ΔRWATA		(2) ΔNPATA		(3) ΔRWATA	
	All banks	Small banks	Large banks	2001–2006	All banks	All banks
$\text{Sec}_{i,t-1}$	−0.0036 (0.0009)*	−0.003 (0.0007)*	−0.015 (−0.011)	−0.0036 (0.0010)*	−0.0002 (0.0001)**	
Credit enhancements$_{i,t-1}$						−0.49 (0.1298)*
$\text{Size}_{i,t-1}$	0.0065 (0.0036)***	0.0041 (−0.0035)	0.0288 (0.0089)*	0.0076 (0.0043)***	0.001 (0.0003)*	0.005 (−0.0037)
$\text{Loan}_{i,t-1}$	−0.1178 (0.0141)*	−0.1297 (0.0163)*	−0.0928 (0.0277)*	−0.135 (0.0171)*	0.0019 (−0.0015)	−0.1538 (0.0159)*
$\text{Cap}_{i,t-1}$	−0.0097 (−0.0711)	0.0214 (−0.069)	−0.4945 (0.1351)*	0.0183 (−0.0821)	−0.005 (−0.0049)	−0.1079 (0.0380)*
$\text{ROA}_{i,t-1}$	−0.0268 (−0.0751)	−0.0857 (−0.0683)	0.4177 (−0.5776)	−0.0122 (−0.0882)	−0.0443 (−0.03)	0.1239 (−0.1019)
$\text{ChOff}_{i,t-1}$	−0.1534 (0.0923)***	−0.1032 (−0.0892)	−0.281 (−0.4573)	−0.1143 (−0.1032)	−0.01 (−0.0164)	−0.6124 (0.1263)*
GDPG_t	0.0005 (−0.0004)	0.0000 (−0.0004)	0.0010 (−0.0011)	0.0003 (−0.0004)	−0.0001 (0.0000)*	−0.0003 (−0.0004)
Constant	−0.0151 (−0.0514)	0.0333 (−0.0492)	−0.4529 (0.1571)*	−0.0227 (−0.0608)	−0.0143 (0.0046)*	0.0446 (−0.0549)
Observations	4837	3621	486	4271	4837	3483
Number of banks	230	181	25	230	230	229
Adjusted R^2	0.056	0.06	0.12	0.064	0.039	0.068

Note: Fixed-effects regressions of bank risk taking on the following regressors: (i) securitization ratio; (ii) size; (iii) loan ratio; (iv) equity capital ratio; (v) ROA; (vi) charge-off ratio; (vii) GDP real growth; and (viii) quarter dummies (not reported). All the balance sheet measures are lagged one quarter. Column 1 represents four specifications of the basic model based on: (i) full sample; (ii) subsample of small banks; (iii) subsample of large banks; and (iv) subperiod 2001:Q2–2006:Q4. Column 2 uses the change in the NPATA ratio (ΔNPATA) as the dependent variable. Column 3 uses a credit exposure proxy (Credit enhancements$_{i,t-1}$) as a substitute for the securitization ratio in the basic regression model. Robust standard errors reported in parentheses are corrected for clustering at the BHC level.

*Significance at 1% level.

**Significance at 5% level.

***Significance at 10% level.

the main regression substituting the credit exposure proxy for the outstanding securitization. The results show that the credit exposure arising from securitized assets has a negative and statistically significant impact on bank risk taking and therefore provides evidence for the proposed recourse hypothesis. In addition, the variation in the effect of securitization across different underlying asset classes found in Table 4 provides further support for the proposed hypothesis. As suggested by Chen, Liu, and Ryan (2008), banks are likely to retain less risk, through both contractual and non-contractual arrangements, in mortgage-backed securitizations due to relatively low and easy externally verifiable credit risk of mortgage loans. This could explain mortgage securitizations having a smaller impact on the risk aversion of the issuers compared to securitizations of home equity lines of credit. Additionally, mortgages are close-ended loans as opposed to revolving loans such as home equity lines of credit, which makes securitizations of the latter more implicit recourse requiring (Higgins and Mason 2004; Chen, Liu, and Ryan 2008).

6. Conclusions

This paper investigated the impact of securitization on the credit risk-taking behavior of US BHCs during the period 2001–2007.

The empirical results indicate a significant negative impact of securitization on bank credit risk taking, suggesting that banks with a greater amount of assets securitized are more risk-averse in their activities. Examining securitization by the type of underlying assets suggests that the negative relationship between securitization and risk taking is primarily driven by securitizations of mortgages, home equity lines of credit, and other consumer loans; among these, credit risk taking is associated most negatively with securitized home equity lines of credit. Securitizations of all other types of assets seem to have no significant impact on bank credit risk-taking behavior. We explain these findings by the 'recourse hypothesis'. This arises because issuing banks commonly provide recourse, explicitly and/or implicitly, in securitization transactions.

Taken as a whole, securitization activities are found to have a negative impact on the credit risk-taking behavior of banks. However, if the proposed recourse hypothesis is correct, the credit risk-reducing effect of securitization might be offset by banks' greater risk arising from the securitized pool. Therefore, the net impact of securitization on the riskiness of issuing banks is ambiguous and will depend on the structure of transactions, in particular, on the relative magnitude of credit support provided by banks. This leads us to suggest that banks view securitization as a financing rather than a risk management mechanism.

According to the European Central Bank Financial Stability Review (2009), regulators acknowledge the potential benefits of securitization and aim at reviving the market by introducing more standardized and simple securitization structures. Further, several recent proposals require originating banks to retain exposure to securitizations through a tranche or a vertical slice of the portfolio to better align the incentives in the market.[21] In this regard, this paper contributes to the ongoing discussions by showing that, while the net risk transfer through securitization for originating banks might be ambiguous due to retained interests, banks do account for the consequently arising exposure reducing credit risk taking.

Notes

1. Securitization has been widely used as a funding, risk management, and performance improvement tool by banks and other institutions over the last two decades. But securitization experienced a spectacular growth during the decade prior to the financial crisis. The market for mortgage-backed securities increased from $2.49 trillion in 1996 to $8.9

trillion outstanding at year-end 2008. The outstanding volume of asset-backed securities reached $2.67 trillion at year-end 2008 from $0.4 trillion in 1996 (Source: Securities Industry and Financial Markets Association).

2. See, for example, Dionne and Harchaoui (2003), Uzun and Webb (2007), Franke and Krahnen (2005), and Haensel and Krahnen (2007).
3. Board of Governors of the Federal Reserve System (2002). For discussion of implicit recourse see also Higgins and Mason (2004), Gorton and Souleles (2005), and Vermilyea, Webb, and Kish (2008).
4. Aggarwal and Jacque (2001) and Thomas and Wang (2004).
5. This might still entail a bias. In particular, a merger or an acquisition might cause significant changes in the acquiring bank's balance sheet composition and therefore have an impact on the analysis results. We control for this by imposing outliers limits on bank asset and loan growth, however, acknowledge that it might still have an impact on the observed results through other bank-level characteristics.
6. The construction of the variables is described in detail in Appendix 1.
7. Minton, Sanders, and Strahan (2004); Bannier and Haensel (2007); Martín-Oliver and Saurina (2007); Uzun and Webb (2007); Jiangli and Pritsker (2008); and Minton, Stulz, and Williamson (2008).
8. Herfindahl–Hirschman Index (HHI) is calculated using four loan categories: (i) real estate loans, (ii) commercial and industrial loans, (iii) consumer loans, and (iv) other loans; a higher value indicates higher loan portfolio concentration.
9. Minton, Stulz, and Williamson (2008) find similar evidence.
10. Non-performing loans are defined as loans past due 90 days or more and still accruing interest and non-accrual loans.
11. Net charge-offs are defined as charge-offs minus recoveries.
12. Jiangli and Pritsker (2008) suggest that this could reflect securitization and/or size effect in allowing banks to extend loans with higher expected losses.
13. We find no significant difference in return on equity between securitizers and non-securitizers, which implies that securitizers have relatively higher equity capital.
14. Using US BHC Data from 1999 to 2005, Minton, Stulz, and Williamson (2008) find that the net buyers of credit protection have dramatically more trading revenue than other banks.
15. Under Basel I, banks assets and off-balance-sheet activities are allocated into four categories according to their credit risk: (i) assets with zero default risk (e.g. government securities and reserves); (ii) low-risk assets (e.g. interbank deposits); (iii) assets with medium default risk (e.g. mortgage loans); and (iv) high-risk assets (e.g. commercial loans). Each category is assigned a relative risk weight, ranging from 0 to 1. Therefore, a bank's total risk-weighted assets (RWA) are derived as:

$$RWA = 0 * \text{Category I} + 0.2 * \text{Category II} + 0.5 * \text{Category III} + 1.0 * \text{Category IV}.$$

16. The Federal Reserve Board Website http://www.federalreserve.gov/newsevents/speech/kroszner20070712a.htm.
17. A number of studies document that large banks are more likely to securitize assets (Karaoglu 2005; Bannier and Haensel 2007). Jiangli and Pritsker (2008) suggest that this may reflect economies of scale for large banks in underwriting and securitization or diseconomies of scale in funding through deposits.
18. Stringent regulatory requirements might further contribute to the risk-taking incentives of owners and lead to them favoring riskier portfolios to compensate for the loss of utility (Koehn and Santomero 1980; Buser, Chen, and Kane 1981).
19. In particular, Demsetz and Strahan (1997) suggest that large BHCs use their diversification advantage to operate with greater leverage and to pursue riskier lending.
20. We use non-performing asset ratio (non-performing assets scaled by total assets) rather than non-performing loan ratio as we aim to test the change in the riskiness of bank's total assets and not just loans. The former additionally incorporates non-performing debt securities and other assets. See Appendix 1 for details.
21. See Fender and Mitchell (2009b) for discussion.
22. In regulatory reporting forms, income statement items are reported on a year-to-date basis. Following Cebenoyan and Strahan (2004), to make measures of risk and profitability more familiar (charge-off ratio, loan loss provision ratio, ROAs, and equity), we annualize the quarterly flow variables by multiplying by four.

Acknowledgements

We are grateful to two anonymous referees for their helpful suggestions that greatly improved the paper. We would like to thank Lorenzo Trapani, Mascia Bedendo, and the participants to the Emerging Scholars in Banking and Finance Conference for valuable comments and discussions. The usual disclaimer applies.

References

Affinito, M., and E. Tagliaferri. 2010. Why do (or did?) banks securitize their loans? Evidence from Italy. Bank of Italy Discussion Paper No. 741.

Aggarwal, R., and K.T. Jacques. 2001. The impact of FDICIA and prompt corrective action on bank capital and risk: Estimates using a simultaneous equations model. *Journal of Banking and Finance* 25: 1139–60.

Ambrose, B.W., M. LaCour-Little, and A.B. Sanders. 2005. Does regulatory capital arbitrage, reputation, or asymmetric information drive securitization? *Journal of Financial Services Research* 28: 113–33.

Anderson, R.C., and D.R. Fraser. 2000. Corporate control, bank risk taking, and the health of the banking industry. *Journal of Banking and Finance* 24: 1383–98.

Avery, R.B., and A.N. Berger. 1990. Risk-based capital and deposit insurance reform. Federal Reserve Bank of Cleveland Working Paper No. 9101.

Bannier, C.E., and D. Haensel. 2007. Determinants of banks' engagement in loan securitization. Frankfurt School Working Paper No. 85.

Berger, A.N. 1995. The relationship between capital and earnings in banking. *Journal of Money, Credit and Banking* 27: 432–56.

Berger, A.N., and G.F. Udell. 1994. Did risk-based capital allocate bank credit and cause a 'credit crunch' in the United States? *Journal of Money, Credit and Banking* 26: 585–628.

Board of Governors of the Federal Reserve System. 2002. SR 02-15: Implicit recourse provided to asset securitizations. http://www.federalreserve.gov/boarddocs/srletters/2002/SR0215a1.pdf

Buser, S.A., A.H. Chen, and E.J. Kane. 1981. Federal deposit insurance, regulatory policy, and optimal bank capital. *The Journal of Finance* 36: 51–60.

Calomiris, C.W., and J.R. Mason. 2004. Credit card securitization and regulatory arbitrage. *Journal of Financial Services Research* 26: 5–27.

Cantor, R.M., and S. Rouyer. 2000. Another perspective on risk transference and securitization. *Journal of Risk Finance* 1: 37–47.

Carey, M. 1998. Credit risk in private debt portfolios. *The Journal of Finance* 53: 1363–87.

Cebenoyan, S.A., and P.E. Strahan. 2004. Risk management, capital structure and lending at banks. *Journal of Banking and Finance* 28: 19–43.

Chen, W., C.-C. Liu, and S.G. Ryan. 2008. Characteristics of securitizations that determine issuers' retention of the risks of the securitized assets. *Accounting Review* 83: 1181–215.

Dell'Ariccia, G., D. Igan, and L.A. Laeven. 2009. Credit booms and lending standards: Evidence from the subprime mortgage market. European Banking Center Discussion Paper No. 2009-14S.

Demsetz, H., and K. Lehn. 1985. The structure of corporate ownership: Causes and consequences. *Journal of Political Economy* 93: 1155.

Demsetz, R.S., and P.E. Strahan. 1997. Diversification, size, and risk at bank holding companies. *Journal of Money, Credit and Banking* 29: 300–13.

Demsetz, R.S., M.R. Saidenberg, and P.E. Strahan. 1996. Banks with something to lose: The disciplinary role of franchise value. *Economic Policy Review* 2: 1–14.

Dionne, G., and T.M. Harchaoui. 2003. Banks' capital, securitization and credit risk: An empirical evidence for Canada. HEC Working Paper No. 03-01.

Esty, B.C. 1998. The impact of contingent liability on commercial bank risk taking. *Journal of Financial Economics* 47: 189–218.

European Central Bank. 2009. Financial stability review, December 2009.

Federal Deposit Insurance Corporation. 2007. *Risk management credit card securitization manual.* http://www.fdic.gov/regulations/examinations/credit_card_securitization/index.html

Fender, I., and J. Mitchel. 2009a. Incentive and tranche retention in securitization: A screening model. Bank of International Settlements Working Paper No. 289.

Fender, I., and J. Mitchell. 2009b. The future of securitization: How to align incentives. *Bank of International Settlements Quarterly Review*, September 2009: 27–42.

Franke, G., and J.P. Krahnen. 2005. Default risk sharing between banks and markets: The contribution of collateralized debt obligations. CFS Working Paper No. 2005/06.

Gorton, G.B., and G.G. Pennacchi. 1995. Banks and loan sales: Marketing nonmarketable assets. *Journal of Monetary Economics* 35: 389–411.

Gorton, G.B., and N.S. Souleles. 2005. Special purpose vehicles and securitization. Federal Reserve Bank of Philadelphia Working Paper No. 05-21.

Greenbaum, S.I., and A.V. Thakor. 1987. Bank funding modes: Securitization versus deposits. *Journal of Banking and Finance* 11: 379–401.

Haensel, D., and J.P. Krahnen. 2007. Does credit securitization reduce bank risk? Evidence from the European CDO market, Mimeo.

Hess, A.C., and C.W. Smith. 1988. Elements of mortgage securitization. *The Journal of Real Estate Finance and Economics* 1: 331–46.

Higgins, E.J., and J.R. Mason. 2004. What is the value of recourse to asset backed securities? A clinical study of credit card banks. Federal Reserve Bank of Philadelphia Working Paper No. 03-6.

Jiangli, W., and M.G. Pritsker. 2008. The impacts of securitization on US bank holding companies. *Proceedings (Federal Reserve Bank of Chicago)* May 2008, 377–93.

Karaoglu, N. 2005. Regulatory capital and earnings management in banks: The case of loan sales and securitizations. FDIC Center for Financial Research Working Paper No. 2005-05.

Keys, B.J., T.K. Mukherjee, A. Seru, and V. Vig. 2010. Did securitization lead to lax screening? Evidence from subprime loans. EFA 2008 Athens Meetings Paper.

Kim, D., and A.M. Santomero. 1988. Risk in banking and capital regulation. *The Journal of Finance* 43: 1219–33.

Koehn, M., and A.M. Santomero. 1980. Regulation of bank capital and portfolio risk. *The Journal of Finance* 35: 1235–44.

Krainer, J., and E. Laderman. 2009. Mortgage loan securitization and relative loan performance. Federal Reserve Bank of San Francisco Working Paper No. 2009-22.

Kroszner, R.S. 2007. Basel II implementation in the United States. Speech given at the New York Bankers Association Annual Washington Visit, Washington, DC.

Laeven, L., and R. Levine. 2009. Bank governance, regulation and risk taking. *Journal of Financial Economics* 93: 259–75.

Loutskina, E. 2005. Does securitization affect bank lending? Evidence from bank responses to funding shocks, Mimeo.

Loutskina, E., and P.E. Strahan. 2006. Securitization and the declining impact of bank finance on loan supply: Evidence from mortgage acceptance rates. NBER Working Paper No. W11983.

Martín-Oliver, A., and J. Saurina. 2007. Why do banks securitize? Mimeo.

Mian, A.R., and A. Sufi. 2009. The consequences of mortgage credit expansion: Evidence from the 2007 mortgage default crisis. NBER Working Paper No. W13936.

Minton, B.A., A. Sanders, and P.E. Strahan. 2004. Securitization by banks and finance companies: Efficient financial contracting or regulatory arbitrage? Mimeo.

Minton, B.A., R.M. Stulz, and R.G. Williamson. 2008. How much do banks use credit derivatives to hedge loans? Fisher College of Business Working Paper No. 2008-03-001.

Niu, F.F., and G.D. Richardson. 2006. Are securitizations in substance sales or secured borrowings? Capital-market evidence. *Contemporary Accounting Research* 23: 1105–33.

Pavel, C., and D. Phillis. 1987. Why commercial banks sell loans: An empirical analysis. *Federal Reserve Bank of Chicago Economic Perspectives* 14: 3–14.

Purnanandam, A.K. 2009. Originate-to-distribute model and the sub-prime mortgage crisis. AFA 2010 Atlanta Meetings Paper.

Saunders, A., E. Strock, and N.G. Travlos. 1990. Ownership structure, deregulation, and bank risk taking. *The Journal of Finance* 45: 643–54.

Shrieves, R.E., and D. Dahl. 1992. The relationship between risk and capital in commercial banks. *Journal of Banking and Finance* 16: 439–57.

Stiroh, K.J. 2006. New evidence on the determinants of bank risk. *Journal of Financial Services Research* 30: 237–63.

Thomas, H., and Z. Wang. 2004. Bank securitization and risk management. Unpublished manuscript.

Uzun, H., and E. Webb. 2007. Securitization and risk: Empirical evidence on US banks. *Journal of Risk Finance* 8: 11–23.

Vermilyea, T.A., E.R. Webb, and A.A. Kish. 2008. Implicit recourse and credit card securitizations: What do fraud losses reveal? *Journal of Banking and Finance* 32: 1198–208.

Appendix 1. Variable names and construction

Variable	FR Y-9C Data Item
Balance sheet structure	
Total assets	BHCK2170
Liquidity ratio	(BHCK0081+BHCK0071+BHCK1754+BHCK 1773)/BHCK2170
Loan ratio	BHCK2122/BHCK2170
Deposits/assets ratio	(BHCK3517+BHCK3404)/BHCK3368
Deposits/loans ratio	(BHCK3517+BHCK3404)/BHCK3516
Equity/assets ratio	BHCK3210/BHCK2170
Loan portfolio composition	
Real estate loan ratio	BHCK1410/(BHCK2122+BHCK2123)
C&I loan ratio	(BHCK1590+BHCK1766)/(BHCK2122+BHCK2123)
Consumer loan ratio	BHCK1975/(BHCK2122+BHCK2123)
Other loan ratio	(BHCK1400−BHCK1410−BHCK1766−BHCK1590−BHCK 1975)/(BHCK2122+BHCK2123)
Loan HHI	(BHCK1410/(BHCK2122+BHCK2123))^2+(BHCK 1590+BHCK1766/(BHCK2122+BHCK2123))^2+ (BHCK1975/(BHCK2122+BHCK2123))^2+((BHCK1400− BHCK14−BHCK1766−BHCK1590−BHCK1975)/(BHCK 2122+BHCK2123))^2
Regulatory capital	
Tier I leverage ratio	BHCK7204
Tier I risk-based capital ratio	BHCK7206
Total risk-based capital ratio	BHCK7205
Risk characteristics	
NPL ratio	(BHCK5525+BHCK5526−BHCK3506−BHCK3507)/ BHCK3516
NPA ratio	(BHCK5525+BHCK5526)/BHCK2170
RWATA ratio	BHCKA223/BHCK2170
Charge-off ratio	(BHCK4635−BHCK4605)BHCK3516
Loan loss provision ratio	BHCK4230/BHCK3516
Operating performance	
Return on assets	BHCK4340/BHCK3368
Return on equity	BHCK4340/BHCK3519
Interest income/net operating revenue	BHCK4074/(BHCK4074+BHCK4079)
Non-interest income/net operating revenue	BHCK4079/(BHCK4074+BHCK4079)
Revenue HHI	(BHCK4074/(BHCK4074+BHCK4079))^2+(BHCK4079/ (BHCK4074+ BHCK4079))^2

Note: Variables used in the study. Data items are taken from FR Y-9C forms.

Bancassurance efficiency gains: evidence from the Italian banking and insurance industries

Franco Fiordelisi and Ornella Ricci

[a] *Dipartimento di Scienze Aziendali ed Economico-Giuridiche, Università di Roma Tre, Via Silvio D'Amico 77, 00145 Rome, Italy*

Bancassurance has rapidly grown in Europe over the past 20 years catching the attention of managers and academia. Most dedicated studies have only been descriptive in nature, while the number of empirical studies is very limited. Potential efficiency gains are a poorly investigated issue, even though cost and revenue synergies are commonly recognised among the main economic rationales for conglomeration. Our paper aims to assess bancassurance performance gains (from both the banking and the insurance standpoints) in the Italian banking and insurance sectors over the period 2005–2006 by estimating cost and profit efficiency using stochastic frontier analysis. With regard to the banking industry, we do not show any strong evidence in favour of entering the life insurance business. The investigation into the insurance industry highlights the competitive viability of bancassurance as a distribution channel, especially in terms of cost efficiency. In terms of profitability, our findings suggest that the mix of products should be continuously revised to adapt to customer needs and the evolution of financial markets. As a consequence, ownership links are not necessarily the best bancassurance strategy, and the parties involved should also consider more flexible forms of cooperation, such as cross-selling agreements and non-equity strategic alliances.

1. Introduction

During the last 20 years, the financial services industry has experienced a general trend towards greater integration and consolidation. In Europe, the combination of banking and insurance activities – known as *bancassurance* – has become particularly successful, catching the attention of both managers and academia. Focusing on the last decade, the bancassurance M&A activity in Europe (ECB 2008) was particularly intensive in 2000 and 2001, registering an opposite trend over the period 2002–2004 and then increasing again in 2005 and 2006 (i.e. the period under investigation). From summer 2007, the global financial crisis triggered by the US subprime mortgages has caused a relevant slowdown in the consolidation process.

As noted by Chen et al. (2009), most studies dealing with bancassurance have only been descriptive in nature (providing a broad insight into economic rationales and the advantages and drawbacks for all the institutions involved) while only few studies provide an empirical assessment of the bancassurance business. Most of these empirical studies focus on the assessment of risk diversification benefits (e.g. Boyd, Graham, and Hewitt 1993; Genetay and Molyneux 1998;

Estrella 2001; Fields, Fraser, and Kolari 2007), while efficiency assessment seems to be a poorly investigated issue. This is surprising since cost and revenue synergies are commonly recognised as a crucial goal for conglomeration and an empirical assessment of the bancassurance potential efficiency gains is a key issue in the analysis of current trends in the financial services industry. The lack of studies dealing with the estimation of scope economies between the banking and the insurance activities is mainly due to econometric difficulties (e.g. Berger and Humphrey 1994) and data unavailability. Some authors (e.g. Vander Vennet 2002) attempt to infer cost and revenue synergies deriving from conglomeration by estimating X-efficiency with a frontier methodology, but they tend to consider the banking or insurance perspective exclusively, failing to give a comprehensive view of the bancassurance phenomenon. On the banking side, we find studies dealing with universal banking or financial conglomeration (e.g. Allen and Rai 1996; Vander Vennet 2002), but none directly refers to the bancassurance business. From the insurance standpoint, bancassurance is considered, in a mutually exclusive way, as a distribution strategy (Hwang and Gao 2005) or as equity relationships between banks and insurers (Barros, Barroso, and Borges 2006). As far as we are aware, there are no empirical studies assessing performance differences between alternative bancassurance models, even though this issue is very important, especially for practitioners.

We aim to answer the following three research questions in our paper. First, are banks that are engaged in the insurance business more cost and profit efficient than competitors who have specialised in traditional and investment banking? Second, are bancassurance companies more cost and profit efficient than independent companies (ICs) operating in the life business? Third, which model of bancassurance performs best? To answer these questions, we focus on the Italian banking and insurance sectors over the period 2005–2006, using a sample of more than 250 annual observations, larger than those analysed in previous studies.[1] The Italian case is particularly interesting since the cooperation between banks and life insurers has been well established for a number of years: for example, the most important bancassurers (e.g. Creditras, Intesa Vita, BNL Vita, MPS Vita) were already operating in the late 1990s. Furthermore, the Italian life insurance market is the fourth largest in Europe and the sixth in the world for the volume of premiums.

The contribution of our paper is manifold. First, we analyse cost and profit efficiency gains focusing on both the banking and the insurance industries: as far as we are aware, there are no other studies running a bilateral analysis of the bancassurance phenomenon. Second, we exploit a unique data set[2] that enables us to investigate both the ownership and the distribution perspectives of the bancassurance phenomenon. In this way, we are able to consider that insurance companies can distribute their products through bank branches, even if they are not bank participated, based on soft forms of integration (such as cross-selling agreements, non-equity strategic alliances or minority stakes). Third, we provide quantitative findings on performance differences between various organisational models of bancassurance.

Overall, our findings do not provide strong evidence in favour of bancassurance efficiency gains from the banking side: companies entering the life business do not outperform their more specialised competitors in either cost or profit. From the insurance standpoint, we show that there are substantial cost economies when life policies are offered by bank branches. We also provide evidence that the typical insurance policies provided by bancassurance companies (i.e. index-/unit-linked products and capital redemption operations) are less profitable than traditional protection policies. This suggests that the mix of products should be continuously adapted to customer needs and the evolution of financial markets. In conclusion, the equity link is not necessarily the best model for a bancassurance strategy: alternative and flexible forms of cooperation (e.g. cross-selling agreements, non-equity strategic alliances or minority stakes) need to be carefully considered.

The remainder of the paper is organised as follows. Section 2 provides an overview of the bancassurance phenomenon and presents a comprehensive literature review. The methodology applied in the empirical analysis is defined in Section 3, while Section 4 describes the sample selection criteria and data sources. Section 5 gives the empirical results, and Section 6 presents the study's conclusions.

2. Literature review

The convergence between the banking and the insurance industries has been encouraged by the deregulation process starting at the end of the 1980s and accompanied by significant tendencies towards disintermediation and securitisation (Locatelli, Morpugno, and Zanette 2003). Commercial banks have attempted to compensate for their interest margin decrease by entering the investment banking or insurance businesses. The life business is a particularly interesting opportunity for various reasons, such as the progressive ageing of the population in all developed countries, the contemporaneous decrease in governments' welfare state protection and also the existence of some similarities and complementarities with banking activity.

The cooperation between banks and insurance companies, starting in the 1980s with simple distribution agreements, has gradually evolved to equity links in the early 1990s, gaining a crucial role in many European life insurance markets. In Italy, nearly 60% of 2006 life premiums were collected through bank branches, a level similar to France, where bancassurance had its origin. In addition to this, three of the top five life insurers were totally or jointly owned by banks (ANIA, 2008).

With some differences among European countries, we can currently observe a variety of organisational models for the cooperation between banks and insurance companies (Hoschka 1994; Van der Berghe and Verweire 2001; Voutilainen 2005; Staikouras 2006).

The early bancassurance model is the cross-selling agreement: thanks to a straightforward partnership, banks sell insurance products through their branches, on behalf of a single company or several companies. This kind of agreement has many advantages: it is simple and reversible, not implying any change in the ownership structure or in the organisational model of the firms involved, as they remain absolutely independent. On the other hand, conflicts of interest between banking and insurance products sharing the same distribution channel are more likely in the absence of coordination between two different sets of management. The second model is the cooperation between two independent partners realised through strategic alliances (non-equity or reinforced by cross-ownerships in the form of minority stakes) or joint ventures (JVs). A JV is surely the stronger form of cooperation, aiming to fully exploit the skills of both participants, reinforcing their areas of specialisation. Generally, insurance companies take care of product design while banks handle distribution. These alliances can reach significant synergies concerning know-how, human capital, cross-selling and scope economies, but it is essential that the two partners are committed to share business strategies and resources. The third model is controlled by ownership that realises the highest level of integration with the banking and insurance activities managed by the same owner. The bank establishes a subsidiary entirely dedicated to the insurance business (captive company) or buys an insurance company already operating in the market. This captive model allows the bank to use information at its disposal, designing products for well-known customer needs and avoiding the danger of 'cannibalisation' (Berghendal 1995), but is the least flexible and reversible. In the Italian case, the most common organisational models are JVs (e.g. Creditras, a JV between the Unicredit banking group and the insurer Ras,[3] Intesa Vita, a JV between Banca Intesa[4] and Alleanza Assicurazioni,[5] and AXA-Mps Vita, a JV between Monte dei Paschi di Siena and AXA) and captive companies (e.g. Eurizon Vita belonging to the Intesa San Paolo banking group or BNL vita belonging to Banca Nazionale del Lavoro[6]).

Shifting attention to the empirical literature dealing with the bancassurance phenomenon, we find only a few studies. Various papers (Boyd, Graham, and Hewitt 1993; Genetay and Molyneux 1998; Estrella 2001; Fields, Fraser, and Kolari 2007) suggest that the bancassurance phenomenon can be explained by the opportunity for improving the risk return profile of a bank's portfolio activities. Despite the evidence in favour of this hypothesis, investors can obtain risk reduction by holding a diversified portfolio of non-diversified banks, so that diversification is not a sufficient economic rationale for bancassurance (Klein and Saidenberg 2000).

Bancassurance gains can also be assessed by focusing on scope (cost and revenue) economies. Cost savings may be due to sharing physical inputs, staff costs and distribution networks; employing common information systems, investment departments, account service centres; reusing managerial expertise or information; obtaining capital with larger issue size (Berger 2001). Revenue synergies may exist when consumers are willing to pay higher prices for one-stop banking, for example, due to the reduction in user transaction and search costs associated with consuming different financial services offered by the same provider, often at the same location (Berger, Humphrey, and Pulley 1994).[7] The empirical estimation of scope economies is problematic due to econometric difficulties[8] resulting in mixed and contrasting results (Altunbas et al. 2001b). Furthermore, the data available in banks' financial statements do not allow us to isolate the output produced thanks to integration or cooperation with insurance companies. It is only possible to disentangle interest-based business from fee-based business where the latter includes insurance in various activities (e.g. investment banking). As a consequence, the scope economies estimation using the available data would not enable us to establish whether bancassurance is a viable strategy for realising cost and revenue synergies. Various empirical studies (Berger and Humphrey 1994, 1997) show that both scale and scope economies are less important than management ability in combining production factors, labelled as X-efficiency. As suggested by Cummins, Weiss, and Zi (2003), X-efficiency can also provide indirect evidence for the existence of scope economies, if diversified firms significantly outperform specialised ones.

Focusing on efficiency, few studies have empirically analysed the integration of the banking and insurance industries. Verweire (1999) was the first to analyse bancassurance gains (focusing on both bank and insurance company performance) using traditional financial ratios. Other studies apply frontier methodologies to estimate bancassurance efficiency gains either in the banking or the insurance industry, but none run a bilateral analysis to explore both sectors together. In banking, Allen and Rai (1996) examine universal banking, defined as the combination of traditional and investment banking; Vander Vennet (2002) analyses financial conglomerates, defined as the combination of traditional and investment banking or insurance; Casu and Girardone (2004) investigate all Italian banking groups, assuming that they generally experienced a trend towards conglomeration. All these studies provide some evidence in favour of a positive relationship between banking efficiency and diversification, but do not focus on bancassurance.

With regard to the insurance industry, few studies (Hwang and Gao 2005; Barros, Barroso, and Borges 2006) use frontier methodologies to explore the bancassurance phenomenon. Hwang and Gao (2005) analyse life insurance companies operating in the Irish market showing that company size, market share and bancassurance activities (defined as the distribution of insurance products by bank branches) are all positively related to cost efficiency. Barros, Barroso and Borges (2006) investigate the Portuguese life insurance industry by including a dummy identifying bank-owned companies in the cost function. Their findings indicate that bancassurance is positively related to cost efficiency, even if this relationship is not statistically significant.

We aim to advance the existing literature by considering both the ownership and the distribution perspective. Furthermore, our study is the first to assess the bancassurance phenomenon focusing on both the banking and the insurance points of view. To account for comparability problems (due to differences in the type of business and financial reporting standards), we assess bancassurance efficiency gains by running two separate analyses for the banking and the insurance industries using the same methodology.

There are also various studies positing that different business models of bancassurance (e.g. captive, JV, strategic alliance, distribution agreement) result in different levels of performance. By carrying out a survey of company managers, Voutilainen (2005) shows that the exploitation of cost and revenue synergies is one of the most important bancassurance aims. Staikouras (2006) provides a theoretical analysis of several drivers of success (such as well-managed corporate culture exchanges, an accurate definition of the corporate governance model, etc.). Lin, Lin and Wu (2009) reach similar conclusions by conducting a number of interviews with bancassurance companies in Taiwan. As far as we are aware, there are no studies currently available providing empirical evidence of the benefits and drawbacks of different bancassurance organisational structures. Our paper is the first to provide such empirical evidence by comparing bancassurance companies (wholly or jointly owned by banks) with other independent firms operating in the life business and also taking into account the distribution perspective. As such, we are able to consider that ownership links are not the only way to access bank branches. They can also be reached by using softer forms of integration. At the same time, we manage to isolate the effect of full or partial control by banks.

3. Methodology

Cost efficiency can be measured using the stochastic frontier analysis, contemporaneously introduced by Aigner, Lovell, and Schmidt (1977) and Meeusen and Van Den Broeck (1977):

$$\ln \mathrm{TC}_{i,t} = x_{i,t}\beta + (v_{i,t} + u_{i,t}), \tag{1}$$

where $\ln \mathrm{TC}_{it}$ is the logarithm of total production cost of the ith bank at time t, x_{it} indicates the natural log of input prices and output quantities, β is a vector of unknown parameters to be estimated, v_{it} is a random error term assumed to be i.i.d $N(0, \sigma_v^2)$ and independent of u_{it}, that is a non-negative random variable accounting for cost inefficiency and distributed as the upper half of $N(0, \sigma_u^2)$. For the deterministic kernel of the frontier, a translog specification[9] is adopted:

$$\ln \mathrm{TC} = a_0 + \sum_k a_k \ln y_k + \sum_j b_j \ln p_j + \frac{1}{2}\left(\sum_k \sum_j c_{kj} \ln y_k p_j + \sum_k \sum_j d_{kj} \ln p_k p_j\right) + \sum_k \sum_j g_{kj} \ln y_k p_j + \varepsilon, \tag{2}$$

where TC is the logarithm of the total production cost, y_k are output quantities and p_j are input prices. As usual, symmetry and linear homogeneity restrictions are imposed, standardising total cost TC and input prices p_j in terms of the last input price. We express all variables as deviations from the overall sample means, so that relevant elasticities evaluated at the sample mean are simply given by the first-order coefficients (as demonstrated by Boucinha, Ribeiro, and Weyman-Jones 2009).

In order to account for possible synergies on the revenue side, we estimate the alternative profit efficiency following Berger and Mester (1997) since there is no reliable publicly available data on bank's and insurance's output prices and, consequently, estimating a standard profit function would be problematic. The alternative profit efficiency specifies profits given the level of outputs, rather than the output prices as in the standard definition. The frontier definition is the same as in the case of cost, except for the replacement of total cost with total profit and for the inefficiency term (u_{it}) that is subtracted (not added as in the cost case), given that the alternative profit frontier represents the maximum performance. Using a translog specification, we face the problem of sample firms with negative profit values (for which logarithms cannot be taken) by redefining the alternative profit efficiency function (e.g. DeYoung and Hasan 1998; Akighbe and McNulty 2003) as follows:

$$\mathrm{PE}_i = \begin{cases} \dfrac{\pi_i}{\pi_{\max}} & \text{if } \pi_i > 0, \\ 0 & \text{if } \pi_i \leq 0. \end{cases} \tag{3}$$

Both in the cost and in the profit case, the definition of the inefficiency component as identically distributed in the sample requires that all the firms share the same production technology and comparable environmental conditions, while in the case of sample heterogeneity efficiency estimates can be strongly biased. Kumbhakar and Lovell (2000) outline the importance of incorporating exogenous variables (both firm-specific factors or environmental conditions) in the frontier model, in order to account for factors that are neither inputs nor outputs but can determine performance differences among firms.

In order to account for data heterogeneity, we follow Coelli, Perelman and Romano (1999) by running two different approaches based on the inclusion of environmental conditions and/or firms-specific factors in the frontier model. Under the first approach (labelled as 'Case 1'), we assume that environmental conditions/firm-specific factors directly influence the production structure, so that each firm faces a different cost or profit frontier. As such, we add the following exogenous factors terms ($\sum_{m=1}^{M} \theta_m \ln z_{m,it}$, where z_m are the environmental/firm-specific factors) to the translog specification reported in Equation (2). The efficiency estimates obtained in Case 1 are measures of efficiency net of exogenous influences.

In the second approach (labelled as 'Case 2' and well known as the 'Technical inefficiency effects model', proposed by Battese and Coelli 1995), we assume that all firms in the sample share the same production technology, but some firm-specific factors (i.e. out of management control, at least in the short term) influence the distance from best practice. As such, we run a translog function where the deterministic kernel of the frontier is the same as in Equation (2) and the inefficiency components $u_{it}s$ are now assumed to be distributed independently, but not identically. For each observation, the inefficiency effect is obtained as the truncation at zero of a normal distribution, with the mean μ_{it}, that is a function of M firm-specific conditions:

$$\mu_{it} = \delta_0 + \sum_{m=1}^{M} \delta_m z_{m,it}. \tag{4}$$

Efficiency estimates in Case 2 incorporate the effect of firm-specific factors and these can be viewed as gross measures of efficiency. Using these models, it is possible to overcome the limitations of a *two-step* approach in which the predicted inefficiency effects are regressed upon a vector of variables supposed to influence firm performance. As outlined in Battese and Coelli (1993) and Battese et al. (1998), this approach suffers from a strong inconsistency: unless the second-step regression coefficients are all equal to zero, the covariates influence the inefficiency level. This is in contrast with the assumption of inefficiency terms identically distributed across the sample (traditionally used in first-stage frontier analysis).

Kumbhakar and Lovell (2000) note that it is difficult to choose if an exogenous variable is a characteristic of the production frontier or a determinant of productive (in)efficiency (i.e. choosing between Case 1 and Case 2 models). This can be done on the basis of theoretical reasons or through statistical hypothesis testing. From the former point of view, Case 2 model is more convenient because, as outlined in Bos et al. (2005), it allows the analysis to account for heterogeneity across firms and still benchmark all the different firms against an identical frontier.

In addition to this, we construct a model (Coelli, Perelman, and Romano 1999) that includes environmental variables both in the translog function and as determinants of inefficiency. Then, we compare the unrestricted model to Case 1 and Case 2 models on the basis of a likelihood ratio test to determine which approach supplies the best fit to the sample data.

4. Data and variables

This section describes the sample and the variables used in our empirical analysis with a separate discussion for the banking and the insurance industry. Section 4.1 presents the sample selection criteria, Section 4.2 discusses the choice of input and output variables and Section 4.3 deals with firm-specific factors included in the frontier model as exogenous sources of inefficiency.

4.1 *Sample selection criteria*

First of all, we define the bancassurance business with respect to the banking side. Starting from the Vander Vennet (2002) definition of a financial conglomerate,[10] we classify a bank as a Bancassurance Combination (hereafter, BC) when: (a) it is engaged in life insurance activity through a consolidated subsidiary (fully or partially controlled) and (b) the ratio of not-interest income to total revenues exceeds 20%, meaning that activities beyond traditional banking (as insurance) have a relevant weight in the bank's income structure. Banks not meeting both conditions are included in another group labelled as 'non Bancassurance oriented institutions' (hereafter, NBIs). Banks specialised in investment banking or in a particular business (e.g. consumer finance, leasing) are excluded. Summarising, BCs are banking groups expanding their scope beyond traditional banking and entering the life business through a consolidated life insurance subsidiary, while NBIs are specialised commercial banks or institutions engaged in both commercial and investment banking. Data for consolidated annual statements and ownership information are drawn from the Associazione Bancaria Italiana (ABI) Banking Data database. Dropping observations with missing (or extreme) values, our banking sample consists of an unbalanced panel of data with 80 annual observations: 47 for BCs (23 in 2005; 24 in 2006) and 33 for NBIs (18 in 2005; 15 in 2006).

Second, we define bancassurance from the insurance standpoint as the Italian life companies[11] that are: (1) wholly owned by banks or controlled by banks with a stake greater than 50% (insurance companies controlled by banks, CBs); (2) jointly owned by a bank and an insurer, with either equal or unequal participation (JVs). ICs are treated as a residual cluster. We collected data on the insurance business from various sources. Data regarding the distribution system have been collected by a unique data set (provided by *Associazione Nazionale delle Imprese di Assicurazione* (ANIA)) containing figures for the percentage of premiums collected by bank branches for every firm in the sample, irrespective of ownership type. Balance sheet and technical account data for the life business (for both specialised and composite companies) are drawn from INFOBILA (i.e.

a database managed by ANIA). Removing observations with missing (or extreme) values, our sample is an unbalanced panel data of 168 annual observations: 25 for CBs (13 in 2005; 12 in 2006); 43 for JVs (21 in 2005; 22 in 2006) and 100 for ICs (49 in 2005; 51 in 2006).

4.2 *Input and output definition*

The definition of input and output variables is tailored to account for differences in the activities undertaken by banking and insurance companies.

In order to define the banking output, various studies apply the intermediation approach (Berger and Humphrey 1997) where banks are viewed as mediators between demand and supply of funds, so that total loans and other earnings assets are outputs while labour, fixed assets and financial capital are inputs. Recently, some studies (Rogers 1998; Vander Vennet 2002) have outlined the importance of accounting for non-traditional output in banking institutions expanding their scope beyond commercial banking, suggesting that the intermediation approach may be an inappropriate way to represent their business. Following Vander Vennet (2002), we define outputs as the total interest income, representing traditional banking, and total not-interest income, representing fee-based activities (such as insurance). Labour, fixed assets and total funding are regarded as bank inputs. Furthermore, consistent with several recent studies (e.g. Altunbas et al. 2000; Girardone, Gardener, and Molyneux 2004; Yildirim and Philippatos 2007; Koetter 2008), bank equity capital is included as a netput (i.e. a quasi-fixed input that cannot be adjusted in the short run). Punctual variable definitions and summary statistics are reported in Table 1.

BCs are, on average, larger institutions than NBIs, as shown by the values for outputs, total cost and profit. Input prices appear quite similar in the two subgroups. However, the average prices of labour and fixed assets are lower for NBIs, while the price of funding is lower for BCs.

Since the intermediation approach is not optimal for representing the insurance business (see Cummins, Tennyson, and Weiss 1999), we apply the value-added approach following the most recent studies (e.g. Fenn et al. 2008). As such, we select a single output, i.e. the net incurred claims plus additions to reserves, that enables us to account for the main insurance activities. Namely, risk pooling and bearing are measured by the incurred benefits (i.e. the payments made to policyholders when an insured event happens), while the intermediation function is captured by the sum of funds not needed for customers claims, added to technical reserves and invested in securities. A number of past studies (e.g. Greene and Segal 2004) have focused on the amount of premium income to measure insurance output. However, this solution has been criticised (e.g. Yuengert 1993), since premiums paid by policyholders result from a combination of producers' and consumers' surpluses, so that differences in the prices of products across firms may result in misleading conclusions about their operational efficiency.

Regarding insurance inputs, we consider labour, business services/materials and financial capital. Regarding labour costs, we consider both acquisition and investment costs: these items include expenses for both labour and business services/material and regard, respectively, the risk pooling activity and the intermediation function. In order to include financial capital, we consider equity and technical provisions as netputs (following Fenn et al. 2008). Total cost (TC) is defined as all expenses reported in the technical account, excluding net incurred claims, in order to avoid confusion with the output measure (see Fenn et al. 2008); revenues are calculated as net earned premiums plus investment income. Total profit (TP) is simply the difference between revenue and cost as defined above.

Definitions and summary statistics for all the variables included in the deterministic portion of the cost and profit frontiers are reported in Table 2.

Table 1. Descriptive statistics of input/output variables and firm-specific factors for the banking sample (mean values over 2005–2006).

Variable	Code	Definition	Total (80-year observation)		BCs (47-year observation)		NBIs (33-year observation)	
			Mean	Standard deviation	Mean	Standard deviation	Mean	Standard deviation
Total cost*	TC	Interest expenses + operating expenses	2,606,703	5,530,092	4,276,466	6,752,460	228,555	167,072
Output 1*	y_1	Total interest income	2,002,659	4,476,682	3,277,323	5,512,076	187,230	121,392
Output 2*	y_2	Not-interest income	1,156,866	2,272,927	1,912,772	2,730,121	80,272	71,076
Input price 1	p_1	Personnel expenses/number of employees	66.2990	7.5824	68.2811	8.6332	63.4760	4.5616
Input price 2	p_2	Capital expenses/total fixed assets	0.4913	0.2351	0.5183	0.2125	0.4528	0.2627
Input price 3	p_3	Interest expenses/deposits and other funding	0.0364	0.0084	0.0353	0.0073	0.0380	0.0096
Total profit*	TP	Total pre-tax profit	552,809	1,152,836	913,606	1,399,068	38,947	61,601
Equity*	E	Total equity	2,863,907	5,255,847	4,611,345	6,312,284	375,132	216,908
Size	LN_TA	Natural log of total assets	16.5610	1.5170	17.4975	1.2494	15.2272	0.5607
Capital and risk-taking	TCR %	Total capital ratio %	0.1077	0.0325	0.0987	0.0117	0.1203	0.0462
Institutional type	COMM	Commercial or cooperative bank	0.5750	0.4975	0.6383	0.4857	0.4848	0.5075
Listing	LISTED	Listed or unlisted institution	0.5000	0.5032	0.7021	0.4623	0.2121	0.4151

Note: BCs, bancassurance combinations; NBIs, non-bancassurance-oriented institutions.
*Values are in euro thousand.

Table 2. Descriptive statistics of input/output variables and firm-specific factors for the insurance sample (mean values over 2005–2006).

			Total (168-year observation)		CB (25-year observation)		IC (100-year observation)		JV (43-year observation)	
Variable	Code	Definition	Mean	Standard deviation	Mean	Standard deviation	Mean	Standard deviation	Mean	Standard deviation
Total cost*	TC	Total expenses excluding net incurred claims	131,121	209,638	162,645	297,644	110,043	187,730	161,812	196,052
Output*	y_1	Claims net of reinsurance + bonus and rebates + additions to reserves	958,259	1,501,068	1,462,725	2,122,881	632,164	986,025	1,423,325	1,861,756
Input price 1	p_1	Net operating expenses + technical charges/total assets	0.0141	0.0111	0.0118	0.0045	0.0157	0.0138	0.0116	0.0037
Input price 2	p_2	Investment charges/total assets	0.015	0.0077	0.0144	0.0076	0.0138	0.0074	0.0179	0.0078
Total profit*	TP	Net earned premiums + investment income - total cost	999,022	1,558,427	1,499,801	2,180,759	678,905	1,073,804	1,452,330	1,902,063
Netput 1*	n_1	Total equity capital at the beginning of the period	323,396	779,532	228,443	372,659	401,997	967,046	195,808	309,461
Netput 2*	n_2	Total technical reserves at the beginning of the period	4,082,029	6,297,881	5,979,725	9,456,252	3,239,935	5,182,425	4,937,074	6,222,843
Distribution	%BANK	% of premiums collected by bank branches	0.4406	0.4361	0.7956	0.2843	0.1648	0.2923	0.8758	0.2421
Market power	MS	Market share in the Italian life insurance industry	0.0117	0.0185	0.0177	0.0257	0.0075	0.0121	0.0182	0.0232
Business mix	%FIN	% of products into the III or VI class of the EU directive	0.4947	0.2846	0.4073	0.2400	0.4338	0.2967	0.6871	0.1740
Specialisation	COMP	Composite company or life specialist	0.3452	0.4769	0.0400	0.2000	0.4600	0.5009	0.2558	0.4415

Note: CB, controlled by banks; IC, independent company; JV, joint venture.
*Values are in euro thousand.

From the value of outputs, total cost, total profit and technical reserves, it can be seen that CBs and JVs are, on average, larger than ICs. Input prices appear quite similar among subgroups. Bancassurance companies, both CBs and JVs, are less capitalised than ICs.

4.3 *Firm-specific factors included to account for heterogeneity*

We select various firm-specific factors to account for differences among sample firms that may influence their efficiency levels. On the banking side, we account for the engagement in bancassurance by including a dummy variable (BANKASS) that assumes the value of 1 for BCs and 0 for NBIs. As shown in Table 1, a number of variables were also selected to account for possible differences among sample banks:

- *Size (LN_TA)* is the natural log of total assets. The relationship between size and efficiency has always received great attention in efficiency studies due to its policy implications. As shown in Table 1, BCs are, on average, larger than NBIs.
- *Capital and risk-taking (TCR%)* is the ratio between regulatory capital and total risk-weighted assets. This variable enables us to account for the capital adequacy in each company. By exploiting the ABI database, we are able to adopt a more sophisticated measure than the ratio between equity and total assets considered in various other studies (e.g. Mester 1996; Altunbas et al. 2000; Fiordelisi and Molyneux 2010) to account for capital adequacy. As shown in Table 1, BCs are more risky than NBIs, showing a lower level of capitalisation with respect to the risk taken.
- *Institutional type (COMM)* is a dummy variable (1 = stock company, i.e. *Società per azioni*; 0 = savings or cooperative bank, i.e. *Banche Popolari* and *Banche di credito cooperativo*). This variable enables us to account for the bank ownership model that various studies (e.g. Altunbas, Evans, and Molyneux 2001a; Bos et al. 2005; Fiordelisi 2007) show to have an impact on the production structure. As shown in Table 1, BCs are more often commercial banks with respect to NBIs.
- *Listing (LISTED)* is a dummy variable (1 = listed companies; 0 otherwise). We posit that this factor can influence firm performance. As shown in Table 1, BCs are listed companies more often with respect to NBIs.
- *Time effect (YEAR)* is a year dummy (0 = 2005; 1 = 2006) to account for the time effect.

With respect to the insurance industry, we first account for the ownership features of sample life companies, introducing two different dummy variables: the first variable (CB) takes the value of 1 for life insurance companies controlled by banks and 0 otherwise; the second variable (JV) assumes the value of 1 for life companies partially controlled by banks (0 otherwise). As shown in Table 2 the following other variables were selected to account for the main possible sources of heterogeneity:

- *Distribution (%BANK)* is the percentage of premiums collected by bank branches (i.e. the exact weight of the banking channel for every company). This variable is superior to a simple dummy variable (used in other studies) since it enables us to accurately assess the distribution perspective in the bancassurance business. As shown in Table 2, the percentage of premiums collected by bank branches is larger for CB or JV companies than for ICs. In any case, IC companies collect a significant percentage (16%) of their premiums through bank branches.

- *Market power (MS)* is the share held by a company in the Italian life insurance market. Both JVs and CBs hold a greater market share than ICs, while there is no significant gap between bancassurance firms.
- *Business mix (%FIN)* is the percentage of policies falling into Class III or VI, as identified by the 96/1992 Directive (respectively, unit-/index-linked and capital redemption operations). This variable is important since bancassurance firms have traditionally focused on these products that are particularly suitable for capturing complementarities between banking and insurance activities. As such, it is not surprising that the percentage of premiums collected by bank branches for unit- and index-linked contracts is nearly 80% (ANIA, 2008). As shown in Table 2, the specialisation in products with a high financial content is evident for JVs.
- *Specialisation (COMP)* is a dummy variable taking the value of 1 if the firm is a composite company also offering property and casualty (P&C) insurance and 0 if it is a life specialist.[12] Almost half of the IC companies are composites, while bancassurance firms are more often life specialists. Under current legislation, insurance companies are not allowed to undertake both life and P&C businesses, except for companies authorised before 1979. Some large Italian companies fall into this special category, so it is important to account for this.
- *Time effect (YEAR)* is a dummy variable to account for the time effect (i.e. 0 = 2005; 1 = 2006).

5. Results

Section 5.1 presents the main empirical findings with respect to the banking industry, and Section 5.2 focuses on the insurance industry. In Section 5.3, we compare the main results from a two-sided perspective.

5.1 *Bancassurance gains: the banking perspective*

First of all we run the likelihood ratio (LR) test to compare Case 1 and Case 2 models against the unrestricted one. The LR statistic is defined as $\lambda = -2\{\ln[L(H_0)] - \ln[L(H_1)]\}$, where $\ln[L(H_0)]$ is the value of the log-likelihood functions under the null hypotheses corresponding to Case 1 and Case 2 models and $\ln[L(H_1)]$ is the value of the log-likelihood function for the alternative unrestricted model.

The test results do not enable us to discriminate between the two models regarding cost efficiency, while we can prefer Case 2 in the profit efficiency estimation.[13] Furthermore, Case 2 is also more convenient than Case 1 to our aims from a theoretical standpoint since it allows us to account for heterogeneity maintaining a common frontier as a benchmark for all sample firms (Bos et al. 2005). As such, we focus on Case 2 results. Regarding cost efficiency (Table 3), we find no substantial differences between BCs and NBIs. Both groups of companies display similar results in terms of volatility and range between the minimum and the maximum value. Concerning the profit efficiency, mean scores are lower than for the cost case and have a larger standard deviation. BCs seem to slightly outperform NBIs on the cost side, while the latter have a higher level of profit efficiency. Since these scores are obtained from Case 2 model estimation, these are gross measures of efficiency (i.e. these incorporate the effect of all the variables included as determinants of firm performance). Consequently, we need to examine the coefficients of single firm-specific factors to assess the impact of engaging (or not) in a bancassurance strategy (Table 3).[14]

Regarding the impact of firm-specific factors, it is useful to recall that a coefficient >0 means a positive effect on the inefficiency component and a negative relationship with efficiency; the opposite applies for a coefficient <0. We show that firm size (LN_TA) has no statistically significant (at

Table 3. Measuring cost and profit efficiency in the Italian banking industry over 2005–2006 including exogenous factors as determinants of performance.

	Cost efficiency				Profit efficiency			
	Mean	Standard deviation	Minimum	Maximum	Mean	Standard deviation	Minimum	Maximum
	Cost and profit efficiency in BCs and NBIs over 2005–2006							
BCs (47 observations)	0.9147	0.0727	0.5682	0.9786	0.6586	0.2786	0.0000	0.9726
NBIs (33 observations)	0.9087	0.1033	0.4769	0.9815	0.6973	0.2510	0.0000	0.9723
Total (80 observations)	0.9123	0.0861	0.4769	0.9815	0.6746	0.2666	0.0000	0.9726

	Cost	Profit
	Firm-specific factors effect on cost and profit inefficiency	
LN_TA	−0.028 (0.078)	−0.992* (0.527)
TCR%	−9.103** (4.45)	−3.123*** (1.06)
COMM	−0.423** (0.179)	−8.859*** (1.072)
LIST	0.349* (0.181)	28.571*** (1.075)
BANKASS	−0.149 (0.179)	−0.079 (0.984)
YEAR	−0.344*** (0.124)	1.368* (0.735)

Notes: BC, bancassurance combinations, NBI, non bancassurance oriented institutions. LN_TA is the natural log of total assets, TCR% is the ratio between regulatory capital and total risk-weighted assets, COMM is a dummy taking the value of 1 for commercial banks and 0 otherwise, LISTED is a dummy taking the value of 1 for listed companies and 0 otherwise, BANKASS is a dummy taking the value of 1 for BCs and 0 otherwise and YEAR is a dummy taking the value of 0 for the year 2005 and 1 for the year 2006. A coefficient >0 means a positive effect on the inefficiency component and then a negative relationship with efficiency; the opposite for a coefficient <0. Values in parentheses are standard errors.
$^{*}p < 0.1$.
$^{**}p < 0.05$.
$^{***}p < 0.01$.

the 10% confidence level or less) relationship with cost efficiency, while it displays a positive and statistically significant (at the 10% level) link with profits. This result is substantially consistent with the previous literature: for example, Worthington (1998) points out that larger organisations direct more inputs into identifying and resolving inefficiency; Vander Vennet (2002) finds that cost efficiency is unrelated to size, while the smallest banks appear less profit efficient; Weill (2004) shows that data envelopment analysis (DEA) scores increase monotonically with size, while there is no clear trend for SFA scores. Cavallo and Rossi (2002) provide evidence that results for the size–efficiency relationship strongly differ among several European countries.

We also find that the capital adequacy variable (TCR%) has a positive and statistically significant (at the 5% confidence level or less) link with both cost and profit efficiency. This is consistent with Mester (1993), who points out that higher capital ratios may prevent moral hazard. If a bank's capital level decreases, managers have an increasing incentive to take on excessive risk, engaging in activities that do not create value for shareholders.[15]

The negative coefficient for the institutional type dummy (COMM, i.e. statistically significant at the 5% level or less) suggests that in our sample stock companies outperform savings and cooperatives. This is consistent with the 'agency' theory (e.g. Rasmusen 1988): cooperative financial institutions are assumed to be less efficient than commercial banks since the former are characterised by the vote per person and managers are usually protected from takeover threats and not motivated by performance remuneration schemes. On both the cost and the profit side, we find a disadvantage for listed institutions (i.e. the LISTED coefficient is positive and significant at the 10% confidence level or less). This may be explained supposing that listed banks have a more complex organisation and higher compliance costs than unlisted institutions. In addition, they may be more exposed to competitive pressure and price competition, possibly to the detriment of high profits.[16]

We also find that cost efficiency improved between 2005 and 2006 while profit efficiency declined (i.e. the coefficient for the YEAR variable is negative and statistically significant at the 1% confidence level for the cost case; positive and statistically significant at the 10% confidence level for profits).

For our aims, the most important variable is the dummy BANKASS. This variable is found not to be statistically significant at the 10% confidence level or less in either the cost or the profit models. As a robustness check, we also control that the BANKASS dummy is not significant if exogenous factors are included in the deterministic kernel of the frontier (i.e. using Case 1). Overall, we find no evidence of cost and profit efficiency gains for bancassurance in itself. Consequently, performance differences between BCs and NBIs are due to factors different from company engagement in the life business: for example, BCs may benefit from larger corporate size than NBIs or may suffer lower level of capitalisation and higher competitive pressure.

5.2 *Bancassurance gains: the insurance perspective*

First of all, we run the LR test to select Case 1 or Case 2 model. Its results do not enable us to discriminate between Case 1 and Case 2 models for both the cost and the profit side.[17] As mentioned earlier, Case 2 is more convenient than Case 1 for our aims from a theoretical standpoint, leading us to be consistent with the banking side analysis and focus on Case 2 results.

Our findings (Table 4)[18] show that bancassurance companies – both fully controlled by banks (hereafter, CBs) and, especially JVs – have a higher average level of cost efficiency than independents (hereafter, ICs). Surprisingly, our results for profit maximisation display the opposite situation: JVs have a substantial disadvantage with respect to both CBs and ICs.

These differences are observed with reference to gross efficiency scores incorporating the effect of firm-specific factors included in the frontier model. Consequently, we need to examine the coefficients of single firm-specific factors to assess the impact of full or partial control by banking institutions (Table 4). First of all, we investigate the firm-specific factors related to the company's distribution model and business mix: the share of premiums collected by bank branches (%BANK) and the weight of policies with a high financial content (%FIN). The former appears positively related to cost efficiency and significant at the 5% confidence level, revealing that insurance companies selling their products in collaboration with a bank benefit from relevant cost economies with respect to other distribution channels. This result is consistent with previous efficiency literature (e.g. Hwang and Gao 2005) and with studies finding a price reduction thanks to bancassurance bundling (Okeahalam 2008). It is also confirmed by the ANIA (2008) report for the Italian life insurance market, signalling that the incidence of acquisition and administrative costs for collected premiums is reduced for bank branches with respect to agents, brokers and financial advisors. The distribution of premiums through bank branches is also positively related to profit efficiency, but the relationship is not statistically significant at the 10% level or less. Consequently, we find no strong evidence in favour of revenue synergies for insurance companies cooperating with banks. Analysis of the weight of policies with a high financial content (%FIN) reveals that index-/unit-linked and capital redemption products are, on average, less costly to manage but also

Table 4. Measuring cost and profit efficiency in the Italian life insurance industry over 2005–2006 including exogenous factors as determinants of performance.

	Cost efficiency				Profit efficiency			
	Mean	Standard deviation	Minimum	Maximum	Mean	Standard deviation	Minimum	Maximum
Panel A – Cost and Profit efficiency for different ownership types over 2005–2006								
CBs (25 observations)	0.9429	0.0305	0.8778	0.9761	0.7734	0.1427	0.4682	0.9316
ICs (100 observations)	0.9086	0.0876	0.6138	0.9876	0.7176	0.1433	0.3789	0.9455
JVs (43 observations)	0.9559	0.0321	0.8241	0.9849	0.6780	0.1280	0.4288	0.9200
Total (168 observations)	0.9258	0.0735	0.6138	0.9876	0.7158	0.1417	0.3789	0.9455

	Cost	Profit
Panel B – Firm-specific factors effect on cost and profit inefficiency		
%BANK	−0.438** (0.187)	−0.055 (0.088)
MS	−5.773*** (2.093)	1.717 (2.906)
%FIN	−0.748** (0.371)	0.639*** (0.14)
COMP	−0.316** (0.149)	−0.154** (0.07)
CB	−0.103 (0.097)	−0.124 (0.099)
JV	−0.014 (0.103)	−0.1 (0.087)
YEAR	−0.169** (0.075)	0.304*** (0.063)

Notes: CB, controlled by banks; IC, independent company; JV, joint venture. %BANK is the percentage of premiums collected by bank branches, MS is the market share in the Italian life insurance market, %FIN is the percentage of products falling into Class III or VI of 96/1992 EU directive, COMP is a dummy taking the value of 1 for composite companies and 0 otherwise, CB is a dummy taking the value of 1 for companies controlled by banks and 0 otherwise, JV is a dummy taking the value of 1 for JVs and 0 otherwise, YEAR is a dummy taking the value of 0 for the year 2005 and 1 for the year 2006. A coefficient >0 means a positive effect on the inefficiency component and then a negative relationship with efficiency, the opposite for a coefficient <0. Values in parentheses are standard errors.

**$p < 0.05$

***$p < 0.01$.

less profitable than traditional protection insurance. These types of product, especially index/unit linked, registered strong growth until a few years ago, driving the success of bancassurance. Then, after the end of the most euphoric phase for capital markets, these products became less attractive for investors. Regarding the other firm-specific factors, the market share (MS) has a positive relationship with cost efficiency. The direction of causality is not investigated in this analysis. As such, it could be that the most efficient firms are able to gain market share from their competitors or that large companies with a key role in the industry pay more attention to the pursuit of cost efficiency and, therefore, are better placed in the market for production factors. In the profit efficiency estimation, the market share coefficient is not significant, suggesting that larger firms are not able to exploit their power to charge higher prices. Finally, the dummy for composite companies (COMP) is positively related to both cost and profit efficiency, representing a possible indirect proof that the collaboration between life and P&C businesses realises economies of scope. This result is also consistent with Fenn et al. (2008), but its relevance is, to some extent, limited by current legislation forcing insurance companies to specialise in just one of the two areas of

Table 5. Estimated parameters for the translog portion of the cost and profit frontiers in the Italian banking industry over 2005–2006.

	Cost efficiency		Profit efficiency	
$Beta_0$ (constant)	−0.149***	(0.03)	1.338***	(0.039)
$\ln(y_1)$	0.686***	(0.072)	0.336***	(0.118)
$\ln(y_2)$	0.385***	(0.031)	0.186***	(0.031)
$\ln(p_1/p_3)$	0.634***	(0.082)	0.268***	(0.097)
$\ln(p_2/p_3)$	0.053*	(0.031)	0.475***	(0.035)
$1/2 \ln(y_1)\ln(y_1)$	0.427***	(0.155)	−1.23***	(0.166)
$\ln(y_1)\ln(y_2)$	−0.398***	(0.129)	0.793***	(0.12)
$1/2 \ln(y_2)\ln(y_2)$	0.34***	(0.11)	−0.48***	(0.117)
$1/2 \ln(p_1/p_3)\ln(p_1/p_3)$	−0.936**	(0.426)	0.447	(0.395)
$\ln(p_2/p_3)$	−0.036	(0.097)	−0.339***	(0.106)
$1/2 \ln(p_2/p_3)\ln(p_2/p_3)$	0.129**	(0.06)	−0.242***	(0.058)
$\ln(y_1)\ln(p_1/p_3)$	0.228*	(0.126)	−1.945***	(0.14)
$\ln(y_1)\ln(p_2/p_3)$	−0.037	(0.066)	0.09	(0.106)
$\ln(y_2)\ln(p_1/p_3)$	−0.208**	(0.1)	1.398***	(0.081)
$\ln(y_2)\ln(p_2/p_3)$	0.044	(0.053)	0.073	(0.067)
$\ln(E)$	−0.109	(0.074)	0.569***	(0.096)
$1/2 \ln(E)\ln(E)$	0.073	(0.054)	−0.055	(0.067)
$Delta_0$ (constant)	−0.572**	(0.231)	−26.506***	(0.744)
LN_TA	−0.028	(0.078)	−0.992*	(0.527)
TCR%	−9.103**	(4.45)	−3.123***	(1.06)
COMM	−0.423**	(0.179)	−8.859***	(1.072)
LIST	0.349*	(0.181)	28.571***	(1.075)
BANKASS	−0.149	(0.179)	−0.079	(0.984)
YEAR	−0.344***	(0.124)	1.368*	(0.735)
sigma-squared	0.061***	(0.014)	29.713***	(1.014)
gamma	0.922***	(0.032)	0.999***	(0.001)
LLF	69.235		−84.283	

Notes: Values in parentheses are standard errors. The null hypothesis of the absence of inefficiency can be rejected at the 1% level. Since the data are expressed as deviations from the overall sample mean, elasticities evaluated at the sample mean are simply given by the first-order coefficients (Boucinha, Ribeiro, and Weyman-Jones 2009). y_1 is output 1 (total interest income), y_2 is output 2 (not-interest income), p_1 is input price 1 (personnel expenses/number of employees), p_2 is input price 2 (capital expenses/total fixed assets), p_3 is input price 3 (interest expenses/deposits and other funding), E is netput 1(total equity), LN_TA is the natural log of total assets, TCR% is the ratio between regulatory capital and total risk-weighted assets, COMM is a dummy taking the value of 1 for commercial banks and 0 otherwise, LISTED is a dummy taking the value of 1 for listed companies and 0 otherwise, BANKASS is a dummy taking the value of 1 for BCs and 0 otherwise, YEAR is a dummy taking the value of 0 for the year 2005 and 1 for the year 2006 and LLF, log-likelihood function.
$^{*}p < 0.1$.
$^{**}p < 0.05$.
$^{***}p < 0.01$.

business. The time variable YEAR reveals an improvement in cost efficiency and a decline in profit efficiency, probably due to the increase in competitive pressures.

The CB and JV coefficients are not found to be statistically significant at the 10% level or less on both the cost and the profit side. These findings suggest that differences in firm performance are mainly due to the distribution system and product mix, rather than to the ownership profile. As a robustness check, we have also verified that results relative to the ownership dummies remain substantially unchanged using Case 1 model. Consequently, bancassurance firms (both CBs and

Table 6. Estimated parameters for the translog portion of the cost and profit frontiers in the Italian insurance industry over 2005–2006.

	Cost efficiency		Profit efficiency	
$Beta_0$ (constant)	−0.228***	(0.013)	0.357***	(0.122)
$\ln(y_1)$	0.202***	(0.016)	0.903***	(0.058)
$\ln(p_1/p_2)$	0.504***	(0.011)	0.526***	(0.035)
$1/2 \ln(y_1) \ln(y_1)$	0.199***	(0.02)	0.343***	(0.054)
$1/2 \ln(p_1/p_2) \ln(p_1/p_2)$	0.2***	(0.014)	−0.025	(0.048)
$\ln(y_1) \ln(p_1/p_2)$	−0.005	(0.016)	−0.152***	(0.043)
$\ln(n_1)$	0.079***	(0.01)	0.119***	(0.038)
$\ln(n_2)$	0.715***	(0.02)	0.055	(0.062)
$1/2 \ln(n_1) \ln(n_1)$	0.057***	(0.014)	0.03	(0.046)
$\ln(n_1) \ln(n_2)$	−0.003	(0.016)	−0.065	(0.052)
$1/2 \ln(n_2) \ln(n_2)$	0.172***	(0.018)	0.299***	(0.055)
$\ln(n_1) \ln(y_1)$	−0.054***	(0.013)	0.039	(0.04)
$\ln(n_2) \ln(y_1)$	−0.156***	(0.02)	−0.317***	(0.052)
$\ln(n_1) \ln(p_1/p_2)$	−0.007	(0.009)	−0.014	(0.033)
$\ln(n_2) \ln(p_1/p_2)$	0.008	(0.018)	0.182***	(0.052)
$Delta_0$ (constant)	−0.579	(0.389)	0.323**	(0.141)
%BANK	−0.438**	(0.187)	−0.055	(0.088)
MS	−5.773***	(2.093)	1.717	(2.906)
%FIN	−0.748**	(0.371)	0.639***	(0.14)
COMP	−0.316**	(0.149)	−0.154**	(0.07)
CB	−0.103	(0.097)	−0.124	(0.099)
JV	−0.014	(0.103)	−0.100	(0.087)
YEAR	−0.169**	(0.075)	0.304***	(0.063)
Sigma-squared	0.045**	(0.023)	0.061***	(0.009)
Gamma	0.94***	(0.035)	0.458	(0.326)
LLF	184.254		6.907	

Notes: Values in parentheses are standard errors. The null hypothesis of the absence of inefficiency can be rejected at the 1% level. Since the data are expressed as deviations from the overall sample mean, elasticities evaluated at the sample mean are simply given by the first-order coefficients (Boucinha, Ribeiro, and Weyman-Jones 2009). y_1 is output 1 (claims net of reinsurance + and rebates + additions to reserves), p_1 is input price 1 (net operating expenses + technical charges/total assets), p_2 is input price 2 (investment charges/total assets), n_1 is netput 1 (total equity capital at the beginning of the period), n_2 is netput 2 (total technical reserves at the beginning of the period), %BANK is the percentage of premiums collected by bank branches, MS is the market share in the Italian life insurance market, %FIN is the percentage of products falling into Class III or VI of 96/1992 EU directive, COMP is a dummy taking the value of 1 for composite companies and 0 otherwise, CB is a dummy taking the value of 1 for companies controlled by banks and 0 otherwise, JV is a dummy taking the value of 1 for JVs and 0 otherwise, YEAR is a dummy taking the value of 0 for the year 2005 and 1 for the year 2006 and LLF, log-likelihood function.
$^{**}p < 0.05$.
$^{***}p < 0.01$.

JVs) strongly rely on distribution by bank branches and these are able to realise relevant cost economies with respect to other possible channels. The cost over-performance of JVs could also be due to specialisation in financial products, which is particularly marked in companies involving both banking and insurance partners. Finally, bancassurance firms are among the largest operators in the industry and benefit from the positive link between market share and cost efficiency. These effects seem to be more relevant than scope economies derived from being a composite company, in favour of ICs.

On the other hand, in terms of profit, only two firm-specific factors play a determinant role in explaining firm performance. As a consequence, the disadvantage found for JVs can be largely explained by the concentration of the business mix on high financial content products that is much more important than in ICs, and also with respect to CBs.

5.3 *Banking versus insurance: evidence from a bilateral analysis*

Our results for the banking industry do not enable us to support the hypothesis that bancassurance provides banks involved in this business with cost or profit efficiency gains. BCs and NBIs display different mean efficiency levels, but these differences are explained by factors other than bancassurance (such as corporate size, ownership structure and capital adequacy). On the insurance side, we find evidence of substantial gains due to a bancassurance strategy. Namely, the use of bank branches reduces distribution costs for life policies. In addition, high financial content products (playing a crucial role in bancassurance companies) are found to be less costly to manage than traditional protection insurance products, but also less profitable. Overall, we find bancassurance advantages only on the cost side, while from the more important profit perspective there are no substantial gains.

The differences in our findings for banking and insurance companies are not surprising. The banks analysed display large asset size and a great variety of businesses: as such, bancassurance efficiency gains are likely to have a small impact on the bank's global cost and income structure and are consequently difficult to detect. On the insurance side, we can capture straightforwardly differences due to bancassurance strategy since our data enable us to focus on the life business (i.e. the business area where banks and insurers have large synergies). Regarding the most performing bancassurance structure, JVs are found to have a greater cost performance in comparison to other types of companies, but also the lowest profitability. In addition to this, performance differences appear more influenced by business variables than by ownership features.

We show that the main bancassurance gain is related to the use of a cheap distribution channel (i.e. bank branches), while the success of insurance products with a high financial content appears more volatile and strictly dependent on current market trends. As a consequence, the mix of products needs to be continuously revised according to customer needs and the evolution of the financial market. In conclusion, equity links between banks and insurance companies do not necessarily represent the best bancassurance strategy, while more flexible and reversible forms of cooperation (such as cross-selling agreements, non-equity strategic alliances and minority stakes) also seem able to enhance performance.

6. Concluding remarks

Our paper empirically assesses cost and profit efficiency gains of bancassurance in the banking and the insurance industries. Cost and revenue synergies are commonly recognised as a crucial economic rationale for conglomeration, but few studies have investigated this issue.

While we find no evidence of bancassurance gains in the banking industry (i.e. BCs and NBIs display similar cost and profit efficiency levels), we show that bancassurance has substantial cost efficiency gains in the insurance industry: captive companies (i.e. owned by banks) and JVs outperform ICs supporting the proposition that the use of bank branches is a cheaper distribution channel than other solutions (e.g. agents, brokers). Regarding profitability, the relationship between performance and the use of bank branches is still positive, but not statistically significant at 10% level or less. A key finding is that high financial content products are less costly and less profitable than traditional protection insurance, probably due also to their reduced appeal after the end of the most euphoric phase for capital markets. If the reductions in welfare state protection and social security are also considered, it seems predictable that there will be a further development of insurance products providing a 'second pillar' in addition to public social protection and guaranteeing more stable income over the life cycle.

If bancassurance success is strictly linked to distribution cost savings, while typical bancassurance policies have cyclical fortune due to financial market trends, it is of crucial importance to assess the effective gains of realising ownership links that are often poorly flexible and reversible. This is a key issue especially during crisis periods, when market operators tend to refocus on the core business and regulators tend to limit the creation of huge and complex financial entities, operating in all financial sectors and increasing their systemic relevance. Analysing the case of Italy over 2005–2006, we concluded that equity links with banking institutions do not seem to directly guarantee any advantage. As a consequence, the mix of products should be continuously revised in the light of customer needs and the evolution of the financial market, and the parties involved should also consider more flexible and reversible forms of cooperation, such as cross-selling agreements and non-equity strategic alliances. In order to have a deeper and more complete view of the phenomenon, further research should be devoted to the effects of bancassurance, using a longer time interval and a larger sample, possibly on a cross-country basis.

Acknowledgements

We are grateful to ABI and ANIA for data provision and to the participants at the London 2009 Emerging Scholars in Banking and Finance Conference for their comments. We would also like to thank Francesca Arnaboldi, John Goddard, Phil Molyneux and Thomas Weyman Jones for their valuable advice and the two anonymous referees for their useful suggestions. The usual disclaimer applies.

Notes

1. The sample size is quite small in studies investigating bancassurance with regard to the insurance side: for example, Hwang and Gao (2005) and Barros, Barroso, and Borges (2006) analyse, respectively, 126 and 110 total annual observations.
2. Data were obtained by the *ABI* and the *ANIA*.
3. Part of Allianz group from October 2007.
4. Merged with San Paolo IMI in January 2007.
5. Merged with Toro in October 2009 (now AlleanzaToro).
6. Acquired by BNP Paribas in 2006.
7. More recent studies have adopted a different standpoint, assessing whether bancassurance bundling reduces the price of financial services, resulting in a cost saving for customers (Okeahalam 2008).
8. The translog specification for the cost (revenue or profit) function, being multiplicative in outputs, presents the unfortunate property of having a predicted cost of zero for each of the specialised firms (Berger and Humphrey 1994). The zero level of output can be substituted with the minimum observed in the sample (Hughes and Mester 1993). Nevertheless, any finding of scope economies can be eliminated by setting the observed minimum sufficiently close to zero that it mirrors exactly what happens in the case of a real specialised firm (Berger and Humphrey 1994).
9. For simplicity, we omit the subscripts referring to time and single firms.
10. Vander Vennet (2002) focuses on financial conglomerates. The author classifies a bank a financial conglomerate when (1) it is engaged in non-traditional activities (investment banking and/or insurance) through an in-house department or a consolidated subsidiary and (2) the ratio of not-interest income to total revenues exceeds 20%.
11. We consider Italian insurance firms operating in the life business and registered in Section 1 of the *Albo delle imprese di assicurazione*, having their headquarters in Italy. We draw ownership information from single companies' web sites.
12. As a robustness check, we try to substitute the dummy with a continuous variable given by the ratio between P&C premiums and total premiums. Results remain qualitatively unaltered.

13. On the cost side, the null hypotheses corresponding to Case 1 and Case 2 models are rejected against the unrestricted one. On the profit side, the null hypothesis corresponding to Case 1 is rejected, while the null hypothesis corresponding to Case 2 can be accepted at the 5% confidence level. Detailed results for the LR tests are available from the authors upon request.
14. Coefficients for input and output variables in the translog portion are reported in Table 5.
15. We do not aim to assess the causality of the relationship between efficiency and capital (see Fiordelisi 2007; Fiordelisi and Molyneux 2010): we simply observe the sign of the relationship. As such, it could be that large capital ratios support efficiency and vice versa.
16. In addition to this, it is important to outline that all banks exhibiting a loss in our sample are listed institutions.
17. On both the cost and the profit side, the null hypotheses corresponding to Case 1 and Case 2 models are rejected against the unrestricted one. Detailed results for the LR test are available from the authors upon request.
18. Coefficients for input and output variables in the translog portion are reported in Table 6.

References

Aigner, D., C. Lovell, and P. Schmidt. 1977. Formulation and estimation of stochastic frontier production function models. *Journal of Econometrics* 6, no. 1: 21–37.

Akighbe, A., and J. McNulty. 2003. The profit efficiency of small US commercial banks. *Journal of Banking and Finance* 27, no. 2: 307–25.

Allen, L., and A. Rai. 1996. Operational efficiency in banking: An international comparison. *Journal of Banking and Finance* 20, no. 4: 655–72.

Altunbas, Y., L. Evans, and P. Molyneux. 2001a. Bank ownership and efficiency. *Journal of Money, Credit and Banking* 33, no. 4: 926–54.

Altunbas, Y., E.P.M. Gardener, P. Molyneux, and B. Moore. 2001b. Efficiency in European banking. *European Economic Review* 45, no. 10: 1931–55.

Altunbas, Y., H. Ming, P. Molyneux, and R. Seth. 2000. Efficiency and risk in Japanese banking. *Journal of Banking and Finance* 4, no. 10: 1605–28.

ANIA. 2008. Fact-pack Mercato Vita. ANIA. www.ania.it (accessed February, 2009)

Barros, C.B., N. Barroso, and M.R. Borges. 2006. Measuring efficiency in the life insurance industry with a stochastic frontier model. Paper presented at the 28th International Congress of Actuaries, May 28–June 2, in Paris, France.

Battese, G.E., and T.J. Coelli. 1993. A stochastic frontier production function incorporating a model for technical inefficiency effects. Working Paper in Econometrics and Applied Statistics, Department of Econometrics, University of New England.

Battese, G.E., and T.J. Coelli. 1995. A model for technical inefficiency effects in a stochastic frontier production function for panel data. *Empirical Economics* 20, no. 2: 325–32.

Battese, G.E, T.J. Coelli, C.J. O' Donnell, and D.S.P. Rao. 1998. *An introduction to efficiency and productivity analysis*. Boston, MA: Kluwer Academic Publishers.

Berger, A. 2001. The integration of the financial services industry: Where are the efficiencies? *North American Actuarial Journal* 4, no. 3: 25–52.

Berger, A., and D. Humphrey. 1994. Bank scale economies, mergers, concentration, and efficiency: The U.S. experience. Working Paper 94-25, Wharton School Centre for Financial Institutions, University of Pennsylvania.

Berger, A., and D. Humphrey. 1997. Efficiency of financial institutions: International survey and direction for future research. Finance and Economics Discussion Series no. 97–11, Board of Governors of the Federal Reserve System (US).

Berger, A., D. Humphrey, and L. Pulley. 1994. Do consumer pay for one stop banking? Evidence from a non standard revenue function. Finance and Economics Discussion Series n. 93-30, Board of Governors of the Federal Reserve System (US).

Berger, A., and L. Mester. 1997. Inside the black box: What explains differences in the efficiencies of financial institutions? Working Paper 97-04, Wharton School Centre for Financial Institutions, University of Pennsylvania.

Berghendal, G. 1995. The profitability of bancassurance for European banks. *International Journal of Bank Marketing* 13, no. 1: 17–28.

Bos, J., F. Heid, M. Koetter, J. Kolari, and C. Kool. 2005. Inefficient or just different? Effects of heterogeneity on bank efficiency score. Deutsche Bundesbank Banking Supervision Discussion Papers no. 15/2005. Deutsche Bundesbank.

Boucinha, M., N. Ribeiro, and T. Weyman-Jones. 2009. An assessment of Portuguese banks' costs and efficiency. Banco de Portugal Estudos e Documentos de Trabalho Working Papers no. 22/2009. Financial Stability Report May 2010, 119–39. Banco de Portugal, Economics and Research Department.

Boyd, J.H., S.L. Graham, and R.S. Hewitt. 1993. Bank holding companies mergers with nonbank financial firms: Effect of the risk of failure. *Journal of Banking and Finance* 17, no. 1: 43–63.

Casu, B., and C. Girardone. 2004. Financial conglomeration: Efficiency, productivity and strategic drive. *Applied Financial Economics* 14, no. 10: 687–96.

Cavallo, L., and S. Rossi. 2002. Do environmental variables affect the performance and technical efficiency of the European banking systems? A parametric analysis using the stochastic frontier approach. *The European Journal of Finance* 8, no. 1: 123–46.

Chen, Z., D. Li, L. Liao, F. Moshirian, and C. Szablocs. 2009. Expansion and consolidation of bancassurance in the 21st century. *Journal of International Financial Markets, Institutions & Money* 19, no. 4: 633–44.

Coelli, T., S. Perelman, and E. Romano. 1999. Accounting for environmental influences in stochastic frontier models: With application to international airlines. *Journal of Productivity Analysis* 11, no. 3: 251–73.

Cummins, D., S. Tennyson, and M. Weiss. 1999. Consolidation and efficiency in the US life insurance industry. *Journal of Banking and Finance* 23, no. 2: 325–357.

Cummins, D., M. Weiss, and H. Zi. 2003. Economies of scope in financial services: A DEA bootstrapping analysis of the US insurance industry. Unpublished Working Paper, The Wharton School of the University of Pennsylvania.

DeYoung, R., and I. Hasan. 1998. The performance of de novo commercial banks: A profit efficiency approach. *Journal of Banking and Finance* 22, no. 5: 565–87.

ECB. 2008. Overview of developments in EU banking structures. EU banking structures, October 2008: 7–16.

Estrella, A. 2001. Mixing and matching: Prospective financial sector mergers and market valuation. *Journal of Banking and Finance* 25, no. 12: 2367–92.

Fenn, P., D. Vencappa, S. Diacon, P. Klumpes, and C. O'Brien. 2008. Market structure and the efficiency of European insurance companies: A stochastic frontier analysis. *Journal of Banking and Finance* 32, no. 1: 86–100.

Fields, L., D. Fraser, and J. Kolari. 2007. Bidder returns in bancassurance mergers: Is there evidence of synergy? *Journal of Banking and Finance* 31, no. 12: 3646–62.

Fiordelisi, F. 2007. Shareholder value efficiency in European banking. *Journal of Banking and Finance* 31, no. 7: 2151–71.

Fiordelisi, F., and P. Molyneux. 2010. The determinants of shareholder value in European Banking. *Journal of Banking and Finance* 34, no. 6: 1189–200.

Genetay, Nadege, and Philip Molyneux. 1998. *Bancassurance*. London, UK: Palgrave Macmillan.

Girardone, C., E. Gardener, and P. Molyneux. 2004. Analysing the determinants of bank efficiency: The case of Italian banks. *Applied Economics* 36, no. 3: 215–27.

Greene, W.H., and D. Segal. 2004. Profitability and efficiency in the U.S. life insurance industry. *Journal of Productivity Analysis* 21, no. 3: 229–47.

Hoschka, Tobias C. 1994. *Bancassurance in Europe*. London, UK: Palgrave Macmillan.

Hughes, J.P., and L.J. Mester. 1993. A quality and risk-adjusted cost function for banks: Evidence on the 'too-big-to-fail' doctrine. *Journal of Productivity Analysis* 4, no. 3: 293–315.

Hwang, T., and S. Gao. 2005. An empirical study of cost efficiency in the Irish life insurance industry. *International Journal of Accounting, Auditing and Performance Evaluation* 2, no. 3: 264–80.

Klein, P.G., and M.R. Saidenberg. 2000. Diversification, organization and efficiency: Evidence from bank holding companies. In *Performance of financial institutions*, ed. P.T. Harker and S.A. Zenios, 153–74. Cambridge: Cambridge University Press.

Koetter, M. 2008. The stability of bank efficiency rankings when risk preferences and objectives are different. *The European Journal of Finance* 14, no. 2: 115–35.

Kumbhakar, Subal C., and C.A. Knox Lovell. 2000. *Stochastic frontier analysis*. Cambridge: Cambridge University Press.

Lin, C.T., Y.F. Lin, and C.R. Wu. 2009. Selecting the preferable bancassurance alliance strategic by using expert group decision technique. *Expert Systems with Applications* 36, no. 2: 3623–9.

Locatelli, R., C. Morpugno, and A. Zanette. 2003. L'integrazione tra banche e compagnie di assicurazione e il modello dei conglomerati finanziari in Europa. In *Le strategie delle grandi banche in Europa*, ed. F. Cesarini, 99–158. Rome, Italy: Bancaria Editrice.

Meeusen, W., and J. Van Den Broeck. 1977. Efficiency estimation from Cobb–Douglas production functions with composed error. *International Economic Review* 18, no. 2: 435–44.

Mester, L. 1993. Efficiency of banks in the Third Federal Reserve District. Working Paper no. 94-13, Wharton School Centre for Financial Institutions, University of Pennsylvania.

Mester, L. 1996. A study of bank efficiency taking into account risk-preferences. *Journal of Banking and Finance* 20, no. 6: 1025–45.

Okeahalam, C. 2008. Does bancassurance reduce the price of financial service products? *Journal of Financial Services Research* 33, no. 3: 147–62.

Rasmusen, E. 1988. Mutual banks and stock banks. *Journal of Law and Economics* 31, no. 2: 395–421.

Rogers, K.E. 1998. Nontraditional activities and the efficiency of US commercial banks. *Journal of Banking & Finance* 22, no. 4: 467–82.

Staikouras, S.K. 2006. Business opportunities and market realities in financial conglomerates. *The Geneva Papers on Risk and Insurance Issues and Practice* 31, no. 1: 124–48.

Van Der Berghe, L., and K. Verweire. 2001. Convergence in the financial services industry. *The Geneva Papers* 26, no. 2: 173–83.

Vander Vennet, R. 2002. Cost and profit efficiency of financial conglomerates and universal banks in Europe. *Journal of Money, Credit and Banking* 34, no. 1: 254–82.

Verweire, K. 1999. Performance consequences of financial conglomeration with an empirical analysis in Belgium and the Netherlands. PhD diss., University of Ghent.

Voutilainen, R. 2005. Comparing alternative structures of financial alliances. *Geneva Papers on Risk and Insurance* 30, no. 2: 327–42.

Weill, L. 2004. Measuring cost efficiency in European banking: A comparison of frontier techniques. *Journal of Productivity Analysis* 21, no. 2: 133–52.

Worthington, A.C. 1998. Efficiency in Australian building societies: An econometric cost function approach. *Applied Financial Economics* 8, no. 5: 459–67.

Yildirim, H.S., and Philippatos, G.C. 2007. Efficiency of banks: Recent evidence from the transition economies of Europe, 1993–2000. *The European Journal of Finance* 13, no. 2: 123–43.

Yuengert, A. 1993. The measurement of efficiency in life insurance: Estimates of a mixed normal-gamma error model. *Journal of Banking and Finance* 17, no. 2–3: 483–96.

Financial deepening and bank productivity in Latin America

Georgios E. Chortareas[a], Jesús G. Garza-García[b] and Claudia Girardone

[a] *Department of Economics, University of Athens, 8 Pesmazoglou Street, Athens 10559, Greece;* [b] *Direction of Financial Stability, Banco de México, Ave. 5 de mayo # 1 piso 1, Col. Centro 06059, Del. Cuauhtémoc, México City, México;* [c] *Essex Business School, University of Essex, Wivenhoe Park, Colchester, CO4 3SQ, UK*

Financial intermediation in Latin America has experienced profound changes due to financial liberalization, which also resulted in further financial deepening. The bulk of the literature on financial deepening focuses on its macroeconomic dimension and its implications for growth. In this paper, we shift our attention to its microeconomic implications by shaping the environment within which banks operate. In particular, we examine the possible effects of financial deepening on bank productivity changes as well as the possibility of a two-way causality. We obtain bank productivity estimates using the non-parametric Malmquist methodology. We find strong evidence of causality from financial deepening to bank productivity and also evidence of reverse causality. Our results suggest that a virtuous circle between financial deepening and financial institutions' productivity may exist.

1. Introduction

During the past few decades, the Latin American financial systems experienced profound changes, including the liberalization of their banking sectors, the privatization of financial institutions and the opening of the markets to attract foreign investments. Such reforms during the early 1990s (particularly external financing), were expected to increase savings and investment in the region and ultimately produce higher growth rates (Aizenman 2005). Such reasoning implicitly relies on the finance–growth nexus. In addition to mobilizing savings and improving capital allocation (Boyd and Prescott 1986), financial deepening reduces the extent and significance of information asymmetries (Stiglitz and Greenwald 2003) and allows for risk transformation and monitoring (Diamond 1984).

The aforementioned effects, however, directly impact the financial system and operate through it. Thus, in this paper we complement the existing literature by turning our attention to the microeconomic implications of financial deepening for financial institutions. In particular, we focus on the possible effects of financial deepening on bank productivity, since the degree of financial depth constitutes a significant dimension of the broad environment within which banks operate. Moreover, the Latin American financial systems are highly bank-based and banks constitute the most important source of finance.

A number of studies produced solid empirical evidence on the nexus between finance and economic productivity and growth[1] where the development of financial institutions is treated as a key component of financial deepening (Levine 1997; Beck, Levine, and Loayza 2000; Guillaumont Jeanneney, Hua, and Liang 2006; Lozano-Vivas and Pastor 2006). Nevertheless, it is less clear how exactly finance influences economic growth (Levine 2004). Arestis, Chortareas, and Desli (2006) draw attention to the fact that the literature rarely attempts to identify the particular mechanism through which this nexus materializes. Regardless of the transmission channel, however, one would expect that the waves of financial deepening cannot raise the tide of the economy without affecting bank performance, particularly in emerging economies where the banking sector is the main supplier of funds to the financial system.

In this paper, we shift our focus from the macroeconomic variables to financial institutions and the possible causal links between financial deepening and bank productivity changes. We consider a set of Latin American countries during a period of financial reforms that enhanced financial depth. We examine whether financial deepening affects banking productivity and if channels of reverse causality exist between the two variables. To the best of our knowledge, there is no work considering explicitly such a link between financial deepening and bank productivity.

On one hand, a high degree of financial deepening may affect banking efficiency and productivity through competition and ultimately a more efficient capital allocation which increases the productivity of investment. Moreover, financial deepening mobilizes savings into investment projects, which normally are passed on by the banking sector (Merton and Bodie 1995). Financial deepening also increases the marginal productivity of capital through the intermediation function of well-informed financial institutions (King and Levine 1993a; Beck, Levine, and Loayza 2000). On the other hand, more efficient and profitable banks may increase the degree of financial deepening by increasing competition, improving their services, increasing their network penetration, enhancing transaction processes, and providing consumers with more financial products (e.g. by increasing the amount of credit).

We measure banking productivity using the non-parametric Malmquist total factor productivity (TFP) index. Subsequently, we employ a panel data framework using the generalized methods of moments (GMM) to test our main hypothesis and the direction of causality between financial deepening and bank productivity change. This approach allows controlling for endogeneity, country-specific effects, and potential simultaneity issues between financial deepening and banking productivity.[2]

The next section provides an overview of the recent evolution of financial deepening in Latin America. Section 3 reviews the literature and Section 4 presents the methodology and data used. Section 5 discusses the results of the study and finally Section 6 concludes.

2. Recent trends in financial development in Latin America

After the financial reforms carried out in the 1990s in the majority of countries in Latin America, the banking industry was expected to become more competitive and an important catalyst for economic growth. The immediate aftermath of the financial reforms brought a much-needed capitalization of the financial sector and a change in the market structure of the banking sector (Aizenman 2005). One of the intended consequences of the financial liberalization in the region was to increase the degree of financial development, for example through credit expansion. To proxy the degree of financial development in the region we rely on the measures of financial deepening[3] typically used in the literature that considers the financial deepening and growth nexus (see, among others, King and Levine 1993a, 1993c; Beck, Levine, and Loayza

Table 1. Financial and economic indicators by country in Latin America.[a,b]

Country	PCR (%)	GDP *per capita* (USD)	TRADE/GDP (%)	GOV/GDP (%)	CPI (%)
Argentina	15	5033	36	12	8.89
Brazil	30	3807	26	20	7.81
Chile	67	5754	69	12	2.89
Colombia	28	2226	43	20	6.56
Cost Rica	31	4353	96	14	11.2
Paraguay	23	1200	84	12	8.82
Peru	21	2492	38	10	2.21
Uruguay	43	4780	50	12	8.96
Venezuela	11	4737	49	13	19.09
Average LA[b]	30	3820	55	14	8.90

Source: Data obtained from the IFS of the International Monetary Fund (IMF) (lines 32D.ZF, 59MB.ZF, RF.ZF, and 99B.ZF).
[a]The reported figures are averages over 2000–2006.
[b]PCR is the credit to the private sector; TRADE is calculated as exports + imports (lines 90C and 98C) and GOV is Government expenditure (line 91F). CPI is the average annual consumer price index (line 64.XZF).

2000; Arestis, Chortareas, and Desli 2006; Guillaumont Jeanneney, Hua, and Liang 2006). We use credit to the private sector in terms of GDP for two reasons.[4] First, since Latin American countries have experienced low ratios of credit to the private sector for the last few decades, it is interesting to analyse how an increase in bank productivity is related to an increase (decrease) of this ratio. Secondly, since these economies are still bank-based, the amount of credit to the private sector, and its relationship to bank productivity, becomes an important variable to take into account.

Table 1 reports a selection of financial and economic indicators relevant to the analysis of financial deepening for each of the countries under study over the period 2000–2006. The first column illustrates the level of credit to the private sector (PCR) in terms of GDP. This measure is calculated as the number of claims to the private sector by the banking system divided by GDP. The overall average of PCR in Latin America is 30% while Chile shows the largest ratio (67%). The countries exhibiting the lowest PCR ratios are Peru, Argentina and Venezuela with ratios of 21%, 15% and 11% respectively. Herrero et al. (2002) argue that the financial systems in Latin America are highly bank-based and the region's financial development and financial efficiency have been relatively low compared to other developing regions.

Table 1 also illustrates a set of macroeconomic variables, which are normally associated with long-run economic growth.[5] The term GDP *per capita* is a measure widely used to identify the degree of wealth in a country. The average for Latin America for the period of study is $3820, however there are wide differences across the countries analysed in this study. For example, Chile shows the highest GDP *per capita* ($5754) followed by Argentina and Uruguay ($5033 and $4780, respectively). The countries with the lowest GDP *per capita* are Peru, Colombia and Paraguay ($1200, $2226 and $1200, respectively).

Another important macroeconomic variable is the degree of openness measured as the amount of trade in terms of GDP (TRADE). The highest value for this variable is found in Costa Rica (96%), followed by Paraguay (84%) and Chile (69%). The lowest values are observed in Peru (38%), Argentina (36%) and Brazil (26%). The average for the whole Latin American region is 55%. The table also reports the total amount of government expenditure in terms of GDP (GOV). The average in Latin America is 14% and is particularly high in Brazil and Colombia; however the

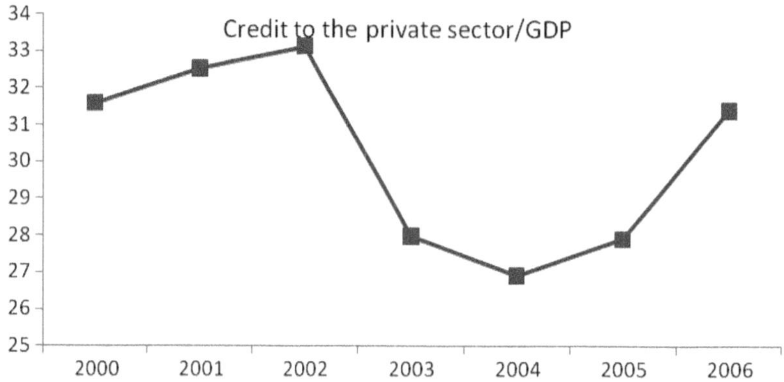

Figure 1. Financial deepening in Latin America. The Latin American average is calculated using the following countries: Argentina, Brazil, Chile, Colombia, Costa Rica, Paraguay, Peru, Uruguay and Venezuela. Source: IFS (International financial statistics of the IMF).

remaining countries show similar lower values. Finally, the level of inflation (CPI) is measured as the average annual consumer price index change and the mean for the region is 8.9%. The lowest ratios are observed in Peru and Chile with 2.21% and 2.89%, respectively. On the other hand, Costa Rica and Venezuela show the highest values in the region with 11.2% and 19.09%, respectively.

Overall, wide differences across the countries under study can be observed. Chile presents the best economic and financial outlook particularly in terms of financial deepening, trade, GDP *per capita* and inflation rate. In contrast, Venezuela shows the lowest financial deepening ratio while suffering from the highest inflation rate. Another noticeable example of these wide differences is the fact that Paraguay's GDP *per capita* is almost three times lower than the average for Latin America.

Figure 1 shows the evolution of financial deepening measured as credit to the private sector in terms of GDP. The graph shows a constant trend from 2000 to 2001 and a sudden drop afterwards, suggesting the drastic decrease in credit soon after the 2001 Argentinean crisis, implying a lack of liquidity reflected in lesser credit to the private sector. From 2003, however, there is an increment in the PCR ratio indicating a recovery in the financial sector and a greater financial deepening.

Figure 2 shows the degree of trade and government expenditure in Latin America in the early 2000s. It shows that there is a slight decline in the ratio over 2000–2001, nevertheless, the ratio recovers and gradually increases in the following years. In terms of government expenditure, the value has been constant during the studied period, oscillating between 10% and 20% on average.

To sum up, the main financial deepening indicator has been gradually increasing after the 2001 sudden drop (Argentinean crisis). Moreover, the inflation rate on average has been kept at single-digit levels, reflecting the macroeconomic discipline that characterized the majority of Latin American countries during the period considered. The degree of openness has increased after 2001 and is close to 50% of GDP. Government expenditure has displayed less variation over time. Finally, the countries under study display wide differences in their GDP *per capita*.

The next section reviews the main literature on the relationship between financial deepening and productivity with a particular focus on the existing work on the finance–growth relationship.

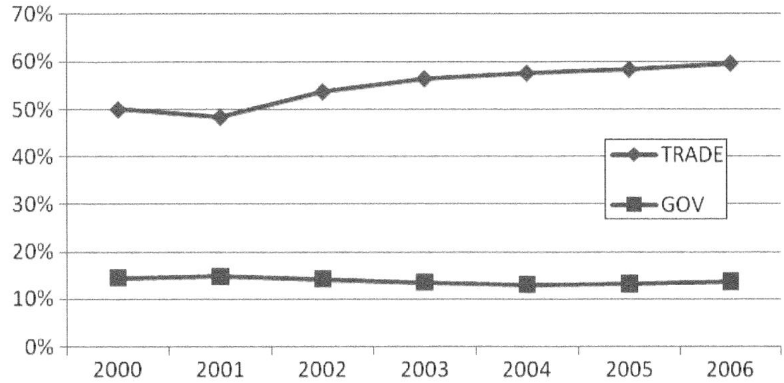

Figure 2. Trade and government expenditure. The Latin American average is calculated using the following countries: Argentina, Brazil, Chile, Colombia, Costa Rica, Paraguay, Peru, Uruguay and Venezuela; the average in Venezuela is for the period 2000–2004 due to data availability.
Source: IFS (International financial statistics of the IMF).

3. Literature review

Economists have extensively debated the role of financial development on economic growth. The idea that financial development affects GDP growth through productivity and technological advancements was convincingly articulated by Schumpeter (1934).[6] Early studies such as that by Goldsmith (1969), suggest that financial development can increase the TFP of the economy through increments in marginal productivity. Other authors suggest that financial development can improve the efficiency of capital allocation by increasing the overall degree of investment (McKinnon 1973; Shaw 1973).

The constantly increasing importance of financial institutions and financial instruments helps to reduce transaction and information costs in the economy, but also poses challenges as manifested by the recent financial crisis. More recently, an abundant literature has also produced convincing evidence for the existence of a positive link between financial deepening and economic growth.[7] The relationship between financial intermediation and growth has been studied through many cross-country studies, at the firm and industry levels (Levine 2004). Less attention has been given, however, to the sources of growth in order to identify the exact mechanisms through which financial development influences economic growth (Rioja and Valev 2004). Jorgenson (2005) suggests that physical accumulation of capital does not necessarily produce long-run economic growth. Therefore, more recent studies attempt to explain the mechanism through which financial deepening impacts economic growth. As Levine (2004, 6) puts it 'if finance is to explain economic growth, we need theories that describe how financial development influences resource allocation decisions in ways that foster productivity growth [...]'. Some authors focused on how financial development affects economic growth through increasing productivity (Levine, Loayza, and Beck 2000; Arestis, Demetriades, and Fattouh 2003; Arestis, Chortareas, and Desli 2006).

Fisman and Love (2003) test how financial deepening affects productivity growth. They find that in the long-run more financially developed countries allocate a higher share of resources towards sectors that rely primarily on external finance. These industries which depend on external financing are most likely to invest in R&D and technology, and access to increased credit may stimulate greater productivity growth. Hartmann et al. (2007) show that financial deepening in Eastern European countries has led to faster capital reallocation; they conclude that deeper credit markets enhance capital reallocation by contributing to an increase in economic productivity growth.

Lower TFP has been explained in developing countries by misallocation of resources across productive units. Thus, the presence of financial frictions increases the misallocation of resources. Contrastingly, as the financial system develops, information and transaction costs associated with capital reallocation decrease while TFP increases (Hsieh and Klenow 2007; Restuccia and Rogerson 2007).

Greenwood and Jovanovic (1990) provide a theoretical analysis of ways in which financial intermediation can enhance productivity and growth by allocating efficiently funds in investment projects with high rates of return. Bencivenga and Smith (1991) suggest that financial intermediaries contribute to the efficient allocation of funds by increasing liquidity and diversifying risk, which in turn influences productivity growth. They acknowledge that regulatory measures such as interest rate ceilings can inhibit this process, particularly in developing nations.

Recent studies focus on the mechanisms that improve productivity to analyse the financial development-economic growth link. Benhabib and Spiegel (1994) find that financial development enhances growth through greater TFP and capital accumulation. Beck and Levine (2002) employ a cross-country panel data to test the relationship between financial structure, industry growth, and new establishment formation. They find that an efficient legal system and financial development are both strong determinants of industry growth, new establishment formation and efficient capital allocation. Guillaumont Jeanneney, Hua, and Liang (2006) study the finance–productivity growth in China for 1993–2001. They use the Malmquist index and its components (namely the technical and efficiency change) to measure productivity and find that financial deepening does affect productivity in China, particularly through efficiency change.

While there exists an abundance of evidence on the effects of financial deepening on productivity in general, to our knowledge there is no evidence on how financial deepening specifically affects the productivity within its direct environment, that is, the productivity of financial institutions. This motivates us to consider the financial depth-banking productivity nexus. Thus, we consider if and how financial deepening affects banking productivity in Latin America.

4. Data and methodology

4.1 *Data and input/output definition*

The data used in this study were obtained from two different sources: the Bankscope database maintained by Fitch/IBCA/Bureau Van Dijk, and the International Financial Statistics (IFS) database provided by the International Monetary Fund. The study includes commercial banks operating in nine Latin American countries: Argentina, Brazil, Chile, Costa Rica, Colombia, Paraguay, Peru, Uruguay and Venezuela. The data are annual and cover the period 2000–2006. We use 1834 commercial bank observations and only banks that appear every 2 years in the database (to account for productivity changes).

The approach to output definition used for the calculation of the TFP index is a variation of the 'intermediation approach', which was originally developed by Sealey and Lindley (1977) and posits that total loans and securities are outputs, whereas deposits along with labour and physical capital are inputs. Specifically, we use the sum of personnel expenses, interest expenses, non-interest expenses and other operating expenses as inputs (Beccalli, Casu, and Girardone 2006); whereas the output variables capture both the traditional lending activity of banks (total loans) and the growing non-lending activities (other earning assets).[8] The descriptive statistics of the inputs and outputs used for the empirical analysis are reported in Table 2 (panel a). The table also illustrates the details of the macroeconomic variables (panel b) that we employ in the second

Table 2. Descriptive statistics of the variables used in the empirical models.[a]

Variables	Mean	Standard deviation	Minimum	Maximum
Panel (a):Bank-based variables (millions in USD)				
Interest rate expenses	241	723.065	0.85	10,476
Personnel expenses	79	270.503	0.10	4046
Other personnel expenses	37	86.332	0.25	1026
Loans	1176	3,266.336	1	55,107
Other earning assets	1290	4,461.955	0.58	67,246
Panel (b): Macroeconomic variables (%)[b]				
PCR	30.2	17.1	8.6	68.8
CPI	8.493	6.373	−1.067	31.115
TRADE	54.7	23.5	21.7	10.64
GOV	13.9	3.5	9.6	22.5
XRATE	716.31	1372.22	0.995	6424
GDP *per capita*	4,017.20	1659.82	913.97	8857

[a]The reported figures are averages over 2000–2006.
[b]PCR is the credit to the private sector in terms of GDP; CPI is the annual change in the consumer price index; TRADE is the sum of export and imports in terms of GDP; GOV is the government expenditure in terms of GDP; XRATE is the annual average exchange rate; GDP *per capita* is the average annual GDP *per capita*.

part of the empirical analysis. It shows some interesting statistics: the average PCR ratio is 30%, having a range of 9–69%. The average value seems significantly low compared to other developed nations. On the other hand, the CPI shows an average value of 8.5% in Latin America for the period 2000–2006, a gradual improvement if compared to previous time periods. Moreover, the minimum value for the CPI variables is −1.067% which is the value for Argentina in 2001. The year after the inflation rate in Argentina soared to nearly 26%. Finally, the TRADE average value is half that of GDP (55%), and the average GOV value is relatively low in terms of GDP (14%) implying that government spending is no longer an essential key in economic and financial development in the region.[9]

4.2 *Main methodological issues*

The methodology employed in this paper follows two stages. First is the computation of the Malmquist index using a bootstrap framework (Section 4.2.1). The second stage implies the estimation of a two-step system GMM regression model using as dependent variables alternatively the TFP index and the PCR, to test for direct and reverse causality (Section 4.2.2).

4.2.1 The Malmquist TFP index

TFP measures changes in total output relative to inputs and the concept derives from the ideas of Malmquist (1953) and the distance function approach.[10] The Malmquist TFP index is the most commonly used measure of productivity change, and the literature accounts for various applications in the specific context of the banking firm productivity (for a systematic introduction to the Malmquist TFP as applied to the banking sector see, e.g. Casu, Girardone, and Molyneux (2004) and more recently, Tortosa-Ausina et al. (2008)). The Malmquist measures TFP change between two data points by calculating the ratio of the distances of each data point relative to a common technology and it requires the inputs and outputs from one time period to be mixed with the technology of another time period. A value of $M > 1$ implies an increase of productivity, a value of $M = 1$ means no change in productivity and $M < 1$ is a reduction in productivity. The distance functions which compose the Malmquist TFP index can be computed using different methods. A standard approach in the literature is the data envelopment analysis (DEA)-like programming originally suggested by Färe et al. (1994), which is the method that will be used in our empirical investigation.

DEA is a deterministic method[11]; thus to provide statistical precision to our estimates we construct the Malmquist productivity indexes using a bootstrap framework. This procedure allows us to: (a) replicate the data-generating process to obtain an empirical approximation of the sampling distribution; and (b) estimate confidence intervals for the estimated parameters (Simar and Wilson 1998, 1999, 2000). In a recent study, Tortosa-Ausina et al. (2008) provide a thorough discussion of the bootstrap procedure and its statistical advantages for the specific case of the Malmquist index (see the appendix for more details).

4.2.2 GMM model

To examine the link between financial deepening and banking productivity change in Latin America as well as the direction of causality we employ dynamic panel data. There are many advantages of using these models. The first advantage resides in the ability to acknowledge both the time and cross-sectional variation in the model. The second benefit of using this methodology is the possibility to avoid any bias between cross-country regressions. The third is the possibility to use instrumental variables producing more precise and accurate estimators.[12] In addition, these methods are useful for panels that are characterized by a relatively low number of years and a large number of cross-sections per year. A recent approach for the employment of dynamic panel data is the GMM approach that was first proposed by Arellano and Bond (1991) and then developed by Arellano and Bover (1995) and Blundell and Bond (1998).

The reduced form equation used in this study is an autoregressive distributed linear specification that can be written as:

$$Q_{i,t} = \alpha_{i,t} + \beta_1 Q_{it-1} + \sum_{k=1}^{3} \beta_k G_{i,t-s} + \sum_{k=4}^{8} \beta_k Z_{i,t} + (\mu_i + \varepsilon_{i,t}) \quad t = 1, \ldots, T;\ s = 0, 1, 2, \tag{1}$$

where $Q_{i,t}$ is the dependent variable, $Q_{i,t-1}$ is the lagged dependent variables, $G_{i,t-s}$ is the current and lagged values of the endogenous variable, $Z_{i,t}$ is a vector of macroeconomic variables, μ_i is the unobserved country-specific and time-invariant effect which allows for heterogeneity, and $\varepsilon_{i,t}$ is a disturbance measure which is independent across observations. For the GMM model to be valid the Hansen J-test and the second order autocorrelation test are analysed. The Hansen J-test assesses the correct identification of the variables used in the model and the model should not have a second order autocorrelation. We can write our estimated model by substituting our chosen variables in Equation (1) as follows:

$$\begin{aligned} \mathrm{TFP}_{i,t} &= \alpha_{i,t} + \beta_1 \mathrm{TFP}_{i,t-1} + \beta_2 \mathrm{PCR}_{i,t} + \beta_3 \mathrm{PCR}_{i,t-1} + \beta_4 \mathrm{PCR}_{i,t-2} + \beta_5 \mathrm{CPI}_{i,t} \\ &\quad + \beta_6 \mathrm{TRADE}_{i,t} + \beta_7 \mathrm{GOV}_{i,t} + \beta_8 \mathrm{XRATE}_{i,t} + \beta_8 \mathrm{GDPpercapita}_{i,t} + \mu_i + \varepsilon_{i,t}, \end{aligned} \tag{2}$$

where TFP is the Malmquist index which measures banking productivity change, PCR is the degree of financial deepening measured as credit to the private sector in terms of GDP,[13] CPI is a measure of the inflation rate, TRADE is the degree of openness, GOV is a variables measuring government expenditure, XRATE is the exchange rate, GDP *per capita* is a measure of wealth, μ_i are the unobserved country-specific effects, and $\varepsilon_{i,t}$ is the disturbance term.

A positive relationship between the banking productivity change index and financial deepening is expected. Greater financial deepening could be increasing the productivity level in the banking sector through, for example, a better allocation of capital or increasing returns because of more lending activities. Three variants are employed in this study: the base model (a) described in equation (2); model (b) with the endogenous dependent variable PCR both at time t and $t-1$; and model (c) where both the first and second lags of PCR are omitted. By estimating the two models (b) and (c) in addition to model (a) we expect to obtain a more detailed picture of the impact, if any, of the two lagged variables of PCR on bank TFP at time t.

Another control variable is the level of trade and government expenditure, and these are normally associated with higher economic growth.[14] There is no *a priori* expected relationship between the degree of openness and government expenditure and banking productivity. Nevertheless, an increased activity in trade and/or government expenditure stimulates further banking activity through a greater flow of capital in the banking sector. The expected sign for the degree of inflation is mixed because higher inflation can be associated both with increases in lending rates and in default risk, thereby potentially affecting banks' efficient operations in opposite ways. Equally, banks can often be constrained by regulatory, institutional, and market factors so that they are unable to keep up raising rates when inflation rates are high and variable. In this latter case the net effect on bank productivity may be weak. The exchange rate (XRATE) does not have an *a priori* expected sign, but it measures country risk. Finally, GDP *per capita* measures the level of wealth and a positive relationship is expected with banking productivity since greater wealth induces greater banking activity through a greater flow of capital into the banking sector.

By reversing the endogenous variable and the dependent variable we are able to test the reverse causality between these variables. The control variables remain as shown in Equation (3):

$$\begin{aligned}\mathrm{PCR}_{i,t} &= \alpha_{i,,t} + \beta_1 \mathrm{PCR}_{i,t-1} + \beta_2 \mathrm{TFP}_{i,t} + \beta_3 \mathrm{TFP}_{i,t-1} + \beta_4 \mathrm{TFP}_{i,t-2} + \beta_5 \mathrm{CPI}_{i,t} + \beta_6 \mathrm{TRADE}_{i,t} \\ &\quad + \beta_7 \mathrm{GOV}_{i,t} + \beta_8 \mathrm{XRATE}_{i,t} + \beta_8 \mathrm{GDPpercapita}_{i,t} + \mu_i + \varepsilon_{i,t}, \qquad (3)\end{aligned}$$

where the variables are defined as in Equation (2) and three variants are again analysed: the base model (d) described in Equation (3); model (e) with the endogenous dependent variable TFP both at time t and $t-1$; and model (f) where both the first and second lags of TFP are omitted. Focusing on the control variables, the level of trade is normally associated with greater financial depth, through for example, a higher demand for new financial products, which could help with risk diversification (see Svaleryd and Vlachos 2002). Bonfiglioli (2008) suggests that the degree of openness affects the efficiency in the economy through several channels such as specialization, comparative advantage, access to larger markets, and increased competition. He argues that increases in government expenditure crowds out private investments which could in turn increase financial deepening and economic growth. However, increased government expenditure focused on stimulating the financial sector may be helpful in fostering the degree of financial deepening.

5. Empirical results

Table 3 reports the bootstrapped estimates of the TFP index over 2000–2006 by country for our sample of Latin American banks.[15] The vast majority of countries have witnessed a decline in productivity growth in their banking sectors over 2000–2003 that, with only a few exceptions appearing to recover afterwards. In several countries the productivity index has increased above

Table 3. TFP change index results.[a]

Country	2000	2001	2002	2003	2004	2005	2006
Argentina	1.046	1.221	1.916	0.503	0.719	1.0463	0.974
Brazil	0.521	1.049	1.284	0.701	0.85	0.997	0.839
Chile	0.975	0.846	0.854	0.846	0.91	1.304	1.06
Colombia	0.839	0.92	0.788	0.846	1.01	0.905	0.915
Cost Rica	1.472	0.904	1.166	0.628	0.911	1.003	1.072
Paraguay	0.955	1.591	2.979	1.058	0.334	0.683	1.455
Peru	1.073	0.822	0.681	1.055	0.805	1.256	1.177
Uruguay	0.721	2.539	2.045	0.273	0.73	1.251	0.094
Venezuela	0.832	1.006	1.449	0.934	0.616	0.845	0.89

[a]All TFP index averages are calculated as geometric means of the chosen bootstrap confidence intervals estimates (1%, 5% and 10%) for each observation. A number <1 indicates decline; a number >1 indicates growth.

unity after 2004, as occurred for example in Chile and Peru. In other countries the index is still below unity in the last available year (2006) yet the estimated figures suggest a productivity improvement overall (e.g. in Colombia). Overall these results appear to suggest that in the aftermath of the crisis, possibly as a result of the financial reforms, there has been a significant improvement in financial sector performance proxied by the Malmquist productivity index in most Latin American countries. These preliminary findings are important for the aims of this study in that it is reasonable to assume that if financial reforms boosted financial deepening and bank productivity growth, then these two variables can be mutually reinforcing (hence the causality test).

The next step of our analysis involves the estimation of dynamic panel data regression models using the previously elaborated bootstrapped productivity index for each bank by country. As noted in the methodological section, we use a GMM framework in order to cope with possible endogeneity in the model and because it provides efficient and more accurate estimators when analysing cross-country data.

In Table 4, the variable PCR and the lagged values of TFP are treated as endogenous whilst CPI, TRADE, GOV, XRATE and GDP *per capita* are strictly exogenous and used as instruments. We construct three models using the endogenous dependent variable including its lags in model (a), the endogenous lagged dependent variable in model (b), and the endogenous dependent variable model (c).

Table 4 presents the estimation results on the relationship between the dependent variable TFP, the endogenous explanatory variable PCR, and the remaining strictly exogenous control variables. In all cases, the Hansen J-test is accepted and there is no second order autocorrelation, therefore allowing the necessary conditions of the GMM model to be correctly identified.

The findings reported in Table 4 suggest that when statistically significant, the relationship between TFP and PCR is consistently positive. In addition, the coefficient for PCR is typically high, ranging from 3.36 for the second lag in model (a) to 8.99 for PCR_{t-1} in model (b) thus suggesting considerable increases in TFP when PCR increases by 1 percentage point. Overall, we find statistical evidence to suggest that on average greater financial deepening has resulted in increased financial sector performance proxied by banking productivity.

Turning to the control variables, CPI is positive and significant in models (a) and (c), suggesting that on average increased inflation is associated with higher banking sector productivity. This result may reflect higher (expected) interest rates in the face of higher inflation which (given the high interest rate margins in the region) result in relatively higher loan rates for commercial banks,

Table 4. Two-step GMM model with bank productivity as dependent variable.[a,b]

	TFP_t (a)	TFP_t (b)	TFP_t (c)
TFP_{t-1}	−0.174	0.169	0.002
PCR_t	4.734	−5.395	4.21***
PCR_{t-1}	−3.931	8.993***	
PCR_{t-2}	3.362*		
CPI	0.0515***	0.023	0.043***
TRADE	0.412	−1.426	0.292
GOV	−1.137	9.677**	−0.16
XRATE	−0.0004*	0.0002	0.0002
GDP *per capita*	0.0001*	−0.0001	0.00004
Constant	−0.595	0.113	−1.072*
AR(1)	−2.11	−2.03	−2.28
p-Value	(0.035)	(0.042)	(0.022)
AR(2)	−1.22	−0.18	−0.21
p-Value	(0.222)	(0.858)	(0.836)
Hansen *J*-test	22.38	23.63	19.08
p-Value	(0.131)	(0.051)	(0.087)
Observations	989	1376	1376
Year dummies	Yes	Yes	Yes
Country dummies	Yes	Yes	Yes

[a]TFP is the banking productivity; PCR is the measure for financial deepening; CPI is the measure of inflation; TRADE is the degree of openness; GOV is the government expenditure; XRATE is the exchange rate; and the GDP *per capita* is the level of wealth.
[b]The two-step estimates are Windmeijer (2005) corrected.
*Significance at 10% level.
**Significance at 5% level.
***Significance at 1% level.

and thus higher profits and productivity levels. The degree of openness, TRADE, is insignificant in every case. The coefficient for the variable GOV that measures government expenditure over GDP, is significant only in model (b) suggesting a positive relationship between government expenditure and banking productivity. Increased government expenditure may be tied to banking productivity through for example greater borrowing which may be directed to increase the banking sector's reserves. Finally, in model (a) both variables XRATE and GDP are significant, though their coefficients are relatively small.

In order to consider the possibility of reverse causality, we also test a model where PCR is the dependent variable and TFP is the explanatory variable and treated as endogenous. We retain the same set of control variables which are exogenous and used as instruments. We consider three models: model (d) with TFP and its lags as the endogenous dependent variable; model (e) with the lagged TFP as the dependent endogenous variable; and model (f) with TFP as the dependent endogenous variable. Table 5 presents the results of this exercise. As for the results reported in Table 4, the Hansen test is accepted and there is no second order autocorrelation for all models, therefore allowing the necessary conditions of the GMM model to be correctly identified.

The three models (d), (e) and (f) show a positive relationship between TFP and PCR. However, there are no statistically significant results between lagged levels of TFP and PCR. The CPI coefficient is invariably negative and significant implying that increases in the inflation is

Table 5. Two-step GMM model with financial deepening as dependent variable.[a]

	PCR_t (d)	PCR_t (e)	PCR_t (f)
PCR_{t-1}	0.651	0.162	0.483***
TFP_t	0.039***	0.089***	0.078***
TFP_{t-1}	−0.002	0.022	
TFP_{t-2}	0.016		
CPI	−0.002*	−0.004***	−0.003***
TRADE	−0.288***	−0.085	−0.162***
GOV	1.215***	1.01***	0.85***
XRATE	0.00003***	−0.00002**	−0.00002**
GDP *per capita*	0.000009*	−0.000004	−0.00001*
Constant	−0.037	0.047	0.108***
AR(1)	−4.61	−2.05	−6.28
p-Value	(0.00)	(0.040)	(0.000)
AR(2)	0.53	−1.02	−0.62
p-Value	(0.594)	(0.306)	(0.538)
Hansen *J*-test	8.84	4.98	11.38
p-Value	(0.065)	(0.289)	(0.077)
Observations	986	1356	1356
Year dummies	Yes	Yes	Yes
Country dummies	Yes	Yes	Yes

[a] See note to Table 4.
*Significance at 10% level.
**Significance at 5% level.
***Significance at 1% level.

harmful to the level of credit to the private sector in an economy, possibly due to higher interest rates. In terms of openness, there is a negative and significant relationship with financial deepening.

Increased TRADE implies a decreased value in PCR, whereas the variable GOV is positive and significant in all models, thus increased government expenditure seems to be an important factor in stimulating further financial deepening. Results for the variable XRATE are mixed: it is negative and significant in models (e) and (f) showing the volatility effects of the change in the exchange rate; yet it is positive in model (d), thus suggesting that this relationship probably needs further investigation. Finally, GDP *per capita* is positive and significant in model (f) and negative and significant in model (d) however the relative magnitude of the coefficients is rather small. It is worth emphasising the presence of a virtuous circle between financial deepening and bank productivity improvements. For each unitary increase in financial deepening, our index of banking productivity increases by approximately four percentage points as Table 4 reveals. Moreover, a multiplier effect emerges as the productivity improvement further enhances financial deepening by a coefficient of 0.078 (Table 5).

These results in general are supportive of a positive causality link between financial deepening and banking productivity changes. We also uncover evidence of a positive reverse causality between banking productivity changes and financial deepening. Such issues can be of importance not only for countries that have experienced a process of financial liberalization but also for many developing countries where such issues remain unresolved, especially those with highly bank-based systems of financial intermediation.

6. Conclusions

During the 1990s the financial markets in Latin America were gradually liberalized in order to enhance competition. Such measures were focused on triggering further financial deepening which in turn could benefit the economy through greater growth. While the literature focuses on the effects of financial deepening on growth and productivity (King and Levine 1993a), less consideration has been given to its direct microcosmic implications for financial institutions, which in turn may be part of the mechanism through which financial deepening affects economic growth. To the best of our knowledge this is the first study to address the potential link between financial deepening and banking industry productivity.

We consider nine Latin American countries and estimate banking productivity for each of them using the Malmquist TFP index. We then test the effects of financial deepening on banking productivity change using a GMM regression framework. Our results reveal an unambiguously positive and statistically significant relationship, suggesting that financial deepening is an important determinant of banking productivity increases. We also uncover evidence of a reverse causality between the two variables, as a number of plausible channels imply.

The results of this paper present a strong argument towards increasing financial deepening as an important stimulator of greater banking productivity. While the region still exhibits relatively low levels of financial deepening, the latter displays an increasing trend in recent years. An expansion of credit to the private sector may be an important determinant of further banking productivity increases in the future. Moreover, the evidence of reverse causality can suggest the existence of a virtuous circle where promoting financial deepening can create conditions favourable for the productivity improvement of financial institutions, which in turn can further boost financial deepening itself. Therefore, policy oriented measures in the region should take in consideration the positive causality between financial deepening and banking productivity change and try to increase the level of credit to the private sector as a stimulant of economic growth.

Acknowledgements

The authors wish to thank Barbara Casu, John Wilson and Dave McMillan (the Guest Editors), two anonymous referees, Fernando Bizuet Cabrera, Dimitris Chronopoulos, Franco Fiordelisi, Jonathan Williams as well as participants to the Emerging Scholars Conference that was held at Cass Business School, London on 9 December 2009 for useful comments and discussion.

Notes

1. On the positive relationship between financial development and economic growth see, among others, Greenwood and Jovanovic (1990), King and Levine (1993a), Acemoglu and Zilibotti (1997), Levine (1997), Beck, Levine, and Loayza (2000), Levine, Loayza, and Beck (2000).
2. See for example Rioja and Valev (2004) on the benefits of applying a (GMM) dynamic panel data in order to address endogeneity and country-specific effects.
3. We should mention that financial development and financial deepening are not the same thing. Moreover, while financial deepening can be used as a proxy measure of financial development, it is not the only proxy available. Financial development can be measured in a variety of ways, including monetary measures, financial institutions assets to GDP, stock market liquidity, regulation and supervision of banks, etc. There is no comprehensive index of financial development that is universally accepted in the literature. Among the various attempts to create an index of financial development are the one proposed by the World Economic Forum in its annual financial development report, and the index recently proposed by Dorrucci, Meyer-Cirkel, and Santabárbara (2009).
4. The empirical section focuses on credit to the private sector in terms of GDP as a proxy of financial deepening due to data availability (Section 4). Moreover, credit to the private sector in terms of GDP is still very low in Latin America compared with other regions and the aftermath of financial liberalization in the region was expected to increase

this ratio (Aizenman 2005). It is interesting therefore to analyse the relationship of credit to the private sector with transmission mechanisms, in this case bank productivity.

5. See Barro (1997) on an analysis of the main determinants of economic growth. The degree of openness, inflation and trade are used in the depth-growth literature (see King and Levine 1993a, 1993c; Beck, Levine, and Loayza 2000; Arestis, Demetriades, and Fattouh 2003).
6. Originally written in 1911 (*Theorie der wirtschaftlichen Entwicklung*) and translated into English in 1934.
7. Some studies which have found a positive relationship between financial development and economic growth include King and Levine (1993a, 1993b, 1993c), Roubini and Sala-i-Martin (1992), Pagano (1993), Jayaratne and Strahan (1996), Levine (1997, 1998), Arestis and Demetriades (1997), Rajan and Zingales (1998), Lindh (2000), Levine, Loayza and Beck (2000), among others.
8. The choice of specifying the model in the form of a single variable on the input side is due to the well-known dimensionality problem associated with the non-parametric DEA approach (see Smith 1997).
9. See Aizenman (2005) for a discussion about the aftermath of the financial liberalization in Latin America. Particularly, it is explained how the privatization of many sectors of the economy contributed to a reduction of government expenditure.
10. Created by the Swedish statistician Malmquist in 1953, this index was first proposed by Caves, Christensen and Diewert (1982). It has since been further developed by Färe (1988) and Färe, Grosskopf, and Lovell (1994) among others. See also Färe et al. (1996) and Färe, Grosskopf, and Russell (1997); and Ray and Desli (1997). Specifically on the distance functions in a multi-input and multi-output framework see Shephard (1970).
11. DEA is a powerful linear programming technique used in non-parametric frontier analysis. Its main disadvantage is that it is a deterministic method, i.e. it does not provide the statistical properties of its estimates. For a systematic introduction to this methodology see *inter alia* Ray (2004).
12. Levine (2004) explains that the GMM methodology is especially useful when analyzing the finance–growth relationship since it is argued that financial development is intrinsically related to greater economic performance.
13. In order to measure financial deepening, credit to the private sector in terms of GDP was the chosen variable since M2/GDP was not available for every country in each year. Furthermore, it has been widely used in the literature as a measure of financial deepening (see Arestis, Chortareas, and Desli 2006; Levine 2004, among others).
14. Following the Solow growth model, the trade level and government expenditure are explanatory variables of economic growth.
15. The bootstrap confidence intervals at 1%, 5% and 10% are available with the authors upon request.

References

Aizenman, J. 2005. Financial liberalizations in Latin America in the 1990s: a reassesment. *The World Economy* 28, no. 7: 959–83.

Acemoglu, D., and F. Zilibotti. 1997. Was Prometheus unbound by chance? Risk diversification and growth. *Journal of Political Economy* 105, no. 4: 709–51.

Arellano, M. and S. Bond. 1991. Some tests of specification for panel data: Monte Carlo evidence and an application to employment equations. *Review of Economic Studies* 58, no. 2: 277–97.

Arellano, M., and O. Bover. 1995. Another look at the instrumental-variable estimation of error component models. *Journal of Econometrics* 68, no. 1: 29–52.

Arestis, P., G. Chortareas, and E. Desli. 2006. Financial development and productive efficiency in OECD countries: An exploratory analysis. *The Manchester School* 74, no. 4: 417–40.

Arestis, P., and P. Demetriades. 1997. Financial development and economic growth: Assessing the evidence. *The Economic Journal* 107, no. 442: 783–99.

Arestis, P., P. Demetriades, and B. Fattouh. 2003. Financial policies and the aggregate productivity of the capital stock. *Eastern Economic Journal* 29, no. 2: 217–42.

Barro, R. 1997. *Determinants of economic growth: A cross-country empirical study*. Cambridge, MA: The MIT Press.

Beccalli, E., B. Casu, and C. Girardone. 2006. Efficiency and stock performance in European banking. *Journal of Business, Finance, and Accounting* 33, nos. 1–2: 245–62.

Beck, T., and R. Levine. 2002. Industry growth and capital allocation: Does having a market- or bank-based system matter? *Journal of Financial Economics* 58, nos. 1–2: 147–80.

Beck, T., R. Levine, and N. Loayza. 2000. Finance and the sources of growth. *Journal of Financial Economics* 58, nos. 1–2: 261–310.

Bencivenga, V., and B. Smith. 1991. Financial intermediation and endogenous growth. *Review of Economic Studies* 58, no. 2: 195–209.

Benhabib, J., and M. Spiegel. 1994. The role of human capital in economic development: Evidence from aggregate cross-country data. *Journal of Monetary Economics* 34, no. 2: 143–74.

Blundell, R., and S.R. Bond. 1998. Initial conditions and moment restrictions in dynamic panel data models. *Journal of Econometrics* 87, no. 1: 115–43.

Bonfiglioli, A. 2008. Financial integration, productivity and capital accumulation. *Journal of International Economics* 76, no. 2: 337–55.

Boyd, J., and E. Prescott. 1986. Financial intermediary-coalitions. *Journal of Economic Theory* 38, no. 2: 211–32.

Casu, B., C. Girardone, and P. Molyneux. 2004. Productivity change in banking: A comparison of parametric and non-parametric approaches. *Journal of Banking and Finance* 28, no. 10: 2521–40.

Caves, D., L. Christensen, and E. Diewert. 1982. Multilateral comparisons of output, input, and productivity using superlative index numbers. *Economic Journal* 92, no. 365: 73–86.

Diamond, D.W. 1984. Financial intermediation and delegated monitoring. *Review of Economic Studies* 51, no. 3: 393–414.

Dorrucci, E., A. Meyer-Cirkel, and D. Santabárbara. 2009. Domestic financial development in emerging economies: Evidence and implications. Occasional Paper 102, European Central Bank, Frankfurt.

Färe, R. 1988. *Fundamentals of production theory: Lecture notes in economics and mathematical systems.* Heidelberg: Springer-Verlag.

Färe, R., S. Grosskopf, Y. He, and J. Horvath. 1996. Industrial productivity growth in China: 1980-1984 vs. 1984-1985. In *Intertemporal production frontiers: With dynamic*, eds. R. Färe and S. Grosskopf. DEA, 98–116. Boston, MA: Kluwer Academic.

Färe, R., S. Grosskopf, and C. Lovell. 1994. *Production frontiers.* Cambridge: Cambridge University Press.

Färe, R., S. Grosskopf, M. Norris, and Z. Zhang. 1994. Productivity growth, technical progress, and efficiency change in industrialized countries. *American Economic Review* 84, no. 1: 66–83.

Färe, R., S. Grosskopf, and R. Russell. 1997. *Index numbers: Essays in honour of Sten Malmquist.* Boston, MA: Kluwer Academic.

Fisman, R., and I. Love. 2003. Trade Credit, financial intermediary development, and industry growth. *Journal of Finance* 58, no. 1: 353–74.

Goldsmith, R. 1969. *Financial structure and development.* New Haven, CT: Yale University Press.

Greenwood, J., and B. Jovanovic. 1990. Financial development, growth, and the distribution of income. *Journal of Political Economy* 98, no. 5: 1076–107.

Guillaumont Jeanneney, S., P. Hua, and Z. Liang. 2006. Financial development, economic efficiency, and productivity growth: Evidence from China. *The Developing Economies* 44, no. 1: 27–52.

Hartmann, P., F. Heider, E. Papaioannou, and M.L. Duca. 2007. The role of financial markets and innovation in productivity and growth in Europe. ECB Occasional Paper Series 72, European Central Bank, Bonn, Germany.

Herrero, A., J. Santillan, S. Gallego, L. Cuadro, and C. Egea. 2002. Latin American financial development in perspective. *Banco de Espana*, Document 0216.

Hsieh, C., and P. Klenow. 2007. Misallocation and manufacturing TFP in China and India. NBER Working Paper 13290, National Bureau of Economic Research, Cambridge, USA.

Jayaratne, J., and P. Strahan. 1996. The finance–growth nexus: Evidence from bank branch deregulation. *Quarterly Journal of Economics* 111, no. 3: 639–70.

Jorgenson, D.W. 2005. Accounting for growth in the information age. In *Handbook of economic growth*, chap. 10, ed. P. Aghion and S. Durlauf, 743–815. Amsterdam: North Holland Elsevier Publishers.

King, R., and R. Levine. 1993a. Finance and growth: Schumpeter might be right. *Quarterly Journal of Economics* 108, no. 3: 717–37.

King, R., and R. Levine. 1993b. Financial intermediation and economic development. In *Financial intermediation in the construction of Europe*, eds. C. Mayer and X. Vives, 156–89. London: CEPR.

King, R., and R. Levine. 1993c. Finance, entrepreneurship and growth: Theory and evidence. *Journal of Monetary Economics* 32, no. 3: 717–37.

Levine, R. 1997. Financial development and economic growth: View and agenda. *Journal of Economic Literature* 35, no. 2: 688–726.

Levine, R. 1998. The legal environment, banks, and long-run economic growth. *Journal of Money, Credit and Banking* 30, no. 3: 596–613.

Levine, R. 2004. Finance and growth: Theory and evidence. NBER Working Paper Series 10766, National Bureau of Economic Research, Cambridge, MA.

Levine, R., N. Loayza, and T. Beck. 2000. Financial intermediation and growth: Causality and causes. *Journal of Monetary Economics* 46, no. 1: 31–77.

Lindh, T. 2000. Short-run costs of financial market development in industrialized economies. *Eastern Economic Journal* 26, no. 2: 221–39.
Lozano-Vivas, A. and J.T. Pastor. 2006. Banking and economic activity performance: An empirical study at the country level. *The Manchester School* 74, no. 4: 469–82.
Malmquist, S. 1953. Index numbers and indifference surfaces. *Trabajos de Estatistica* 4, no. 1: 209–42.
McKinnon, R. 1973. *Money and capital in economic development.* Washington, DC: Brookings Institution.
Merton, R.C. and Z. Bodie. 1995. A conceptual framework for analyzing the financial environment. In *The global financial system: A functional perspective*, chap. 1, ed. D.B. Crane, K.A. Froot, S.P. Mason, A. Perold, R.C. Merton, Z. Bodie, E.R. Sirri, and P. Tufano, 3–31. Boston: Harvard Business School Press.
Pagano, M. 1993. Financial markets and growth: An overview. *European Economic Review* 32, nos. 2–3: 613–22.
Rajan, R., and L. Zingales. 1998. Financial dependence and growth. *American Economic Review* 88, no. 3: 559–86.
Ray, S.C. 2004. *Data envelopment analysis: Theory and techniques for economics and operations research.* Cambridge: Cambridge University Press.
Ray, S.C., and E. Desli. 1997. Productivity growth, technical progress, and efficiency change in industrialised countries: Comment. *The American Economic Review* 87, no. 5: 1033–39.
Restuccia, D., and R. Rogerson. 2007. Policy distortions and aggregate productivity with heterogenous plants. NBER Working Papers 13018, National Bureau of Economic Research, Cambridge, USA.
Rioja, F., and N. Valev. 2004. Finance and the sources of growth at various stages of economic development. *Economic Enquiry* 42, no. 1: 127–40.
Roubini, R., and X. Sala-i-Martin. 1992. Financial repression and economic growth. *Journal of Development Economics* 29, no. 1: 5–30.
Schumpeter, J. 1934. *The theory of economic development: An inquiry into profits, capital, credit, interest, and the business cycle.* Cambridge, MA: Harvard University Press.
Sealey, C., and J. Lindley. 1977. Inputs, outputs and a theory of production and cost at depositary financial institutions. *The Journal of Finance* 32, no. 4: 1251–66.
Shaw, E. 1973. *Financial deepening in economic development.* New York: Oxford University Press.
Shephard, R.W. 1970. *Theory of cost and production functions.* Princeton: Princeton University Press.
Simar, L., and P.W. Wilson. 1998. Sensitivity analysis of efficiency scores: How to bootstrap in nonparametric frontier models. *Management Science* 44, no. 1: 49–61.
Simar, L., and P.W. Wilson. 1999. Estimating and bootstrapping Malmquist indices. *European Journal of Operational Research* 115, no. 3: 459–71.
Simar, L., and P.W. Wilson. 2000. Statistical inference in nonparametric frontier models: The state of the art. *Journal of Productivity Analysis* 13, no. 1: 49–78.
Smith, P. 1997. Model misspecification in data envelopment analysis. *Annals of Operations Research* 72, no. 1: 233–52.
Stiglitz, J.E., and B. Greenwald. 2003. *Towards a new paradigm in monetary economics.* Cambridge: Cambridge University Press.
Svaleryd, H., and J. Vlachos. 2002. Markets for risk and openness to trade: How are they related? *Journal of International Economics* 57, no. 2: 369–95.
Tortosa-Ausina, E., E. Grifell-Tatje, C. Armero, and D. Conesa. 2008. Sensitivity analysis of efficiency and Malmquist productivity indices: An application to Spanish savings banks. *European Journal of Operational Research* 184, no. 3: 1062–84.
Wilson, P.W. 2006. FEAR: *A software package for frontier efficiency analysis with R.* Department of Economics, Clemson University, Clemson, SC.
Windmeijer, F. 2005. A finite sample correction for the variance of linear efficient two-step GMM estimators. *Journal of Econometrics* 126, no. 1: 25–51.

Appendix. The Malmquist productivity index and the bootstrapping process.

The Malmquist productivity index measures TFP change between two data points by calculating the ratio of the distances of each data point relative to a common technology. The methodology is relatively standard and implies the identification of distance functions for a generic firm with respect to two different time periods t and $t+1$ (Shephard 1970; Färe et al. 1994). The Malmquist (output oriented) TFP index can be written as follows:

$$M_{t,t+1}(y^t, y^{t+1}, x^t, x^{t+1}) = \left[\frac{D^{t+1}(y^{t+1}, x^{t+1})}{D^t(y^t, x^t)} \times \frac{D^t(y^{t+1}, x^{t+1})}{D^{t+1}(y^{t+1}, x^{t+1})}\right]^{1/2}, \tag{A1}$$

where M is the Malmquist productivity index, D is the distance function made up of a vector of inputs (x) and a vector of outputs (y). A value of $M > 1$ implies productivity growth, a value of $M = 1$ means no change in productivity and $M < 1$ is a decline in productivity.

The bootstrapping process for the Malmquist is based on the fact that the index is a function of distance estimators. Tortosa-Ausina et al. (2008) provide a summary of the bootstrap procedure that essentially involves four main steps: (1) compute the Malmquist indexes for each decision-making unit (DMU) by using linear programming models to estimate the distance functions; (2) compute a pseudo data set to form the reference bootstrap technology as proposed in Simar and Wilson (1999); compute the bootstrap estimate of the Malmquist for each DMU by applying the original estimators to the pseudo sample obtained in step 2; (3) repeat steps 2–3 1000 times in order to provide a set of estimates. For the purposes of the empirical analysis carried out in this study, we use Wilson's (2006) FEAR 1.1 that is a software package for computing non-parametric estimates and calculate confidence intervals using the bootstrap framework.

Islamic mutual funds' financial performance and international investment style: evidence from 20 countries

Andreas G.F. Hoepner[a,b], Hussain G. Rammal[c] and Michael Rezec[a]

[a]*School of Management, University of St Andrews, The Gateway, North Haugh, St Andrews, KY16 9SS, UK;* [b]*Principles for Responsible Investment, PRI Secretariat, c/o UN Global Compact, DC2-612, United Nations, New York, NY 10017, USA;* [c]*International Graduate School of Business, University of South Australia, GPO Box 2471, Adelaide, SA 5001, Australia*

We pursue the first large-scale investigation of a strongly growing mutual fund type: Islamic funds. Based on an unexplored, survivorship bias-adjusted data set, we analyse the financial performance and investment style of 265 Islamic equity funds from 20 countries. As Islamic funds often have diverse investment regions, we develop a (conditional) three-level Carhart model to simultaneously control for exposure to different national, regional and global equity markets and investment styles. Consistent with recent evidence for conventional funds, we find Islamic funds to display superior learning in more developed Islamic financial markets. While Islamic funds from these markets are competitive to international equity benchmarks, funds from especially Western nations with less Islamic assets tend to significantly underperform. Islamic funds' investment style is somewhat tilted towards growth stocks. Funds from predominantly Muslim economies also show a clear small cap preference. These results are consistent over time and robust to time varying market exposures and capital market restrictions.

1. Introduction

An important contemporary issue for financial institutions and financial markets are Islamic financial services, which are rapidly growing worldwide. In 2007, Islamic law (Shari'ah) compliant assets are estimated to have grown by 37% to $729bn.[1] They are expected to reach the $1 trillion mark in 2010. While many assets are based in countries such as Saudi Arabia, Malaysia or Kuwait, Western financial institutions and governments have also developed a strong interest in Islamic finance (Cihák and Hesse 2010; McKenzie 2009). The British government praises the UK as 'the leading centre for Islamic finance outside of the Gulf Cooperative Council (GCC) and Malaysia' and has defined clear policy objectives for its development (HM Treasury 2008, 5). The UK is the world leader for Islamic finance education. Islamic financial services are offered in Britain by nearly two dozen banks including Barclays, HSBC, Lloyds and RBS. The market leader, HSBC's Islamic finance division Amanah, has realized an annual asset growth of more than 50% in 2007/2008. As Shari'ah law prohibits many high-risk activities, Islamic financial services have been much less affected by the credit crisis than their conventional counterparts, which adds to their appeal. Western countries such as the USA, France, Germany or Switzerland are also promoting their Islamic financial services to attract especially petro-dollars (McKenzie 2009).

One multibillion-dollar industry within Islamic finance is Islamic investment. Dow Jones, FTSE, MSCI Barra and Standard & Poor's offer hundreds of Islamic equity indices. Similarly, more than 700 Islamic mutual funds are currently offered, which specialize in a variety of different assets (e.g. equities, Islamic bonds, real estate, commodities). The few previous studies of their financial performance investigate samples of less than 60 funds and also lack nearly any control for investment style. In this study, we utilize the largest existing data set of Islamic funds (which is unexplored to date) to analyse 265 Islamic equity funds from 20 countries over a 20-year sample period. Specifically, we investigate the following research questions.

(1) Does the financial performance of Islamic equity mutual funds significantly differ from the respective equity market benchmark(s)?
(2) Which investment styles are preferred by Islamic equity mutual funds?
(3) If national differences exist in Islamic equity funds' financial performance and investment style, how can these be explained?

Based on a standard Carhart model, we find more than half of our equal weighted national Islamic equity fund portfolios to significantly underperform their national equity market benchmarks. At the national level, Islamic funds display a tilt towards growth and small cap stocks. However, Islamic mutual funds from the same country tend to invest in a variety of different international regions. Hence, we cannot sufficiently assess their financial performance and investment style without controlling for their exposure to regional and global equity market benchmarks and investment styles. To control for these regional and global factors, we also develop a three-level Carhart model, which uses 12 factors to control for equity market and investment style exposure at three levels: (i) in a nation, (ii) in all other nations of a region (iii) and in all other regions of the world.

This more sophisticated three-level Carhart factor model leads to considerably different results. We find only two-fifths of our national Islamic equity fund portfolios to significantly underperform international equity benchmarks, while a quarter of them significantly outperforms. Islamic funds' preference for growth stocks weakens in the 12-factor model and only funds from predominantly Muslim economies are still tilted towards small cap stocks. These results are consistent over time and robust to time varying market exposures and capital market restrictions.

Interestingly, clear systematic national differences appear in our results. We find Islamic funds from the six largest Islamic financial centres in our study (the GCC countries and Malaysia) to perform competitive to international equity market benchmarks. Two of these nations' Islamic fund portfolios even significantly outperform. In contrast, Islamic fund portfolios from most other nations with often barely developed Islamic financial services significantly underperform their benchmarks. This result can be explained with learning effects resulting from the development of markets, which have also been found for conventional mutual funds (Christoffersen and Sarkissian 2009).

The nations with lesser developed Islamic financial services can further be structured into two groups. While the fund portfolio from only one of the predominantly Muslim countries among these nations significantly trails its benchmarks, Islamic funds from seven Western nations underperform on average. This implies that incorporation in an Islamic economy benefits Islamic funds' financial performance. As funds from Islamic economies tend to have a home bias, a possible reason for this relevance of home country religion might be that the financial value of a stock's Shari'ah compliance is positively related to the influence of Shari'ah law on consumers in its home economy. We find support for this explanation in our observation that Islamic funds from those Islamic economies perform best, whose dominant Islamic school of thought most literally follows the letters of Qur'an.

The home bias of funds from Islamic economies with often comparatively small corporations can also explain why these funds exhibit a small cap preference at the regional and global level in contrast to the remaining funds. Their small cap investment style at the national level might result from larger corporations being usually more diversified, which increases the risk that they operate in sectors forbidden by Shari'ah law.

We structure our text as follows. Section 2 provides a brief background on Islamic mutual funds. Section 3 describes our Islamic fund and benchmark data. Section 4 presents the methods and discusses the results of our main analyses. Section 5 covers our robustness test, before Section 6 concludes.

2. Background

The background section starts with a brief discussion of relevant characteristics of Islamic mutual funds. Subsequently, we discuss Islamic funds' financial performance and investment style from a theoretical and from an empirical perspective.

2.1 *Islamic mutual funds*

Islamic funds are defined by their compliance with Islamic law, commonly known as Shari'ah law. '[W]hile Islam promotes improving ones economics condition, it has to be done within a framework of good values and good economic/business practices' (Ebrahim 2008, 118). Inter alia, Shari'ah law prohibits mutual funds from *Riba al Nasiah*, *Maysir*, *Gharar* and *Haram* products or services and it requires *Haram purifcation*.

Riba al Nasiah represents the receipt of interest on capital. Hence, Islamic mutual funds cannot invest in conventional bonds, warrants, preferred stock, certificates of deposit and some derivatives. *Maysir* and *Gharar* can be translated as gambling and uncertainty, respectively. Their prohibition commonly prevents Islamic funds from leverage, short selling and any derivate product. In addition to *Riba al Nasiah*, *Maysir* and *Gharar*, products or services that adversely affect dignity or promote the exploitation of one another are *Haram* (*forbidden*). Examples are pork, (non-medical) alcohol, gambling, non-Islamic financial services, pornography, tobacco or weapons. Given the sheer size of contemporaneous multinational companies, many of them receive (very) small proportions of their revenue from a prohibited activity. Contemporary Shari'ah scholars therefore tend to allow investment in stocks with tolerable proportions of revenues from prohibited activities under the condition of *Haram purifcation*.[2] This condition requires investors to donate the equivalent proportion of their distributions from such companies to charities to purify their earnings from prohibited activities (Derigs and Marzban 2008; Ebrahim and Rahman 2005; El-Gamal 2006; Jaffer 2004; Rahail 2008).

2.2 *Theoretical perspectives on Islamic funds' financial performance and investment style*

Several theoretical implications result from Shari'ah law and characteristics of Islamic funds. First, Islamic mutual fund managers are restricted in their ability to exploit superior information or winning markets (e.g. using leverage). However, the average mutual fund manager has not been found to display superior skills (Bollen and Busse 2001; Kosowski et al. 2006). Hence, the opposite argument might also apply that Shari'ah law limits the potential damage caused by a manager (Abdullah, Hassan, and Mohamad 2007).

Second, like socially responsible investment, Shari'ah compliant investment refuses to purely pursue profits. Some argue that such a distraction by concerns about responsibility would be detrimental for financial performance (e.g. Geczy, Stambaugh, and Levin 2005). They are supported by evidence suggesting standard sin stocks (alcohol, gambling, tobacco) excluded by Islamic funds to deliver significantly positive abnormal returns (Hong and Kacperczyk 2009). However, others consider responsible, non-financial investment criteria to represent advanced risk management (e.g. Lee and Faff 2009). Evidence to support this argument comes from the cases of Enron, Tyco and Worldcom. Before their scandals, these companies were excluded from the Dow Jones Islamic Market (DJIM) Index (Ghoul and Karam 2007).

Third, the Shari'ah compliance of products and services is likely financially more beneficial in economies, whose customers and agents experience a higher utility from adherence to Shari'ah law. Hence, Islamic mutual funds might experience a better financial performance in predominantly Muslim economies than elsewhere. Fourth, Christoffersen and Sarkissian (2009) find financial centres with a high density of financial intermediaries and competitors to have a significantly positive effect on mutual fund managers' learning gains and their eventual financial performance. They explain the performance relevance of being located in a financial centre with better information and knowledge spillover effects. If such learning processes also drive Islamic funds' financial performance, we expect funds from nations with the most developed Islamic financial markets to perform better than their peers elsewhere.

Fifth, Islamic mutual funds' investment styles are probably more homogeneous than their conventional counterparts' styles due to Shari'ah law's narrow framework of eligible activities. Islamic funds could have somewhat lower betas than conventional, possibly leveraged funds. Islamic funds also likely invest over-proportionally in smaller stocks, as large stocks have a higher risk of receiving intolerable revenues from prohibited activities. Similarly, we expect Islamic funds to be more exposed to growth stocks than value stocks, as the former are considered to have a lower leverage than the latter (Campbell and Vuolteenaho 2004). However, we cannot see any theoretical reason why Islamic funds should be more exposed to momentum than contrarian investment strategies or vice versa.

2.3 *Empirical indications on Islamic funds' financial performance and investment style*

Empirical evidence on Islamic funds is scarce with extant studies analysing the financial performance of less than 60 funds (Abderrezak 2008; Abdullah, Hassan, and Mohamad 2007; Elfakhani, Hassan, and Sidani 2005; Kraeussl and Hayat 2008). The longest investigation to date has been undertaken by Abdullah, Hassan, and Mohamad (2007). They estimated the Jensen (1968) alpha of a portfolio of 14 Malaysian Islamic funds over the period 1992–2001 and found these to significantly underperform the market benchmark. Three other studies investigate samples of less than 6 years and face challenges in their fund or benchmark data:

Kraeussl and Hayat (2008) estimate Jensen alphas for 59 international Islamic equity funds identified via Bloomberg over the 5-year period to August 2006. They found their 31 Malaysian funds to significantly underperform the respective equity market benchmark, while 21 globally investing funds had an insignificant performance difference and 7 'other' funds even significantly outperformed their market benchmark. However, their results have to be interpreted with some care, as they had to replace missing net asset values by the average of the previous and subsequent observation.

Elfakhani, Hassan, and Sidani (2005) investigate 46 international Islamic funds identified by Falaika or Standard & Poors (S&P) over a 68-month sample to August 2002. As they regressed their international Islamic funds on the S&P 500, their results are mainly meaningful for their portfolio of seven North American funds, whose alpha is insignificant. Using sensibly matched equity market benchmarks, Abderezzak (2008) re-investigated the sample of Elfakhani, Hassan, and Sidani (2005) and found only Asian domestic funds to significantly underperform.

Contrary to the other studies, Abderezzak (2008) investigated Islamic funds' investment styles in addition to their financial performance for a sub-sample of 19 US, European or global funds. But as his data access was limited to two US investment style benchmarks, his results were only fully sensible for his six US funds. Four of these six funds display the expected small cap style, while the six funds have no clear preference for a value or growth style.

In summary, previous studies provide some indication that a few Islamic mutual funds might trail their conventional benchmarks and display a preference for small cap stocks. However, the financial performance and investment style of hundreds of Islamic mutual funds is unexplored to date.[3] Consequently, we consider our analysis of 265 funds from 20 countries to be the first large-scale investigation of Islamic equity mutual funds' financial performance and investment style.

3. Data

Data are the main shortage in analyses of Islamic mutual funds. Previous studies lacked time-series data on both hundreds of Islamic mutual funds and international investment style benchmarks. We address both shortages. In the first part of this section, we analyse the descriptive statistics of our sample of 265 Islamic equity funds from 20 countries. Since the characteristics of these 20 countries could explain differences in Islamic funds' financial performance and investment style, we analyse our sample countries' financial market and Islam related properties in the second part. The third part describes our international investment style benchmarks.

3.1 *Islamic mutual fund data*

As of May 2009, we have access to by far the largest, worldwide database of Islamic mutual funds: Eurekahedge. It currently lists 758 Islamic mutual funds (alive or dead), which more than doubles the funds listed on Falaika, the only other provider of return data on hundreds of Islamic funds. Of these, 455 funds are equity funds.[4] Of these equity funds, Eurekahedge reports monthly return data for 304. However, in a few dozen cases, Eurekahedge lists several asset classes of the same mutual fund. In these cases, we follow Da, Gao, and Jagannathan (2009) and calculate an equal-weighted average of these fund classes' simple returns. This leaves us with a survivorship bias-adjusted sample of 265 Islamic equity mutual funds, whose monthly return data we convert in US$. Our sample starts with the launch of the first Islamic mutual fund in September 1990 and ends in April 2009. As Islamic mutual funds are spread over all continents except Latin America, our sample has a wide geographic distribution. It includes funds from the following five regions and 20 countries: (i) Africa: Egypt, Morocco, South Africa; (ii) Asia-Pacific: Australia, Indonesia, Malaysia, Pakistan, Singapore; (iii) Europe: Germany, Ireland, Liechtenstein, Luxembourg, UK (including British Virgin, Cayman and Channel Islands); (iv) GCC: Bahrain, Kuwait, Qatar, Saudi Arabia, UAE; (v) North America: Canada, USA.

Based on Eurekahedge's simple return data, we construct equal-weighted fund of fund portfolios for each nation.[5] This leads to 20 national portfolios, whose continuously compounded monthly returns are computed subsequently. Eurekahedge's simple return data are supplied net of annual management fees but they unfortunately exclude distributions. This is a considerable problem, as estimating mutual funds' financial performance using return data excluding distributions against common market benchmarks, whose return data includes distributions, would lead to significantly downwards biased financial performance estimates. Hence, our investigation of our first research question, if the financial performance of Islamic equity mutual funds significantly differs from the respective equity market benchmark(s), lacks considerable reliability unless we can sufficiently address this problem. Unfortunately though, Islamic mutual fund data are generally exposed to this problem, as the return data offered by Eurekhedge's only competitor, Falaika, do not consider distributions either (Abderrezak 2008). Thus, this limitation cannot be overcome, as any current analysis of hundreds of Islamic mutual funds is inevitably exposed to it. However, we can mitigate the effect of this limitation and investigate the remaining loss of information value.

We mitigate the effect of this limitation by using benchmark return data exclusive of dividends, which ensures that our estimated Islamic fund performance is not systematically downwards biased. We investigate any possibly remaining systematic loss of information value by estimating the financial performance of Islamic funds with our main regression model presented in Equation (3) based on fund and benchmark return data (i) exclusive and (ii) inclusive of distributions. For four British, four Luxembourgian and five US Islamic funds with Eurekahedge plain return data, we can retrieve fund prices net of annual management fees and inclusive of distributions from Datastream.

Based on these funds, we calculate equal-weighted returns of a British, Luxembourgian and US national fund portfolio excluding and including distributions. Based on return data exclusive of distributions, our financial performance estimates of the British, Luxembourgian and US Islamic fund portfolio are −0.0134 (1% significant), −0.0034 (5% significant) and −0.0055 (1% significant), respectively. Based on return data inclusive of distributions, the financial performance estimates of our British, Luxembourgian and US Islamic fund portfolio are −0.0161 (1% significant), −0.0090 (5% significant) and −0.0133 (1% significant), respectively. As the financial performance estimates' size differs between the estimation exclusive and inclusive of distributions, we recommend care in the interpretation of the size of our financial performance estimates based on Eurekahedge's data. Most importantly, however, we find the significance level of our financial performance estimates to be unaffected by the current impossibility to access return data inclusive of distributions for hundreds of Islamic funds.

In summary, while information value is lost due to the fact that Eurekahedge's return data do not include distributions with regard to the precise size of financial performance estimates, no meaningful information value appears lost regarding the significance level of financial performance estimates. Thus, we consider an investigation of our first research question, if the financial performance of Islamic equity mutual funds *significantly* differs from the respective equity market benchmark(s), based on Eurekahedge's return data to be reliable.

Descriptive statistics for our Islamic mutual fund portfolios are shown in Table 1. Over 90% of our funds are domiciled in the Asia-Pacific (42.6%), GCC (34.0%) or European (17.0%) regions. Each region is dominated by a particular country (Malaysia, Saudi Arabia, UK). The UK with its overseas territories hosts the third highest percentage of our sample funds (about 9%), which highlights its relevance in the market for Islamic mutual funds. Most countries have relatively low mean and lower median funds ages, which reflects the youth of the industry.[6] Large funds of hundreds of millions of US$ exist to date only in Saudi Arabia, Malaysia and the USA.

Table 1. Descriptive statistics of Islamic mutual fund sample.

Country/ region	Total no. of funds	Dead funds	Mean age	Median age	Min age	Max age	Mean size in $ Million	Median size in $ Million	Min size in $ Million	Max size in $ Million	Investment region in %: Asia Pacific	Emerging	Europe	Global	GCC/ Africa	North America
Africa	10	1	6.9	3.5	0.8	18.4	35.17	36.0	1.0	75.0					100	
Egypt	5	0	2.6	2.6	0.8	4.4	36.00	36.0	35.0	37.0					100	
Morocco	1	1	12.3	12.3	12.3	12.3	40.00	40.0	40.0	40.0					100	
South Africa	4	0	6.0	3.5	1.8	15.3	29.50	21.0	1.0	75.0					100	
Asia-Pacific	113	8	4.2	3.6	0.5	16.2	18.11	10.0	2.0	421.0	90	1		9		
Indonesia	21	3	2.9	2.0	0.5	9.0	10.38	11.0	3.0	25.0	100					
Singapore	7	1	5.9	5.0	1.5	13.6	13.60	6.0	4.0	39.0	43			57		
Malaysia	76	4	4.7	4.2	0.8	16.2	45.13	15.0	2.0	421.0	91	1		8		
Pakistan	8	0	3.8	3.6	1.8	6.3	17.43	10.0	4.0	45.0	100					
Australia	1	0	3.5	3.5	3.5	3.5	4.00	4.0	4.0	4.0	100					
Europe	45	13	3.9	2.9	0.8	11.5	15.08	12.4	1.0	80.0	15	2	9	47	16	11
Luxembourg	7	2	6.4	5.8	1.6	11.5	20.00	21.0	10.0	28.0		14		86		
Germany	4	0	6.3	6.3	6.3	6.3	n/a	n/a	n/a	n/a	25		25	25		25
Ireland	9	1	3.1	2.5	1.4	8.5	14.30	4.3	3.0	80.0	44		12	44		
Liechtenstein	1	1	2.0	2.0	2.0	2.0	2.00	2.0	2.0	2.0			100			
UK	24	9	4.6	2.9	0.8	11.3	24.00	20.5	2.0	68.0	8		4	42	29	17
GCC	90	2	3.7	3.6	0.9	16.8	51.37	24.0	1.0	2453.0	6	3	3	21	63	3
Bahrain	8	2	4.0	4.0	1.8	7.8	16.50	5.0	1.0	77.0			13	25	50	12
Kuwait	20	0	4.1	3.6	1.7	8.6	45.50	24.0	8.0	142.0	5			10	80	5
Saudi Arabia	58	0	6.0	4.5	0.9	16.8	135.60	24.0	1.0	2453.0	7	5	3	26	57	2
UAE	2	0	2.6	2.6	0.9	4.3	33.50	33.5	29.0	38.0					100	
Qatar	2	0	1.8	1.8	1.2	2.4	25.75	25.75	7.5	44.0					100	
North America	7	0	8.3	7.5	0.8	19.3	789.50	789.5	623.0	956.0						100
USA	6	0	10.2	8.6	0.8	19.3	789.50	789.5	623.0	956.0						100
Canada	1	0	6.4	6.4	6.4	6.4	n/a	n/a	n/a	n/a						100

Notes: This table reports national and regional descriptive statistics for all Islamic Fund portfolios in our sample. The first two columns show the total number of funds and the dead funds included in it. The next four columns display the mean, median, minimum and maximum age of our sample funds in the respective nation or region. The following four columns provide the equivalent information for fund size. In case Eurekahedge does not report the size for any fund in a portfolio, we report n/a. Otherwise, we report the descriptive statistics based on the number of funds, for which Eurekahedge reports size data. The last six columns report the geographical investment focus of the national and regional portfolios based on Eurekahedge's six categories.

The average Islamic equity fund prefers to invest globally, in the Asia-Pacific region or in the GCC countries. However, Islamic funds from the same nation tend to invest in a variety of different regions. For instance, most funds from Saudi Arabia invest in the GCC countries or globally, but some focus their investment on the Asia-Pacific region, on Europe or on North America. British, German and Irish Islamic funds have especially diverse geographic investment foci. A substantial part of them focuses its investment on the Asia-Pacific region or the Middle East. This diversity in geographic investment focus implies that assessing Islamic funds' financial performance only with national, regional or global benchmarks does not fully capture their equity market exposure.

Approximately 9% of our sample funds have died. This is somewhat below the annual attrition rates found for conventional mutual funds and might reflect the strong recent growth in Islamic financial services (Carhart et al. 2002). However, attrition rates vary considerably between our sample countries. While attrition rates in most nations are very low, a quarter of our sample countries including the UK have attrition rates of over 20%, which likely has a negative effect on the financial performance of these nations' Islamic fund portfolios.

3.2 *Sample country characteristics*

Since national differences in Islamic funds' financial performance and investment style might result from national characteristics, Table 2 provides an overview on our sample countries' relation to Islam and their financial markets. The population of half of our sample countries is predominantly Muslim. All of these countries but Indonesia incorporate Islam in their constitution. However, differences exist in the predominant school of Islamic thought. For instance, Saudi Arabia and Qatar follow the Hanbali school with its literal interpretations of Quran, while Pakistan is dominated by the liberal Hanafi school. Islamic financial markets with assets worth more than $10bn exist in seven sample countries. The largest six of these financial markets are all located in the Islamic world (Bahrain, Kuwait, Malaysia, Saudi-Arabia, UAE and Qatar). The seventh largest Islamic financial market is the UK. Interestingly, the UK is the only predominantly Christian country in this group and also represents the only developed Islamic financial market with Islamic fund attrition rates over 20%. This observation suggests that Islamic investment services might develop smoother in Muslim economies.

Assets in predominantly Islamic economies are often, but not necessarily, more likely Shari'ah compliant. While the vast majority of Muslim economies hosts Shari'ah compliant assets over-proportionally, Morocco's and the UAE's financial markets comprise a slightly under-proportional degree of them. Similarly, many Christian economies' assets are clearly under-proportional Shari'ah compliant, whereas Canada and South Africa host compliant assets over-proportionally.

Table 2 also displays relevant financial market restrictions, which limit inbound or outbound investment during our sample period. Outbound restrictions limit the ability of a mutual fund to invest abroad and directly affect its international investment style and likely also financial performance. Inbound restrictions limit foreigners to invest in the respective nation. They indirectly affect the investment style and financial performance of the nation's mutual funds, as they often substantially restrict the demand of national assets. Hence, Islamic funds from economies with inbound restrictions tend to operate in less competitive but also less liquid national stock markets. Malaysia, Morocco and South Africa are the only countries in our sample to impose outbound restrictions. In contrast, inbound restrictions are more common. They have been or are in place in all GCC countries, Egypt, Indonesia, Malaysia, Pakistan and Singapore.

Table 2. Overview on sample countries' relevant characteristics.

Country/ region	% of Muslims in population	Islamic School of Thought	Islamic assets (in $bn)	Index of Shari'ah compliance of listed stocks (DJIM based)	Relevant financial market restrictions
Africa					
Egypt	90%	Hanafi/ Shafi	5.7	0.33	The Capital Market Law 95 of June 1992 and the Banking Law of June 2003 grant foreigners full access to capital markets. However, under Egyptian laws and regulations companies can adopt by-laws limiting or prohibiting foreign ownership of shares
Morocco	98.7%	Maliki	<5	−0.03	The Casablanca Stock Exchange places no restrictions on foreign participation. In contrast, the market is buoyed by strict restrictions on the ability of Moroccan individuals and institutions to invest abroad
South Africa	1.5%	n/a	<5	0.37	South African investment funds can invest 25% of their retail assets in other countries
Asia-Pacific					
Indonesia	86.1%	Shafi	<5	0.41	In September 1997, the Government of Indonesia removed the 49% limit on foreign ownership of companies' shares listed on the Jakarta and Surabaya Stock Exchanges
Singapore	14.9%	n/a	<5	−0.32	In January 2002, Singapore removed all trading restrictions on foreign-owned stockbrokers.
Malaysia	60.4%	Shafi	65.7	0.11	As reaction to the Asian financial crisis, Malaysia imposed strict controls on the repatriation of foreign portfolio capital in September 1998. These controls were eased in subsequent years and fully removed in May 2001. Similarly in September 1998, the Malaysian government required all foreign holdings of Malaysian Ringgit to be repatriated, virtually prohibited offshore Ringgit transactions and imposed tight controls on foreign investments. In December 2002, Malaysia abolished the foreign currency limit on its residents' foreign investments. In April 2005, Malaysian mutual funds were allowed to invest abroad 100% of their net asset value (NAV) attributable to foreigners and 30% of their NAV attributable to residents. Since March 2007, mutual funds are allowed to invest up to 50% of their NAV attributable to residents
Pakistan	95%	Hanafi	6.3	n/a	Since 1991, the Government of Pakistan commenced the process of privatization of previously nationalized financial institutions and actively seeks foreign investment in the Karachi Stock Exchange
Australia	1.7%	n/a	<5	0.12	
Europe					
Luxembourg	1.1%	n/a	<5	n/a	
Germany	3.7%	n/a	<5	−0.52	

(Continued)

Table 2. Continued.

Country/ region	% of Muslims in population	Islamic School of Thought	Islamic assets (in $bn)	Index of Shari'ah compliance of listed stocks (DJIM based)	Relevant financial market restrictions
Ireland	0.01%	n/a	<5	−1.88	
Liechtenstein	3.4%	n/a	<5	n/a	
UK	2.7%	n/a	18.1	−0.005	
GCC					
Bahrain	81.2%	Maliki	37.1	0.89	The Bahrain Stock Exchange (BSE) allows persons from the GCC to own up to 100% of listed Bahraini companies. Non GCC firms/persons may own up to 49% of listed Bahraini companies and 100% of foreign companies
Kuwait	85%	Maliki	54.0	0.45	Since September 2000, Kuwait allows foreigners to invest in the Kuwait Stock Exchange
Saudi Arabia	100%	Hanbali	91.2	n/a	The trading of shares in the Saudi Stock Exchange (SSE) is limited to the nationals of Saudi Arabia and people belonging to the GCC. Since November 1997, foreign investors can enter the Saudi stock market through mutual funds offered by (specific) Saudi banks
UAE	96%	Hanbali/Maliki	48.2	−0.21	Foreign investors may hold up to a 49% interest in limited liability companies, although company by-laws in many cases prohibit foreign ownership
Qatar	77.5%	Hanbali	19.3	0.20	Qatar's regulations allow foreigners to invest in all Qatar Exchange listed companies unless this would lead the foreign ownership of a company to exceed 25%
North America					
USA	0.6%	n/a	<5	0.25	
Canada	1.9%	n/a	<5	0.31	

Notes: This table provides an overview on sample country characteristics potentially relevant to Islamic funds' financial performance and investment style. The first column displays our sample countries sorted by region. Countries, whose constitution incorporates Islam, are displayed in italics. Columns two and three state a nation's percentage of Islamic citizens and their dominant Islamic school of thought (Hanafi, Hanbali, Maliki, Shafi), respectively. Hanafi has the most followers. It emphasizes the reason and is considered the most liberal of the four schools of thoughts. Contrarily, Hanbali is considered to be the most literal of the four schools, since it closely follows the letters of Quran to ensure consistency in its interpretations. Maliki has the third most followers. It is predominantly guided by the practices of the people of Madinah at the time of the Prophet Muhammad, as they are thought to be closest to the Prophet. Shafi is the second most followed school of thought and considered to have the most systematic methodology. Followers of all four schools of thought are Sunni Muslims. Shia Muslims are the dominant group in Azerbaijan and Iran. Columns four and five display the estimated value of Islamic assets in our sample countries and an index of the Shari'ah compliance of our sample nation's listed stocks. The index value is the natural logarithm of the ratio of a country's weight in the DJIM to the country's weight in Dow Jones' underlying asset universe of all countries covered in the DJIM. A positive index values signal an over-proportional Shari'ah compliance of a nation's listed stocks, while negative values indicate the opposite. We exclude the USA, whose weight in the DJIM is around 50%, from the DJIM and the underlying asset universe in our calculation of the remaining countries' index values, as its inclusion would have lead the US index value to dominate all other values (e.g. if the USA has a large positive value, all other values would nearly inevitably be negative). Column six describes relevant financial market restrictions in our sample countries. The information provided in this table is based on BBC, CIA World Factbook, Federation of Malaysian Unit Trust Managers, Global Competition Review, Global Islamic Finance Group, Islamic Finance, Kuwait's Ministry of Commerce and Industry, Magud and Reinhart (2006), McKenzie (2009), Meesook et al. (2001), Religious Population, US Commercial Service, Reuters and the US State Department's Investment Climate Statements.

3.3 *Benchmark data*

We construct our benchmark factors with the online research tool of Style Research Limited, which is based on the Worldscope database and has been used in previous research (Bauer, Koedijk, and Otten 2005; Renneboog, Ter Horst, and Zhang 2008).

To assess Islamic mutual funds exposure to a national, regional and global equity market, we employ the price indices of value weighted portfolios of all stocks in the respective market.[7] We use the common investment style benchmark factors suggested by Fama and French (1993) and Carhart (1997). These measure a portfolio's exposure to equities with a different size, book value to market value ratio and momentum. We construct benchmark factors for each style at the national, regional and global level. The size factor SMB (small minus big) is constructed as the return difference between the stocks in the lower half of a market capitalization ranked stock universe and the stocks in the upper half of the same universe. The book to market ratio factor HML (high minus low) is based on a stock universe ranked according to book value to market value ratio. It represents the return of the top 30% minus the bottom 30%. The momentum factor MOM is based on a stock universe ranked according to each stock's return over the previous 12 months. It represents the return difference between the top 30% (previous winners) and the bottom 30% (previous losers). The MOM factor is updated monthly, while the SMB and HML factor are update annually at the end of June in line with Fama and French (1993). All portfolios are value weighted and based on 1-month lagged information.[8] As risk-free asset returns, we retrieve the 1 or 3 month(s) treasury bill or the inter-bank interest rate for each nation.[9] Finally, we compute continuously compounded monthly returns of each asset.[10]

4. Analysis, results and discussion

We present and discuss our results in order of increasing sophistication of our econometric model. We start with the capital asset pricing model (CAPM) and Carhart model and proceed to the unconditional and conditional three-level Carhart model.

4.1 *CAPM and Carhart model*

We start our analysis by estimating a simple national CAPM as specified in Equation (1)

$$r_{\mathrm{p},t} = \alpha_p + \beta_{\mathrm{nat,p}} r_{\mathrm{natm},t} + \varepsilon_{\mathrm{p},t}, \tag{1}$$

where $r_{\mathrm{p},t}$ and $r_{\mathrm{natm},t}$ represent the excess return of a portfolio (p) and the national equity market benchmark (natm) over the risk-free asset return (r_{f}), respectively. $\beta_{\mathrm{nat,p}}$ is the portfolio's systematic exposure to the national equity market benchmark. $\alpha_{\mathrm{p},t}$ denotes Jensen's (1968) alpha, which can be interpreted as portfolio's systematic return component above or below the return achieved by the equity market benchmark for the same level of systematic risk. $\varepsilon_{\mathrm{p},t}$ captures the random components of a portfolio's excess return for each observation (t) (Lintner 1965; Mossin 1966; Sharpe 1964).

As shown in Table 3, we find nine of our 20 countries' Islamic equity fund portfolios to experience significantly negative Jensen alphas (Egypt, Germany, Liechtenstein, Luxembourg, Morocco, Saudi Arabia, South Africa, UK and USA). In contrast, not a single nation's Islamic funds outperform the market benchmark on average. If our subsequent, more robust estimations would lead to similar results, the theoretical view would be supported that Shari'ah law restricts fund manager skills or distracts mutual funds from the pursuit of profits. All Islamic mutual fund

Table 3. National financial performance and investment style (CAPM and Carhart).

Country/ region	CAPM model		Carhart model					Adj R^2 CAPM	Adj R^2 Carhart
	α_p	$\beta_{nat,p}$	c_p	$\beta_{nat,p}$	$\gamma_{nat,p}$	$\delta_{nat,p}$	$\lambda_{nat,p}$		
Africa									
Egypt	−0.0079**	0.6468***	−0.0075**	0.6587***	0.1768**	−0.0781*	0.0509	0.842	0.852
Morocco	−0.0149***	0.4179***	−0.0136***	0.4238***	0.3521***	0.2304***	−0.0886	0.220	0.320
South Africa	−0.0092***	0.8348***	−0.0081***	0.8657***	0.2299***	0.0571	0.0465	0.850	0.865
Asia									
Indonesia	−0.0013	0.3290***	0.0005	0.3579***	0.1200*	−0.1824**	0.0454	0.611	0.648
Singapore	−0.0024	0.3019***	−0.0003	0.3240***	0.2939***	−0.2351***	0.0724**	0.267	0.371
Malaysia	−0.0034	0.3564***	−0.0039*	0.3289***	−0.0666	0.0464	−0.0682	0.427	0.437
Pakistan	−0.004	0.4985***	−0.0047	0.5096***	0.0774	−0.0058	0.0303	0.720	0.714
Australia	−0.0155	0.4260***	−0.0146	0.3598***	0.4764*	−0.2159	−0.3538	0.124	0.113
Europe									
Luxembourg	−0.0081***	0.6592***	−0.0078***	0.6747***	−0.0094	−0.0933***	0.0412*	0.656	0.683
Germany	−0.0101***	0.6523***	−0.0088***	0.7710***	0.1209*	−0.0985	0.1300**	0.695	0.726
Ireland	0.00136	0.4784***	0.0001	0.5166***	0.1109**	−0.0057	0.0128	0.562	0.570
Liechtenstein	−0.0078*	0.4065***	−0.0097**	0.4122***	0.8321***	−0.3200**	−0.8538***	0.104	0.345
UK	−0.0081***	0.7038***	−0.0087***	0.7014***	0.1158**	−0.2092***	−0.0615**	0.702	0.728
GCC									
Bahrain	−0.0003	0.4156**	−0.0028	0.6102***	0.0552	−0.1173***	0.0358*	0.294	0.465
Kuwait	−0.0019	0.5879***	−0.0024	0.5813***	0.0782	0.0255	−0.0148	0.653	0.648
Saudi Arabia	−0.0248*	0.8974***	−0.0252*	1.0249***	0.1671	0.2014	−0.0520	0.425	0.418
UAE	0.00301	0.7146***	0.0083*	0.8310***	0.0496	−0.1637**	0.0334	0.807	0.832
Qatar	−0.0061	0.6924***	−0.0059	0.6913***	0.1931	−0.0792	0.0369	0.829	0.813
North America									
USA	−0.0045***	0.8568***	−0.0052***	0.8288***	0.1574**	−0.0841**	0.0434*	0.840	0.855
Canada	−0.0029	0.7245***	−0.0040*	0.7669***	0.0208	0.0429	−0.0252	0.732	0.736

Notes: This table illustrates the results of the national CAPM and Carhart model for each national portfolio of Islamic funds, which are displayed in Equations (1) and (2), respectively. Column two and three list a portfolio's Jensen alpha and market risk exposure as estimated by the CAPM model. The next two columns are the equivalent of the Carhart model followed by the estimated coefficients of the SMB (small cap), HML (value), and MOM (momentum) investment style benchmark factors. Negative coefficients indicate exposure to the respective opposite investment styles: large cap, growth, and contrarian. The last two columns present the Adjusted Rsquared statistics of each model. Coefficient covariances and standard errors are made heteroscedasticity and autocorrelation consistent based on Newey and West (1987).

*indicates the 10% significance level.

**indicates the 5% significance level.

***indicates the 1% significance level.

portfolios' betas are significantly below one. This is likely explained by two characteristics of Islamic equity funds. First, the vast majority of Islamic funds do not appear to limit their investment to their national boundaries. Second, Shari'ah law forbids Islamic funds to use leverage in their investment strategies.

To investigate the national investment style of Islamic equity funds, we estimate a Carhart (1997) model, which adds the national investment style benchmark factors $SMB_{nat,t}$, $HML_{nat,t}$ and $MOM_{nat,t}$ to our CAPM as shown in Equation (2),

$$r_{p,t} = \alpha_p + \beta_{nat,p} r_{natm,t} + \gamma_{nat,p} SMB_{nat,t} + \delta_{nat,p} HML_{nat,t} + \lambda_{nat,p} MOM_{nat,t} + \varepsilon_{p,t}, \qquad (2)$$

where $\gamma_{nat,p}$, $\delta_{nat,p}$ and $\lambda_{nat,p}$ measure the exposure of a portfolio to the respective investment style.

Our results are presented in Table 3. They show that more than half of our 20 countries' Islamic equity fund portfolios significantly underperform after controlling for national investment style. The 11 underperforming national portfolios predominantly originate from Africa (Egypt, Morocco, South Africa), Europe (Germany, Liechtenstein, Luxembourg, UK) and North America (Canada, USA). Only one national portfolio from Asia (Malaysia) or the GCC countries (Saudi Arabia) underperforms after controlling for national investment styles.

Our controls allow us to explain substantially more of the return behaviour of several countries' Islamic fund portfolios (e.g. Bahrain, Morocco). In terms of style, we find more than half of our Islamic fund portfolios to display a significantly over-proportional investment in national small cap stocks. We expected this result, since large, often well-diversified companies have a higher risk of receiving intolerable proportions of their revenue from prohibited activities. Islamic funds are also tilted towards growth stocks. This might result from the lower leverage of growth stocks compared with value stocks. Regarding a momentum or contrarian investment style, we neither theoretically reasoned nor empirically observe any systematic preference.

4.2 *Three-level Carhart model*

As Islamic funds from the same nation invest in a variety of regions, national, regional or global benchmark factors alone do not offer a full picture of their financial performance and investment style. However, the Carhart (1997) model is commonly applied only at one level: the national, regional or global.

Gregory and Whitaker (2007, 1327) recently 'proposed a new measure for the performance of international funds', which represents a Carhart model at the national and global level. They constructed an eight-factor model by adding the difference returns between each of the four national benchmark factors and its global counterpart to a global Carhart model. Correcting a national factor for the influence of its global equivalent is very important to avoid a high correlation between both factors and hence potential multicollinearity bias in a regression's results.

Gregory and Whitaker's subtraction of a global factor from a national factor can mitigate multicollinearity problems in several cases. However, it does not ensure the absence of (strong) multicollinearity, as it does not account for the degree, to which a global factor affects its national counterpart. Precisely, Gregory and Whitaker's subtraction under- (over-)corrects the national factors, if a single regression of the national factor on the global factor results in a coefficient of above (below) one. The size of this under- or overcorrection subsequently determines the probability of multicollinearity problems in Gregory and Whitaker's model.[11]

A precise statistical correction for the influence of a global factor on its national equivalent is offered by Elton et al.'s (1993) orthogonalization approach. This approach cleans a factor X from the impact of other factors Y by regressing it on them and replacing factor X by the sum of the intercept and the residuals of the regression. This ensures that the correlation between the cleaned X factor and factors Y is asymptotically zero. For instance, if we orthogonalized the return of the UK equity market from the return of the world equity market, the resulting cleaned UK equity factor would comprise purely UK-specific return characteristics.

Based on these ideas of Gregory & Whitaker (2007) and Elton et al. (1993), we develop a three-level Carhart model, which simultaneously assesses the financial performance and investment style of an asset at the national, regional and global level. Our baseline model is a national four-factor Carhart model. To this model, we add the same four regional factors, which have been orthogonalized from their national equivalents ($r_{\text{regm},t}$, $\text{SMB}_{\text{reg},t}$, $\text{HML}_{\text{reg},t}$ and $\text{MOM}_{\text{reg},t}$). We extend the resulting 8-factor model to a 12-factor model by adding the same four global factors, which have been orthogonalized from their national and regional counterparts ($r_{\text{glom},t}$, $\text{SMB}_{\text{glo},t}$, $\text{HML}_{\text{glo},t}$ and $\text{MOM}_{\text{glo},t}$).[12] The result is our three-level Carhart model as displayed in Equation (3),

$$\begin{aligned} r_{\text{p},t} = {} & \alpha_{\text{p}} + \beta_{\text{nat,p}} r_{\text{natm},t} + \beta_{\text{reg,p}} r_{\text{regm},t} + \beta_{\text{glo,p}} r_{\text{glom},t} + \gamma_{\text{nat,p}} \text{SMB}_{\text{nat,t}} + \gamma_{\text{reg,p}} \text{SMB}_{\text{reg,t}} \\ & + \gamma_{\text{glo,p}} \text{SMB}_{\text{glo,t}} + \delta_{\text{nat,p}} \text{HML}_{\text{nat},t} + \delta_{\text{reg,p}} \text{HML}_{\text{reg},t} + \delta_{\text{glo,p}} \text{HML}_{\text{glo},t} + \lambda_{\text{nat,p}} \text{MOM}_{\text{nat},t} \\ & + \lambda_{\text{reg,p}} \text{MOM}_{\text{reg},t} + \lambda_{\text{glo,p}} \text{MOM}_{\text{glo},t} + \varepsilon_{\text{p},t} \end{aligned} \tag{3}$$

where the subscripts nat, reg or glo indicate that a factor or coefficient represents the national, regional or global level, respectively.[13]

As shown in Table 4, our three-level Carhart models have in most cases substantially higher adjusted R^2 than our national Carhart models. The additional explanatory power of our model is particularly strong for those national portfolios from the GCC countries or Europe, whose geographic investment foci are especially diverse. For instance, the adjusted R^2 of the Bahrain, Saudi Arabia, Ireland and UK portfolio rise from 0.465, 0.418, 0.570 and 0.728 in the national Carhart model to 0.888, 0.843, 0.794 and 0.890 in our three-level Carhart model, respectively. These results highlight the strength of the three-level Carhart model, which hence might be informative to many other applications of asset pricing or investment beyond Islamic mutual funds.

Controlling for Islamic mutual funds' international investment style explains a substantial part of their significant negative abnormal returns. Only 7 of the 11 portfolios with a significantly negative Jensen alpha in their national Carhart model (Germany, Liechtenstein, Luxembourg, Morocco, South Africa, UK, USA) and Australia underperform in our three-level Carhart model. Four portfolios significantly outperform (Ireland, Qatar, Singapore, UAE). The remaining eight national portfolios, which comprise 74.3% of the funds in our sample (i.e. 197 of 265 funds), display a financial performance statically indifferent from international equity benchmarks (Bahrain, Canada, Egypt, Indonesia, Kuwait, Malaysia, Pakistan, Saudi Arabia). Based on these results, we cannot conclude anymore that Islamic funds generally underperform their equity market benchmarks. Hence, while the theoretical view that Shari'ah compliance distracts Islamic mutual funds' from the pursuit of profit might apply to some of our sample funds, it appears too simplistic to generally explain international Islamic equity fund performance.

Instead, our results imply that Islamic funds' financial performance might be conditional on two national characteristics. First, Islamic equity fund portfolios from the six countries with the best developed Islamic financial markets (Bahrain, Kuwait, Malaysia, Qatar, Saudi Arabia, UAE) do not deliver significantly negative abnormal returns and in the cases of Qatar and UAE even outperform their international benchmarks. In contrast, Islamic funds from 8 of the 14 countries with lesser developed Islamic financial markets in our sample significantly trail their benchmarks (Australia, Germany, Liechtenstein, Luxembourg, Morocco, South Africa, UK, USA). This result

Table 4. International financial performance and investment style (three-level Carhart model).

Country/ region	Intercept	Market exposures			SMB exposures			HML exposures			MOM exposures			
	α_p	$\beta_{nat,p}$	$\beta_{reg,p}$	$\beta_{glo,p}$	$\gamma_{nat,p}$	$\gamma_{reg,p}$	$\gamma_{glo,p}$	$\delta_{nat,p}$	$\delta_{reg,p}$	$\delta_{glo,p}$	$\lambda_{nat,p}$	$\lambda_{reg,p}$	$\lambda_{reg,p}$	Adj R^2
Africa														
Egypt	−0.0018	0.6234***	0.1058*	0.1611	0.1500**	0.2519**	0.0428	−0.0610	−0.1689***	−0.0717	0.0311	−0.0199	0.0709	0.839
Morocco	−0.0115***	0.4223***	0.0377	0.1380	0.3488***	0.0825*	−0.0132	0.2307***	−0.0994*	0.1108	−0.0796	−0.0212	−0.0015	0.303
South Africa	−0.0103***	0.8383***	−0.0650	0.0525	0.2459***	0.0254	0.1770*	0.0498	0.0395	0.1578**	0.0486	−0.0010	−0.0213	0.866
Asia														
Indonesia	−0.0005	0.3306***	0.2210***	−0.0849	0.1670**	0.3102**	−0.0738	−0.1811***	−0.0532	−0.0602	0.0609	−0.1120**	−0.1041*	0.703
Singapore	0.0087***	0.2753***	0.2939***	0.5068***	0.1614***	0.0806	0.1997	−0.1182**	−0.3440***	−0.5075***	0.0690**	0.0403	−0.0451	0.678
Malaysia	−0.0027	0.3200***	0.0737	0.0676	−0.0910	0.0974	0.2978*	0.0838	−0.1280**	−0.1969**	−0.0712	−0.0527	0.0039	0.443
Pakistan	−0.0031	0.5318***	0.0725	0.0993	0.1592*	0.1257	0.1675	−0.0454	−0.1429	−0.4619	0.0374	−0.2147**	0.1027	0.724
Australia	−0.0371**	0.6258*	−0.5027	−1.7047**	0.4627	−0.2354	−2.1131	0.0674	−0.6798	−0.7334	−0.1764	−0.6936**	0.2971	0.155
Europe														
Luxembourg	−0.0034**	0.6789***	0.8543***	0.4463***	−0.0053	−0.1153*	−0.0780	−0.0060	−0.3446***	−0.4756***	0.0194	0.0018	−0.0244	0.905
Germany	−0.0087***	0.6061***	0.9695***	0.4782***	−0.1439***	0.1777	0.6758***	0.0185	0.0873	−0.1926	0.1596***	0.1472	0.0577	0.839
Ireland	0.0117***	0.4270***	0.6098***	0.4751***	−0.0343	0.0905	−0.1532	−0.0131	0.2170***	0.1302	0.0002	0.0125	0.1791**	0.794
Liechtenstein	−0.0266**	0.2530	1.2253**	−1.3591	0.4395	0.1241	0.0013	−0.2277	0.7497	0.3164	−0.9588**	−0.0025	0.0928	0.436
UK	−0.0145***	0.6147***	0.3764***	0.6192***	0.0251	−0.0916	0.0180	−0.1287***	−0.1031*	−0.2773***	−0.0089	0.0471	0.0012	0.890
GCC														
Bahrain	0.0032	0.4996***	0.4967***	0.3872***	0.0429	0.0636	−0.0522	−0.0798***	0.0819***	−0.2637**	0.0462***	−0.0441**	0.0502	0.888
Kuwait	0.0030	0.6786***	0.2025**	0.1817**	0.0067	0.0333	−0.3210	0.0204	0.1004	−0.6539**	−0.0038	−0.0422	−0.1683*	0.699
Saudi Arabia	0.0039	1.0100***	1.6277***	1.8272***	0.2532	0.2837*	0.4793	0.1069	0.0724	−0.1774	−0.0232	−0.0374	−0.4956	0.843
UAE	0.0147**	0.7884***	0.1084	0.0912	−0.0130	−0.3057**	−0.2866	−0.1109	−0.1836*	−0.0406	0.0270	0.1463***	0.0090	0.877
Qatar	0.0225**	0.5224***	0.3253*	0.4993**	0.4614*	−0.3292	−0.1664	−0.2431*	−0.1385	0.8810**	0.2069	0.1609	−0.0503	0.806
North America														
USA	−0.0049***	0.8282***	3.0164***	0.2294***	0.0725	−0.7345	−0.1282*	−0.0838**	0.5064*	0.0740*	0.0287	0.0095	0.0614*	0.877
Canada	0.0013	0.7917***	0.0781	0.6866**	0.0116	−0.0950	0.1237	0.0621*	0.0908	−0.2886	−0.0186	0.0019	−0.1127	0.764

Notes: This table reports the results of our three-level Carhart model, which we develop in Equation (3). In short, our three-level Carhart model estimates the exposure of a portfolio to (i) its national (subscript nat) equity market and investment style benchmarks, (ii) its regional (reg) equity market and investment style benchmarks, which are cleaned from the effects of its national equivalents, (iii) and the global equity market (glo) and investment style benchmarks, which are cleaned from the effects of its national and regional equivalents. After the intercept alpha, 12 coefficients are reported in groups of three. These display the national, regional and global coefficients attached to the respective equity market benchmark, the SMB, the HML and the MOM factor. The last coefficient presents the adjusted R^2 statistic. Coefficient covariances and standard errors are made heteroscedasticity and autocorrelation-consistent based on Newey and West (1987).

*indicates the 10% significance level.

**indicates the 5% significance level.

***indicates the 1% significance level.

implies that the development of Islamic financial centres has a positive effect on Islamic fund performance. A very similar finding has recently been made by Christoffersen and Sarkissian (2009) for conventional financial centres and mutual funds. Following their in-depth explanation, we assume that the high density of intermediaries and competitors in the six Islamic financial centres has a positive effect on Islamic fund managers' learning gains and eventually on their funds' performance.

Second, among the 14 nations with the lesser developed Islamic financial markets in our sample, the fund portfolios from seven predominantly Christian economies significantly underperform their international benchmarks (Australia, Germany, Liechtenstein, Luxembourg, South Africa, UK, USA). In contrast, the fund portfolio from only one of the four predominantly Muslim economies in this group underperforms (Morocco). This implies that incorporation in an Islamic economy benefits Islamic funds' financial performance. As funds from Islamic economies tend to have a home bias similar to the one of conventional investors (Ahearne, Griever, and Warnock 2004; French and Poterba 1991), a possible reason for this relevance of home country religion might be that the financial value of a stock's Shari'ah compliance is positively related to the influence of Shari'ah law on consumers in its home economy. This explanation is supported by the observation that Islamic funds from those Islamic economies perform best (Qatar, UAE), whose dominant Islamic school of thought most literally follows the letters of Qur'an.[14]

The three-level Carhart model also allows a precise assessment of Islamic funds' geographical investment focus and international investment style. Islamic funds from Singapore, Bahrain, Kuwait, Saudi Arabia, Germany, Ireland, Luxembourg, the UK and the USA invest at the national, regional and global levels. Funds from the other countries tend to invest at their national level and at the regional or global level, whereby the regional investment might be limited to small cap stocks.

Funds from Islamic economies display a clear tendency to small cap investment at the national, regional and global levels. This observation supports our argument that an Islamic fund invests less likely in large companies due to their higher risk of receiving intolerable proportions of revenue from prohibited activities. At the regional and global level, this observation might also be explained by the home bias of funds from Islamic economies, as these economies often host comparatively small corporations. Islamic funds' preference for growth stocks in our national Carhart model has weakened after controlling for international investment style. Nevertheless, the average Islamic fund remains titled towards growth stocks, which likely results from the lower leverage of growth stocks compared to value stocks. As in the national Carhart model, Islamic funds show no tendency towards either momentum or contrarian investment in our three-level Carhart model.

4.3 *Conditional three-level Carhart model*

Major macroeconomic variables have found to be useful predictors of equity market returns. If fund managers would vary their equity market exposure over time according to these public information variables, they could achieve a significant improvement in their alpha based on public information. Such a potential achievement would be unrelated to and hence artificially inflate the financial performance resulting from a mutual fund's decision to pursue an Islamic investment strategy. Hence, we control for this opportunity by conditioning our model on lagged public information variables based on Ferson and Schadt's (1996) approach. Specifically, we add the product of the non-orthogonalized global equity market excess return over the risk-free rate ($r_{\text{globalm},t}$) and a column vector of lagged public information variables (z_{t-1}) to Equation (3).

We choose the same type of lagged information variables as Renneboog, Ter Horst, and Zhang (2008) in their analysis of socially responsible mutual funds' time varying factor exposure and collect them from Datastream. These variables are: (i) the yield of the 3-month US treasury bill; (ii) the term spread calculated as the difference between the 10-year US government bond yield and the 3-month US treasury bill; (iii) the default spread being the difference between Moody's US BAA rated corporate bond yield and its AAA rated equivalent; (iv) the dividend yield of Datastream's world equity market index. Following Cortez, Silva and Areal (2009), we increase the information value of our lagged information variables by detrending them from their 12-month moving average and address multicollinearity by transforming the results in mean zero values.[15] Our resulting conditional model is displayed in Equation (4):

$$r_{\mathrm{p},t} = \alpha_{\mathrm{p}} + \beta'_{\mathrm{lev,p}} r_{\mathrm{levm},t} + \gamma'_{\mathrm{lev,p}} SMB_{\mathrm{lev},t} + \delta'_{\mathrm{lev,p}} HML_{\mathrm{lev},t} + \lambda'_{\mathrm{lev,p}} MOM_{\mathrm{lev},t} + \theta'_{p}(z_{t-1} r_{\mathrm{globalm},t}) + \varepsilon_{\mathrm{p},t} \quad (4)$$

where $r_{\mathrm{levm},t}$, $\mathrm{SMB}_{\mathrm{lev},t}$, $\mathrm{HML}_{\mathrm{lev},t}$ and $\mathrm{MOM}_{\mathrm{lev},t}$ are column vectors, which include the respective factor at the national, regional and global levels. Consequentially, $\beta'_{\mathrm{lev,p}}$, $\gamma'_{\mathrm{lev,p}}$, $\delta'_{\mathrm{lev,p}}$ and $\lambda'_{\mathrm{lev,p}}$ are row vectors of the coefficients attached to these factors. θ'_{p} is a row vector of coefficients attached to the product of the lagged information variables and the excess return of the global equity market.

Table 5 displays the alpha and beta coefficients of our conditional three-level Carhart model. Generally, these coefficients ensure us that our results are robust to managerial timing activities and hence do not represent an artefact of them. Particularly, a comparison of our conditional model to its unconditional equivalent shows that only three alpha coefficients change their significance in inconsistent directions, which does not indicate any systematic relationship. Hence, most Islamic mutual fund managers either do not time their global equity market exposure based on lagged public information about macroeconomic variables or they fail to significantly benefit from it.

Comparing the difference in the conditional and unconditional global equity market exposures of national portfolios allows us to distinguish between both explanations. In the vast majority of countries, the difference is marginal, which implies that Islamic mutual funds managers, on average, do not attempt to time their global market exposure based on lagged public information. However, the conditional global equity market exposure of Islamic funds from Bahrain, Qatar and Saudi Arabia is substantially lower than their unconditional equivalent. This suggests that Islamic fund managers from these nations vary their portfolio's exposure according to public information variables but do not gain from it, as their abnormal returns in the unconditional model are not substantially better than in its conditional equivalent.

5. Robustness tests[16]

We pursue two further robustness tests in addition to our conditional three-level Carhart model. First, our results might be an artefact of our sample period. If this would be the case, our results should be considerably different over other sample periods. To investigate this possibility, we re-estimate our three-level Carhart model over various sample periods. We find our results to be highly consistent over time.

Second, the financial performance and investment style of Islamic funds in many of our sample countries might not result from the funds' Shari'ah compliance but from the sample countries' capital market restrictions. To test this explanation, we investigate the effect of the capital market restrictions listed in Table 2 on Islamic funds' financial performance and investment style during

Table 5. International financial performance and investment style (conditional three-level Carhart model).

	Intercept	Market exposures			
Country	α_p	$\beta_{nat,p}$	$\beta_{reg,p}$	$\beta_{glo,p}$	Adj R^2
Africa					
Egypt	−0.0015	0.5898***	0.0972	0.0889	0.824
Morocco	−0.0125***	0.4023***	0.0600*	0.2312**	0.307
South Africa	−0.0101***	0.8269***	−0.0270	0.0152	0.865
Asia					
Indonesia	0.0000	0.3096***	0.1284**	−0.0387	0.759
Singapore	0.0094***	0.2660***	0.2883***	0.5082***	0.675
Malaysia	−0.0025	0.3236***	0.0651	0.0737	0.435
Pakistan	−0.0061*	0.5176***	0.2434	0.1565	0.731
Australia	−0.0424**	0.5510	−0.3580	−2.1355**	0.049
Europe					
Luxembourg	−0.0031*	0.6689***	0.8723***	0.4449***	0.904
Germany	−0.0085***	0.5119***	0.8475***	0.4833***	0.863
Ireland	0.0125***	0.3830***	0.5369***	0.5510***	0.807
Liechtenstein	−0.0149	0.7049	1.8756**	−0.0860	0.574
UK	−0.0131***	0.5980***	0.2979***	0.5845***	0.893
GCC					
Bahrain	0.0035	0.4021***	0.4334***	0.2667***	0.908
Kuwait	0.0044	0.4972***	−0.0789	−0.2018	0.745
Saudi Arabia	0.0125**	0.5743***	0.7509**	0.8779***	0.935
UAE	0.0126*	0.7949***	0.0840	0.1065	0.876
Qatar	0.0208*	0.2475	0.0724	−0.0348	0.798
North America					
USA	−0.0046***	0.8738***	3.1877***	0.2568***	0.886
Canada	−0.0014	0.8344***	0.1394	0.5444*	0.771

Notes: This table reports the results of the conditional three-level Carhart model displayed in Equation (5). For brevity, we only report the alpha followed by the national, regional and global beta instead of all 17 coefficients. Coefficient covariances and standard errors are made heteroscedasticity and autocorrelation-consistent based on Newey and West (1987).
*indicates the 10% significance level.
**indicates the 5% significance level.
***indicates the 1% significance level.

our respective nations' sample periods. We perform this analysis by adding a dummy variable to our three-level Carhart model, which is set to one during restrictions and to zero thereafter or before. When a country imposed multiple capital market restrictions, such as Malaysia, we run one regression for each restriction. We do not find capital market restrictions to have any meaningful effect on our financial performance and investment style results in all of our sample countries except Singapore. In Singapore, the inbound restrictions before January 2002 are very likely the reason for the significant outperformance of its Islamic fund portfolio.

6. Conclusion

In this study, we analyse and compare the financial performance and investment style of Islamic equity funds from 20 countries. As Islamic funds often have diverse investment regions, we develop a (conditional) three-level Carhart model to simultaneously control for a fund's exposure to different national, regional and global equity markets and investment styles.

Our findings do not allow us to conclude that Islamic funds in general under- or outperform equity markets. Instead, we find national characteristics to explain the heterogeneity in Islamic fund performance. Islamic funds from the six largest Islamic financial centres in our study (the GCC countries and Malaysia) perform competitive or even outperform international equity market benchmarks. Contrary, Islamic fund portfolios from most other nations with less developed Islamic financial services significantly underperform their benchmarks. Especially Islamic funds from predominantly Christian economies trail their benchmarks.

Our results have several implications. First, Islamic funds benefit from proximity to Islamic financial centres, as this seems to allow them to develop more expertise. Second, Islamic funds appear to have a financial advantage in Muslim economies. This might result from a higher utility, which consumers and agents in those economies receive from the Shari'ah compliance of assets. Third, governments can increase the attractiveness of Islamic funds in their jurisdiction by developing Islamic financial markets.

Islamic funds' international investment style appears somewhat tilted towards growth investing, which might result from growth stocks' under-proportional leverage. Funds from predominantly Muslim economies also display a clear small cap preference. This preference likely reflects the higher risk of large, well diversified corporations to operate in sectors forbidden by Shari'ah law.

We see at least three interesting routes for future research. First, once sufficient data for the majority of Islamic funds' host nations become acquirable, comparing the performance of Islamic funds with size- and age-matched conventional funds should lead to more insights into the attractiveness of active Islamic investment. Second, an in-depth exploration of the specific processes, by which developed Islamic financial markets support Islamic mutual funds, could substantially improve our understanding of Islamic financial services and allow government to grow these more effectively. Third, it has been beyond the scope of this paper to investigate Islamic mutual funds, which do not predominantly invest in stocks. However, hundreds of Islamic mutual funds focus their investment strategies on Islamic bonds, real estate or commodities. These funds' financial performance and investment styles appear academically unexplored to date and hence may be promising routes for future research.

Acknowledgements

Our paper substantially benefited from suggestions by Iqbal Asaria, Shahid Ebrahim, John Wilson and two anonymous referees. We would also like to thank Mohsen Derregia, Dewi Fitriasari, Phil Molyneux and seminar participants at Nottingham, St Andrews and the Emerging Scholars in Banking and Finance conference at Cass Business School for their comments. Finally, we are very grateful to Andrew Gibson Miller of Eurekahedge and Robert Schwob of Style Research Limited for provision of data. All remaining errors are our sole responsibility. The views expressed in this paper are not necessarily shared by the Principles for Responsible Investment.

Notes

1. The estimated growth is partly related to an extended estimation coverage. Nevertheless, Islamic financial services' market value was only about \$150bn in the mid-1990s. Hence, it grew nearly 400% until the end of 2007 with average annual growth rates of about 14% (McKenzie 2009).
2. The Shari'ah Supervisory Board of the Dow Jones Islamic Index, for instance, tolerates corporations, whose total debt, sum of cash and interest bearing securities, or accounts receivable are less than one-third of the corporation's market capitalization (Dow Jones 2009). Other Islamic indices use similar ratios (Derigs and Marzban 2008).

3. The literature on Islamic investment indices is somewhat more extensive. Most notably, Derigs and Marzban (2009) find ex-post optimized Shari'ah compliant indices to deliver a lower financial return than ex-post optimized conventional indices. Results of Forte and Miglietta (2007) highlight the unique characteristics of Islamic investments, as they do not observe FTSE's Islamic index to be significantly co-integrated with its socially responsible or conventional counterpart. Girard and Hassan (2008), however, do not find international FTSE Islamic indices to trail their conventional peers. These three papers are recommended as gateway into this literature.
4. We follow Bollen (2007) and Renneboog, Ter Horst, and Zhang (2008) by defining equity mutual funds as investing at least 75% in stocks. As Eurekahedge does not provide asset allocation data for Islamic funds, our sample comprises all funds classified by Eurekahedge as equity as well as all of Eurekahedge's balanced funds, whose benchmark consist to at least 75% of an equity index.
5. It is common practice to analyse portfolios of assets with religious or ethical characteristics based on equal-weighted rather than value-weighted portfolios. This practice ensures a focus on the assets' religious or ethical characteristics and substantially reduces the risk of bias due to idiosyncratic return characteristics of a specific asset (Hong and Kacperczyk 2009; Renneboog, Ter Horst, and Zhang 2008). In the case of Islamic mutual funds, the available data furthermore do not allow for a precise computation of value-weighted portfolios. Eurekahedge, for instance, provides only static fund size data, which are very generously rounded and somewhat incomplete.
6. In the case of two countries (Liechtenstein, Qatar), our data set comprises more than 20 but less than 30 observations. Thirty observations are commonly considered to be the minimum threshold to assume an approximately normal distribution of ordinary least squares (OLS) regression residuals based on the central limit theorem. Since we cannot assume a normal distribution of regression residuals for these two countries, we pursue Jarque and Bera (1987) tests of the normality of these nations' regression residuals in all our main estimation models. Our results do not allow us to reject the normality of the regression residuals in any specification even at the lenient 10% significant level. Hence, we assume the residuals of our regressions for Liechtenstein and Qatar to be approximately normally distributed based on our tests instead of the central limit theorem.
7. Style Research Limited provides return indices, which assume distributions to have been reinvested, and dividend yields but no price indices. However, as discussed in the previous section, we require equity market returns exclusive of dividends to match these with our Islamic mutual fund returns. Hence, we manually compute price indices by reducing the return indices by the monthly reinvested dividend yield.
8. As Style Research does not offer the construction of the size and book to market factor precisely according to Fama and French (1993), we follow the slightly amended procedure of Renneboog, Ter Horst, and Zhang (2008). Renneboog, Ter Horst, and Zhang (2008, 307) found that their 'factors are virtually identical' to the ones of Fama and French (1993).
9. Matching Islamic equity mutual funds against conventional equity mutual funds as common in the socially responsible investment literature (e.g. Kreander et al. 2005) is not possible for large parts of our sample, as the usual databases cover an insufficient number of conventional mutual funds from many nations in Asia or Africa.
10. As we do not have sufficient data on any benchmark asset for Liechtenstein, we employ Germany's benchmark assets for it. For Luxembourg, we employ the equity market benchmark and the investment style benchmarks of the Benelux countries due to the same reason.
11. For instance, in case the global factor and the national factor were perfectly correlated, whereby the absolute returns of the global factor would always be half of the national factor's returns, subtracting the global from the national factor would lead to a corrected national factor, which is identical to the global factor. Hence, multicollinearity problems would be certain in this case.
12. As our baseline model is a national four-factor Carhart model, we expect the coefficients of the orthogonalized regional and global factors in our three-level Carhart model to be more variable than their national equivalents.
13. The other symbols in Equation (3) are defined equivalent to the previous equations.
14. UAE and Qatar are the only two predominantly Islamic economies, whose Islamic funds significantly outperform their international equity benchmarks on average. UAE and Qatar are also two of three Islamic countries in our sample, who closely follow the most literal Islamic school of thought (Hanbali). The third 'Hanbali' country is Saudi-Arabia. As shown in Table 5, Saudi Arabia's Islamic funds could outperform their equity market benchmarks on average, if their fund managers would be more successful in timing their market risk exposure based on economic fundamentals. Hence, we carefully conclude that the most literal Islamic school of thought, Hanbali, might have a positive effect on Islamic fund performance.
15. The mean zero value transformation of Cortez, Silva, and Areal (2009) addresses some but not all multicollinearity in our sample. Hence, we also pursue a three-step orthogonalization procedure. First, we orthogonalize the product involving the treasury bill from its terms spread equivalent. Second, we orthogonalize the product including the dividend yield from its cleaned treasury bill and its term spread equivalent. Third, we orthogonalize the product based

on the default spread from its cleaned dividend yield, cleaned treasury bill and term spread equivalent. Eventually, we use the product involving the cleaned default spread, the cleaned dividend yield, the cleaned treasury bill and the term spread.

16. The results of the further robustness tests are available upon request.

References

Abderrezak, F. 2008. The performance of Islamic equity funds: A comparison to conventional, Islamic and ethical benchmarks. MA Thesis, University of Maastricht, Maastricht, NL.

Abdullah, F., T. Hassan, and S. Mohamad. 2007. Investigation of performance of Malaysian Islamic unit trust funds. *Managerial Finance* 33, no. 2: 142–53.

Ahearne, A.G., W.L. Griever, and F.E. Warnock. 2004. Information costs and home bias: An analysis of us holdings of foreign equities. *Journal of International Economics* 62, no. 2: 313–36.

Bauer, R., K.G. Koedijk, and R. Otten. 2005. International evidence on ethical mutual fund performance and investment style. *Journal of Banking & Finance* 29, no. 7: 1751–67.

Bollen, N.P.B. 2007. Mutual fund attributes and investor behavior. *Journal of Financial and Quantitative Analysis* 42, no. 3: 683–708.

Bollen, N.P.B. and J.A. Busse. 2001. On the timing ability of mutual fund managers. *Journal of Finance* 56, no. 3: 1075–94.

Campbell, J.Y. and T. Vuolteenaho. 2004. Bad beta, good beta. *American Economic Review* 94, no. 5: 1249–75.

Carhart, M.M. 1997. On persistence in mutual fund performance. *Journal of Finance* 52, no. 1: 57–82.

Carhart, M.M., J.N. Carpenter, A.W. Lynch, and D.K. Musto. 2002. Mutual fund survivorship. *Review of Financial Studies* 15, no. 5: 1439–63.

Christoffersen, S.E.K. and S. Sarkissian. 2009. City size and fund performance. *Journal of Financial Economics* 92, no. 2: 252–275.

Cihák, M. and H. Hesse. 2010. Islamic banks and financial stability: An empirical analysis. *Journal of Financial Services Research* 38, nos. 2–3: 95–113.

Cortez, M.C., F. Silva, and N. Areal. 2009. The performance of European socially responsible funds. *Journal of Business Ethics* 87, no. 4: 573–88.

Da, Z., P. Gao, and R. Jagannathan. 2009. Informed trading, liquidity provision, and stock selection by mutual funds. NBER Working Paper 14609.

Derigs, U. and S. Marzban. 2008. Review and analysis of current Shariah-compliant equity screening practices. *International Journal of Islamic and Middle Eastern Finance and Management* 1, no. 4: 285–303.

Derigs, U. and S. Marzban. 2009. New strategies and a new paradigm for Shariah-compliant portfolio optimization. *Journal of Banking & Finance* 33, no. 6: 1166–76.

Dow Jones. 2009. Dow Jones Islamic Market (DJIM) indexes. Dow Jones & Company. http://www.djindexes.com/islamic/index.cfm?go=overview (accessed September 10, 2009).

Ebrahim, M.S. 2008. The financial crisis: Comments from Islamic perspectives. *IIUM Journal of Economics and Management* 16, no. 2: 111–8.

Ebrahim, M.S. and S. Rahman. 2005. On the pareto-optimality of futures contracts over forward contracts: Implications for emerging Muslim economies. *Journal of Economic Behavior and Organization* 56, no. 2: 273–95.

Elfakhani, S., M.K. Hassan, and Y. Sidani. 2005. Comparative performance of Islamic versus secular mutual funds. Working Paper, University of New Orleans. http://www.business.uno.edu/econ/workingpapers/2006WP/10-IslamicMutualFunds.pdf (accessed August 10, 2007).

El-Gamal, M. A. 2006. *Islamic finance: Law, economics and practice*. Cambridge: Cambridge University Press.

Elton, E.J., M.J. Gruber, S. Das, and M. Hlavka. 1993. Efficiency with costly information: A reinterpretation of evidence from managed portfolios. *Review of Financial Studies* 6, no. 1: 1–22.

Fama, E.F. and K.R. French. 1993. Common risk factors in the returns on stocks and bonds. *Journal of Financial Economics* 33, no. 1: 3–53.

Ferson, W. and R. Schadt. 1996. Measuring fund strategy and performance in changing economic conditions. *Journal of Finance* 51, no. 2: 425–61.

Forte, G. and F. Miglietta. 2007. Islamic mutual funds as faith-based funds in a socially responsible context. Working Paper, Department of Finance, Bocconi University. http://papers.ssrn.com/sol3/papers.cfm?abstract_id=1012813#Paper-Download (accessed May 25, 2008).

French, K.R. and J.M. Poterba. 1991. Investor diversification and international equity markets. *American Economic Review* 81, no. 2: 222–6.

Geczy, C.C., R.F. Stambaugh, and D. Levin. 2005. Investing on socially responsible mutual funds. Working Paper, The Rodney L. White Center of Financial Research, The Wharton School, University of Pennsylvania. http://papers.ssrn.com/sol3/papers.cfm?abstract_id=416380 (accessed November 24, 2006).

Ghoul, W. and P. Karam. 2007. MRI and Sri mutual funds: A comparison of Christian, Islamic (morally responsible investing), and socially responsible investing (SRI) mutual funds. *Journal of Investing* 16, no. 2: 96–102.

Girard, E. and M.K. Hassan. 2008. Is there a cost to faith-based investing: Evidence from FTSE Islamic indices. *Journal of Investing* 17, no. 4: 112–21.

Gregory, A. and J. Whittaker. 2007. Performance and performance persistence of 'ethical' unit trusts in the UK. *Journal of Business Finance & Accounting* 34, no. 7–8: 1327–44.

HM Treasury. 2008. The development of Islamic finance in the UK: The government's perspective. British Crown. http://www.hm-treasury.gov.uk/d/islamic_finance101208.pdf (accessed September 10, 2009).

Hong, H. and M. Kacperczyk. 2009. The price of sin: The effects of social norms on markets. *Journal of Financial Economics* 93, no. 1: 15–36.

Jaffer, S. 2004. *Islamic asset management: Forming the future for Shariah-compliant investment strategies*. London: Euromoney Books.

Jarque, C.M. and A.K. Bera. 1987. A test for normality of observations and regression residuals. *International Statistical Review* 55, no. 2: 163–72.

Jensen, M.C. 1968. The performance of mutual funds in the period 1945–1964. *Journal of Finance* 23, no. 2: 389–416.

Kosowski, R., A. Timmermann, R. Wermers and H. White. 2006. Can mutual fund 'Stars' Really pick stocks: New evidence from a bootstrap analysis. *Journal of Finance* 61, no. 6: 2551–95.

Kraeussl, R. and R. Hayat. 2008. The performance of Islamic equity funds. Working Paper, Vrije University Amsterdam. http://papers.ssrn.com/sol3/papers.cfm?abstract_id=1320712 (accessed February 9, 2009).

Kreander, N., R.H. Gray, D.M. Power, and C.D. Sinclair. 2005. Evaluating the performance of ethical and non-ethical funds: A matched pair analysis. *Journal of Business Finance & Accounting* 32, no. 7–8: 1465–93.

Lee, D.D. and R.W. Faff. 2009. Corporate sustainability performance and idiosyncratic risk: A global perspective. *The Financial Review* 44, no. 2: 213–37.

Lintner, J. 1965. The valuation of risk assets and the selection of risky investments in stock portfolios and capital budgets. *Review of Economics and Statistics* 47, no. 1: 13–37.

Magud, N. and C.M. Reinhart. 2006. Capital controls: An evaluation. NBER Working Paper 11973. http://www.nber.org/papers/w11973.pdf/ (accessed January 26, 2010).

McKenzie, D. 2009. Islamic finance 2009. International Financial Services London. http://www.ifsl.org.uk/output/ReportItem.aspx?NewsID=32 (accessed September 9, 2009).

Meesook, K., I.H. Lee, O. Liu, Y. Khatri, N. Tamirisa, M. Moor, and M.H. Krysl. 2001. *Malaysia: From crisis to recovery*. Washington, DC: International Monetary Fund.

Mossin, J. 1966. Equilibrium in a capital asset market. *Econometrica* 34, no. 4: 768–83.

Newey, W.K. and K.D. West. 1987. A simple, positive semi-definite, heteroskedasticity and autocorrelation consistent covariance matrix. *Econometrica* 55, no. 3: 703–8.

Rahail, A. 2008. *Islamic finance: A practical guide*. London: Globe Law and Business.

Renneboog, L., J. Ter Horst, and C. Zhang. 2008. The price of ethics and stakeholder governance: The performance of socially responsible mutual funds. *Journal of Corporate Finance* 14, no. 3: 302–22.

Sharpe, W.F. 1964. Capital asset prices: A theory of market equilibrium under conditions of risk. *Journal of Finance* 19, no. 3: 425–42.

The effect of liquidity on the price discovery process in credit derivatives markets in times of financial distress

Sergio Mayordomo[a], Juan Ignacio Peña[b] and Juan Romo[c]

[a] *Department of Research and Statistics, Comisión Nacional del Mercado de Valores (CNMV), C/ Miguel Ángel 11, 28010 Madrid, Spain;* [b] *Department of Business Administration, Universidad Carlos III de Madrid, C/Madrid 126, 28903 Getafe, Madrid, Spain;* [c] *Department of Statistics, Universidad Carlos III de Madrid, C/Madrid 126, 28903 Getafe, Madrid, Spain*

This paper analyses the role of liquidity in the price discovery process. Specifically, we focus on the credit derivatives markets in the context of the subprime crisis. We present a theoretical price discovery model for the asset swap packages (ASPs), bond and credit default swap (CDS) markets and then we test the model with data from 2005 to 2009 on Euro-denominated non-financial firms. Our empirical results show that the ASP market clearly leads the bond market in the price discovery process in all cases, while the leadership between ASPs and CDSs is very sensitive to the appearance of the subprime crisis. Before the crisis, the CDSs market leads the ASP market, but during the crisis, the ASP market leads the CDS market. The liquidity, measured as the relative number of market participants, helps to explain these results.

1. Introduction

The purpose of this paper is to analyse the role of liquidity in the price discovery process. Specifically, we focus on the credit derivatives markets in the context of the subprime crisis. Liquidity is defined in terms of the relative number of participants in a given market, i.e. the number of agents operating in one market relative to the number of participants in another market. Our results suggest that this is the main factor that determines the leadership of the price discovery process between the two markets. We present a theoretical model that helps to understand how the process of price discovery works in the asset swap, bond and credit default swap (CDS) markets. Then we present an empirical application with data from 2005 to 2009 that confirms the theoretical model's insights.

The importance of liquidity in the corporate bond market is not a new topic. Collin-Dufresne, Goldstein, and Martin (2001), Perraudin and Taylor (2003), Elton et al. (2001), Delianedis and Geske (2001) and Chen, Lesmond, and Wei (2007) among others find that liquidity is an additional factor to credit risk which is present in credit spreads. Longstaff, Mithal, and Neis (2005) and Tang and Yan (2007) also support the presence of a liquidity premium in CDS spreads. Tang and Yan (2007) find that both the liquidity level and the liquidity risk[1] are significant factors in determining CDS spreads. De Jong and Driessen (2006) show that not only liquidity in a given market affects credit spreads, but there are also liquidity risk and liquidity spillover effects from the treasury bonds and equity markets.

According to Yan and Zivot (2007), an efficient price discovery process is characterized by the fast adjustment of market prices from the old equilibrium to the new equilibrium with the arrival of new information. The new equilibrium is achieved by means of the interactions of buyers and sellers. Thus, the financial instrument price's that contributes more and newer information to the price discovery process should be the one with the highest number of informed market participants. Assuming that in a given market, the higher the overall number of market participants, the higher the number of informed agents and given that the overall number of market participants is a measure of market liquidity, we state that liquidity is the common element in price discovery analyses that determines which market reveals information more efficiently. The price discovery analysis has been applied to a wide number of financial instruments such as stocks, commodities and credit markets among others. Working (1948), Stein (1961) and Garbade and Silver (1983) (GS henceforth) can be considered among the pioneers on this topic. GS posits a formal model to analyse the process of price discovery and show empirically that this process is led by the markets where the number of participants is higher, in their case, the futures market in comparison with the spot market. More recently, a number of analyses that study price discovery on the basis of either Hasbrouck's (1995) or Gonzalo and Granger's (1995) (GG henceforth) methodologies have appeared. Both methodologies are supported by an empirical test based on a vector autoregression (VAR) with an Error Correction Term model. In one of these applications to the commodities market, Figuerola-Ferretti and Gonzalo (2010) (FFG henceforth) develop an econometric approach in order to match the theoretical model of GS (1983) and the econometric methodology of GG based on the permanent-transitory (PT) decomposition. They find that the prices of futures on non-ferrous metals are 'information dominant' with respect to the spot prices in the most liquid futures markets.

The applications of the price discovery methodology to credit derivatives markets are relatively new, if we compare them with the applications to the futures and spot markets, due to the recent development of CDS market.[2] These applications analyse the efficiency of both CDS and bond markets in terms of price discovery. Blanco, Brennan, and Marsh (2005) and Zhu (2006) use American and European corporate bonds and CDSs and obtain that the CDS market reflects the information more accurately and quickly than the bond market. The same results are found in Baba and Inada (2007) who repeat the same analysis for subordinated CDS and subordinated bond spreads of Japanese mega-banks. In other analyses of price discovery based on emerging markets sovereign bonds and CDS, Ammer and Cai (2007) find that bond spreads lead CDS premiums more often than has been found for investment-grade corporate credits.[3] Based on iTraxx companies, Dötz (2007) finds that both markets make net contributions to price discovery, with the CDS market dominating slightly over the bond market.[4] In general terms, liquidity and credit risk factors are considered as the main determinants of the role of leadership in credit markets.

The analysis of price discovery is extended in Norden and Weber (2004), Forte and Peña (2009) and Coudert and Gex (2010) to the stock market. All of them find that the stock market leads the CDS and bond markets, while there is a leading role of the CDS market with respect to the bond market.[5]

However, a formal theoretical model that analyses the process of price discovery in credit derivatives markets is still lacking. We fill this gap presenting a theoretical model based on the participation of different market players and match this model with GG's econometric methodology by means of FFG's econometric approach. Our model is an extension of the GS model allowing for the simultaneous participation of agents in different markets. This is our first contribution.

Moreover, we find another gap in the price discovery literature in credit markets, namely, no analysis of the price discovery process between ASPs and CDSs has been carried out up to now.[6] Price discovery in credit markets has focused on bond and CDS spreads. We analyse the price discovery process between ASPs and CDSs in the time period from 2005 to 2009 and find that the leadership, in terms of price discovery, between ASPs and CDSs is very sensitive to the appearance of the subprime crisis. During the period before the crisis, the CDSs appear clearly as the more efficient market in 87.5% of the cases. During the crisis, ASP spreads reveal more efficiently credit risk than before up to the point that in 71.88% of the cases ASP spreads lead CDS spreads in the price discovery process. This is our second contribution.

De Wit (2006), Felsenheimer (2004) and Francis, Kakodkar, and Martin (2003) among others suggest that ASP spreads should be a more accurate measure of credit risk than bond spreads. Actually, according to Schonbucher (2003), ASPs are liquid instruments and it is even easier to trade an ASP than the underlying defaultable bond alone. We give support to this idea by means of our empirical price discovery analysis for asset swap and bond spreads up to the point that according to GS (1983) terms, we find that the bond market is a 'pure satellite' of the asset swap market. This finding is our third contribution.

To summarize, our analysis and results are significant contributions to an important contemporary issue in the discipline of Financial Institutions and Markets research for the following reasons. First, we present a simple theoretical model which helps to understand the process of price discovery in credit derivatives markets in the context of the recent financial crisis. Second, our empirical results may be of special interest for market regulators and investors because they provide a number of insights into the relative reliability of market-based credit risk measures. Given the fact of the relatively low liquidity of CDS market in comparison with bonds and ASPs, our results cast doubts on the representativeness of market prices quoted in the CDS market in periods of financial distress as the current crisis. The key implication of this result is that inferences on the creditworthiness of a given firm based solely in CDS spreads during periods of high market turbulence and low liquidity are bound to be misleading. Third, given that we find that, in all cases, the ASP spread reflects credit risk more efficiently than the bond spread, our results suggest that it is more appropriate to use the ASP spread as a credit risk indicator instead of the bond spread.

This paper is divided into four sections, in Section 2 we describe the price discovery model and the hypotheses to test. Section 3 describes the data. Section 4 presents the price discovery results. Section 5 concludes.

2. Price discovery model

First of all, we report a brief definition of the two credit derivatives employed in this paper. A CDS is a traded insurance contract which provides protection against credit risk until the occurrence of a credit event or the maturity date of the contract, whichever is first, in exchange for periodic premium payments (the CDS premium or CDS spread) and/or an upfront payment. In the event of default, CDSs are settled in one of two ways: by physical settlement or by cash settlement. A buyer of CDS protection on a single name makes regular payments of the CDS' full running spread to the protection seller. The CDS contract that we analyse is unfunded and so investors do not make an up-front payment (ignoring dealer margins and transaction costs). Thus, the traded CDS premium or the market CDS spread is an at-market annuity premium rate $\bar{s}$ such that the market value of the CDS is zero at origination.

An ASP contains a defaultable coupon bond with coupon $\bar{c}$ and an interest-rate swap (IRS) that swaps the bond's coupon (fixed leg) into Euribor plus the asset swap spread rate s^A (floating leg).

The asset swap's fixed leg represents the buyer's periodic fixed rate payments, while its floating leg represents the seller's payment. The asset swap spread is chosen so that the value of the whole package is the par value of the defaultable bond and for this reason it is also known as a par to par swap. The interest rate swap (IRS) included in the asset-swap package has zero cost and so the asset swap's cost is equal to the price of the defaultable bond included in the package. As the asset swap spread valuation is obtained using the bond's face value (FV), an up-front payment must be added to the bond's price at the investment period t to ensure that the value of the whole package is FV. The asset swap spread is computed by setting the present value of all cash flows equal to zero and the up-front payment represents the net present value of the swap.

The goal of the price discovery model is to analyse the dynamics and interaction between CDS and ASP spreads in an equilibrium non-arbitrage model.[7] The procedure is based on the behaviour of market participants in the corresponding market place. We adapt and extend to the credit derivatives markets, the model of price discovery developed by GS and focuses on the case where the arbitrageurs present a finite elasticity demand/supply of arbitrage services. We modify the model of the price discovery developed by GS by considering five different types of market participants instead of three. Each agent who participates in the market place can be classified into one of the following groups:

(i) The first group is formed by arbitrageurs. Whenever there exists an adequate grade of liquidity, they try to exploit possible discrepancies among CDS and ASP prices. Thus, they invest whenever a security is trading above/below the 'correct price'.[8]
(ii) Agents that only take positions in the asset swap market. They can be understood either as long-run investors such as portfolio managers who feel attracted by asset swap characteristics or as investors who must hold any capital requirement. Examples of these agents are insurance firms or pension funds that invest in bonds or asset swaps as a 'buy and hold' strategy.
(iii) Agents that only participate in the CDS market either as protection sellers or buyers. For instance, the collateralized debt obligation (CDO) issuer usually enters the CDS market as a protection seller.[9] These participants in the CDS market can also be understood in most cases as speculators.[10] Some examples of these agents are hedge funds that benefit from CDS leverage effect, contrary to the ASPs or bonds, whose buyers incur an outlay at the investment date.
(iv) Agents that participate in both financial markets as market makers. According to Acharya, Schaefer, and Zhang (2007), most of the financial institutions that make markets in corporate bonds are also the liquidity providers in other related segments of the fixed-income markets, specifically in credit markets such as CDSs and CLOs or CDOs. This type of agents can also be considered as financial intermediaries who manage portfolios for different customers or simply as investors in credit markets. We consider that these individuals take a given position in one market or the other, attending to their reservation prices for the corresponding market.
(v) Agents that use the CDS market to hedge their positions in corporate debt. These agents buy bonds or asset swaps that at the same time are hedged by means of e CDSs.[11] They employ CDSs to hedge their bond or ASP positions contrary to the individuals in group (iii) who do not have any underlying bond or ASP.

GS, as well as FFG, consider three types of agents and two markets in such a way that the only individuals who operate in both markets are the arbitrageurs. We offer a more general model that includes participants who operate in both markets and hedgers. It means that both markets are not only linked by arbitrageurs as in GS but by the two additional groups of individuals. This aspect is of special relevance for understanding price discovery in credit markets, given that price setters in the CDS market are frequently the same as in bonds or asset swap markets and the link is not only given by the arbitrageurs.

2.1 *Arbitrageur's demand*

The procedure employed by arbitrageurs to exploit potential mispricings between the CDS and the ASP is based on a cash-and-carry strategy. The arbitrageur strategy is constructed from the following portfolios depending on if asset swap spread is above (below) the CDS spread:

Portfolio I

- Long (short) position in a CDS with an annual full running premium equal to $\bar{s}_t$ which is paid (received) quarterly.

Portfolio II

- Long (short) position in an ASP whose cost is equal to the bond's par value. The investor pays to (receives from) the counterparty, the bond's coupon at the coupon dates in exchange for receiving (paying) every quarter the 3-month Euribor rate ($E_{3m,t}$) plus the asset swap spread (s_t^A). The quarterly payment dates coincide with the CDS premium payment dates.[12]
- Loan (deposit) with a principal equal to the bond's FA at 3-month Euribor.[13] Interest payment dates coincide with both the CDS premium and the asset swap floating leg payment dates.

Portfolio II is equivalent to a synthetic short (long) position in a CDS and so, there should be an equivalence relationship between CDS and asset swap spreads. Otherwise, arbitrage opportunities may appear.[14]

At origination, the cost of both portfolios is zero, and so the net payoff is also zero. A quarter after origination and every subsequent quarter, in case of no default, a combination of long positions on both the CDS and ASP leads to a net payment for the investor equal to the difference between ASP and CDS spreads, $s_t^A - \bar{s}_t$,[15] both of them converted into quarterly terms using an 'actual/360' day count convention.[16] This difference is known as the basis.

However, in case of default, the investor's net payment differs from the basis. On the one hand, the IRS included into the ASP remains alive after default, and it should be serviced or unwound at market value. On the other hand, the CDS accrued premium as well as loan's accrued interests must be paid. Moreover, not only the underlying bond but a given number of bonds, even cheaper than the underlying, can be delivered which gives the holder of a CDS a cheapest-to-deliver (CTD) bond option. Then, the net payment is different from the basis.

In order to find the non-arbitrage equilibrium condition, the following assumptions must be imposed:

A1. No limitations on short sales of the ASP.[17]
A2. No limitations on borrowing and no restrictions on participating in the ASPs and CDSs market (market segmentation does not affect the arbitrageur).
A3. No tax effects.
A4. No additional costs except the ones required to fund an ASP position.

Arbitrageurs can be identified as hedge fund investors whose demand takes place after identifying securities that are trading above/below the correct price. Among the strategies employed to exploit arbitrage opportunities in fixed-income markets hedge funds employ merger arbitrage, fixed-income arbitrage, capital structure arbitrage, volatility arbitrage or what is known, from our point of view erroneously, as statistical arbitrage that is based on the cointegration methodology proposed by Engle and Granger (1987).[18] Of the above strategies, the one employed to exploit transitory mispricings in CDS and ASP spreads is the one based on the cointegration methodology. The idea is that, given two cointegrated assets, an investor can profit by buying one cointegrated asset and selling the other in case of transitory mispricings. The investor is betting that the spread between the two cointegrated assets will narrow, given the cointegration's adjustment process towards an economic equilibrium. Thus, if the ASP spread is too high relative to the long-term equilibrium, arbitrageurs will take long positions both in CDSs and ASPs. This long-term no-arbitrage equilibrium condition is also known as the equivalence or parity relationship between ASP and CDS spreads. Thus, we define the arbitrageurs demand on the basis of the following long-run equivalence relationship:

$$s_t^A = \beta_2 \bar{s}_t + \beta_3. \tag{1}$$

According to Blanco, Brennan, and Marsh's (2005) terminology, β_2 includes non-transient factors besides credit risk.[19] The parameter β_3 includes factors or imperfections that generate a constant difference between both spreads such as institutional factors causing differences in funding or transaction costs, or other costs in general.

The demand of arbitrageurs will depend on the grade to which the equivalence relationship holds and on their elasticity of demand which is denoted as H:

$$H(\beta_2 \bar{s}_t + \beta_3 - s_t^A), \quad H > 0. \tag{2}$$

We assume that there exist an unspecified number of arbitrageurs and β_2 is allowed to be different from 1.[20] The possibility of a default means that the cash-and-carry strategy, which is based on long positions in the CDS and short positions in the synthetic CDS or vice versa, is not completely riskless. In case of default, the investor's net payment differs from the basis and the arbitrageur could even incur losses, which means that the strategy is not exempt of risk. Another argument that reinforces the idea that the strategy is not riskless is that the CDS and the synthetic CDS are not exactly the same asset and thus their prices can change in a different way at a given time period. Moreover, although we assume that there are no restrictions on corporate bond and ASP short sales, these may appear in real world.[21] These restrictions make it difficult to exploit arbitrage opportunities whenever short sales are needed and this fact limits the arbitrageurs demand. Moreover, there could be constraints in the short-run availability of arbitrage capital or restrictions to market participation. For this reason, it seems more realistic to assume that H is finite. GS also consider as more realistic a finite value for H in the commodities markets.

2.2 *Demand schedule of market participants*

The behaviour of the other agents in the market place is defined according to their demand schedules. Thus, the demand schedule for the jth participant who deals only in ASP market is

$$E_{j,t} - A^{\text{ASP}}(R_{j,t}^{\text{ASP}} - s_t^A), \quad A^{\text{ASP}} > 0, \; j = 1, \ldots, N_{\text{ASP}}, \tag{3}$$

where according to the GS notation we define $E_{j,t}$ as the ASP endowment of the jth participant immediately prior to period t, N_{ASP} is the number of participants who deal only in the asset swap market. Let $R_{j,t}^{\mathrm{ASP}}$ be the reservation price at which participant jth is willing to hold the endowments of ASPs $E_{j,t}$ while A^{ASP} represents the elasticity of demand which is assumed to be the same for the total N_{ASP} participants. Let $A^{\mathrm{ASP}}(R_{j,t}^{\mathrm{ASP}} - s_t^A)$ be the variation in the endowments prior to period t. An increase in the asset swap spread implies an increase in the ASP buyers' returns given that they are equal to the sum of the floating rate and the asset swap spread. Therefore, there is an increase in the ASP endowments prior to period $t+1$, $E_{j,t+1}$, whenever $R_{j,t}^{\mathrm{ASP}} < s_t^A$. Notice that it is his reservation price with respect to the ASP spread what defines an investor as an ASP seller or buyer.

The demand schedule for the participants who deal only in the CDS market is as follows:

$$E_{i,t} - A^{\mathrm{CDS}}(\bar{s}_t - R_{i,t}^{\mathrm{CDS}}), \quad A^{\mathrm{CDS}} > 0, \; i = 1, \ldots, N_{\mathrm{CDS}}, \tag{4}$$

where $E_{i,t}$ is the CDS endowment of the ith participant immediately prior to period t, N_{CDS} is the number of participants who deal only in the CDS market, $R_{i,t}^{\mathrm{CDS}}$ is the reservation price at which participant ith is willing to hold the endowments of CDSs $E_{i,t}$ while A^{CDS} represents the elasticity of demand which is the same for the total number of participants N_{CDS}. The individuals operating only in the CDS market are buyers or sellers depending on their reservation prices. These agents can be considered as speculators that bet on the probability of default. The individuals with $\bar{s}_t > R_{i,t}^{\mathrm{CDS}}$ will be net suppliers of CDSs or protection sellers. They benefit from the periodic payments that receive and are willing to provide default protection at this price.[22] As $\bar{s}_t > R_{i,t}^{\mathrm{CDS}}$, the CDS endowments of these individuals decrease with respect to those immediately prior to period t. This supply of CDSs could be absorbed by an individual i_2^{th} with a reservation price such that $\bar{s}_t < R_{i_2,t}^{\mathrm{CDS}}$ or by the debt hedgers or by the other individuals that participate in both markets at the same time. The individuals with $\bar{s}_t < R_{i_2,t}^{\mathrm{CDS}}$ are net buyers of CDSs or net default protection buyers.

The demand schedule of individuals who participate in both financial markets as market makers is defined from the reservation price in the corresponding market such that the endowments of ASPs are not conditioned by the endowments of CDSs. The ASPs and CDSs' demand schedule of these agents is as follows:

$$E_{k,t}^{B,\mathrm{ASP}} - A^{B,\mathrm{ASP}}(R_{k,t}^{B,\mathrm{ASP}} - s_t^A), \quad A^{B,\mathrm{ASP}} > 0, \; k = 1, \ldots, N_{\mathrm{BOTH}} \tag{5}$$

$$E_{k,t}^{B,\mathrm{CDS}} - A^{B,\mathrm{CDS}}(\bar{s}_t - R_{k,t}^{B,\mathrm{CDS}}), \quad A^{B,\mathrm{CDS}} > 0, \; k = 1, \ldots, N_{\mathrm{BOTH}}, \tag{6}$$

where the notation in Equations (5) and (6) is equivalent to the one employed in Equations (3) and (4).

The demand schedule of hedgers is conditioned by their positions in ASPs. We assume that the positions in ASPs of these agents are completely hedged. Thus, the endowments and demand of CDSs are independent of the CDSs premium and they are equal to the endowments and demand of ASPs. The endowments of ASPs increase as the ASP spread increases:

$$E_{h,t}^{H,\mathrm{ASP}} - A^{H,\mathrm{ASP}}(R_{h,t}^{H,\mathrm{ASP}} - s_t^A), \quad A^{H,\mathrm{ASP}} > 0, \; h = 1, \ldots, N_H. \tag{7}$$

Notation for Equation (7) is equivalent to the one in Equations (3) and (5) and it represents the debt hedgers demand schedule for both ASPs and CDSs.

2.3 *Clearing market conditions*

Using all the above demand schedules for the five types of individuals, we set the clearing market conditions for both markets.[23]

The ASP market will clear at the value of s_t^A that solves the supply/demand equation:

$$\sum_{j=1}^{N_{\text{ASP}}} E_{j,t} + \sum_{k=1}^{N_{\text{BOTH}}} E_{k,t}^{B,\text{ASP}} + \sum_{h=1}^{N_H} E_{h,t}^{H,\text{ASP}}$$
$$= \sum_{j=1}^{N_{\text{ASP}}} [E_{j,t} - A^{\text{ASP}}(R_{j,t}^{\text{ASP}} - s_t^A)] + \sum_{k=1}^{N_{\text{BOTH}}} [E_{k,t}^{B,\text{ASP}} - A^{B,\text{ASP}}(R_{k,t}^{B,\text{ASP}} - s_t^A)]$$
$$+ \sum_{h=1}^{N_H} [E_{h,t}^{H,\text{ASP}} - A^{H,\text{ASP}}(R_{h,t}^{H,\text{ASP}} - s_t^A)] - H(\beta_2 \bar{s}_t + \beta_3 - s_t^A). \tag{8}$$

The CDS market will clear at the value of $\bar{s}_t$ that solves the supply/demand equation:

$$\sum_{i=1}^{N_{\text{CDS}}} E_{i,t} + \sum_{k=1}^{N_{\text{BOTH}}} E_{k,t}^{B,\text{CDS}} + \sum_{h=1}^{N_H} E_{h,t}^{H,\text{ASP}}$$
$$= \sum_{i=1}^{N_{\text{CDS}}} [E_{i,t} - A^{\text{CDS}}(\bar{s}_t - R_{i,t}^{\text{CDS}})] + \sum_{k=1}^{N_{\text{BOTH}}} [E_{k,t}^{B,\text{CDS}} - A^{B,\text{CDS}}(\bar{s}_t - R_{k,t}^{B,\text{CDS}})]$$
$$+ \sum_{h=1}^{N_H} [E_{h,t}^{H,\text{ASP}} - A^{H,\text{ASP}}(R_{h,t}^{H,\text{ASP}} - s_t^A)] - H(\beta_2 s_t + \beta_3 - s_t^A). \tag{9}$$

We solve the previous equations in order to find the CDS and ASP prices that clear both markets. For this purpose and as in GS, we assume that the mean reservation price for the N_{CDS} individuals in the CDS market is $R_t^{\text{CDS}} = N_{\text{CDS}}^{-1} \sum_{i=1}^{N_{\text{CDS}}} R_{i,t}^{\text{CDS}}$ and for the N_{ASP} individuals in the ASP market, it is given by $R_t^{\text{ASP}} = N_{\text{ASP}}^{-1} \sum_{j=1}^{N_{\text{ASP}}} R_{j,t}^{\text{ASP}}$. For the individuals who are present in both markets, we have that the mean reservation prices are $R_t^{B,\text{CDS}} = N_{\text{BOTH}}^{-1} \sum_{k=1}^{N_{\text{BOTH}}} R_{k,t}^{B,\text{CDS}}$ and $R_t^{B,\text{ASP}} = N_{\text{BOTH}}^{-1} \sum_{k=1}^{N_{\text{BOTH}}} R_{k,t}^{B,\text{ASP}}$, as well as for the hedgers, the reservation price is defined as $R_t^{H,\text{ASP}} = N_H^{-1} \sum_{h=1}^{N_H} R_{h,t}^{H,\text{ASP}}$. As in GS, we assume that the elasticities are the same for all market participants in ASP and CDS markets ($A^{\text{ASP}} = A^{B,\text{ASP}} = A^{\text{CDS}} = A^{B,\text{CDS}} = A^{H,\text{ASP}}$).[24] Solving Equations (8) and (9) for s_t^A and $\bar{s}_t$ as a function of the mean reservation prices, we obtain:[25]

$$s_t^A = \frac{C + H\beta_2 F + A\,(N_{\text{CDS}} + N_{\text{BOTH}})(N_H R_t^{H,\text{ASP}} + N_{\text{BOTH}} R_t^{B,\text{ASP}} + N_{\text{ASP}} R_t^{\text{ASP}})}{B}, \tag{10}$$

$$\bar{s}_t = \frac{\begin{gathered}-D + HF + A\{(N_{\text{CDS}}(N_H + N_{\text{BOTH}} + N_{\text{ASP}})R_t^{\text{CDS}} \\ + N_H[N_{\text{BOTH}}(-R_t^{H,\text{ASP}} + R_t^{B,\text{ASP}} + R_t^{B,\text{CDS}}) + N_{\text{ASP}}(-R_t^{H,\text{ASP}} + R_t^{\text{ASP}})] \\ + N_{\text{BOTH}}(N_{\text{BOTH}} + N_{\text{ASP}})R_t^{B,\text{CDS}}\}\end{gathered}}{B} \tag{11}$$

where the grouped elements that appear in Equations (10) and (11) are defined as follows:

$$B = A(N_{\text{CDS}} + N_{\text{BOTH}})(N_H + N_{\text{BOTH}} + N_{\text{ASP}})$$
$$+ H(N_{\text{CDS}} + N_{\text{BOTH}} + \beta_2 N_{\text{BOTH}} + \beta_2 N_{\text{ASP}}) \tag{12a}$$

$$C = H\beta_3(N_{\text{CDS}} + N_{\text{BOTH}}) \tag{12b}$$

$$D = H\beta_3(N_{\text{ASP}} + N_{\text{BOTH}}) \tag{12c}$$

$$F = N_{\text{CDS}} R_t^{\text{CDS}} + N_{\text{BOTH}}(R_t^{B,\text{ASP}} + R_t^{B,\text{CDS}}) + N_{\text{ASP}} R_t^{\text{ASP}}. \tag{12d}$$

In order to derive the dynamic price relationship, the model in Equations (10) and (11) must be characterized with a description of the evolution of the reservation prices. Immediately after the market clearing in period $t-1$, a given market participant in CDSs is willing to hold an amount $E_{i,t}$ or $E_{k,t}^{B,\text{CDS}}$, depending on the investor's type, at price $\bar{s}_{t-1}$. A given participant in the ASP market is willing to hold an amount $E_{j,t}$, $E_{k,t}^{B,\text{ASP}}$ or $E_{h,t}^{H,\text{ASP}}$, depending on the investor's type, at price s_{t-1}^{A}. It implies that the corresponding reservation prices after that clearing are $\bar{s}_{t-1}$ and s_{t-1}^{A} for participants in CDS and ASP markets, respectively. Thus, the reservation prices behave according to the following process:

$$R_{i,t}^{\text{CDS}} = \bar{s}_{t-1} + v_t + w_{i,t}^{\text{CDS}}, \quad i = 1, \ldots, N_{\text{CDS}} \tag{13a}$$

$$R_{j,t}^{\text{ASP}} = s_{t-1}^{A} + v_t + w_{j,t}^{\text{ASP}}, \quad j = 1, \ldots, N_{\text{ASP}} \tag{13b}$$

$$R_{k,t}^{B,\text{CDS}} = \bar{s}_{t-1} + v_t + w_{k,t}^{B,\text{CDS}}, \quad k = 1, \ldots, N_{\text{BOTH}} \tag{13c}$$

$$R_{k,t}^{B,\text{ASP}} = s_{t-1}^{A} + v_t + w_{k,t}^{B,\text{ASP}}, \quad k = 1, \ldots, N_{\text{BOTH}} \tag{13d}$$

$$R_{h,t}^{H,\text{ASP}} = s_{t-1}^{A} + v_t + w_{h,t}^{H,\text{ASP}}, \quad h = 1, \ldots, N_H \tag{13e}$$

such that:

$$\text{cov}(v_t, w_{l,t}) = 0, \quad \forall l \tag{13f}$$

$$\text{cov}(w_{e,t}, w_{l,t}) = 0, \quad \forall l \neq e, \tag{13g}$$

where v_t is a white noise with finite variance that is a common component for all participants and $w_{i,t}$, $w_{j,t}$, $w_{k,t}$ and $w_{h,t}$ are also white noises with finite variance that represent the idiosyncratic component for participants i, j, k and h, respectively.

As GS states, the price change for the above individuals, for instance $R_{i,t}^{\text{CDS}} - \bar{s}_{t-1}$ for the individuals who operate only in the CDS market, reflects the arrival of new information between period $t-1$ and period t which changes the price at which the ith participant is willing to hold the quantity $E_{i,t}$ of the CDS. The price changes have a component common to all participants (v_t) and a component idiosyncratic to the ith participant ($w_{i,t}$). Thus, the mean reservation price can be also expressed as follows:

$$R_t^{\text{CDS}} = \bar{s}_{t-1} + v_t + w_t^{\text{CDS}} \tag{14a}$$

$$R_t^{\text{ASP}} = s_{t-1}^{A} + v_t + w_t^{\text{ASP}} \tag{14b}$$

$$R_t^{B,\text{CDS}} = \bar{s}_{t-1} + v_t + w_t^{B,\text{CDS}} \tag{14c}$$

$$R_t^{B,\text{ASP}} = s_{t-1}^{A} + v_t + w_t^{B,\text{ASP}} \tag{14d}$$

$$R_t^{H,\text{ASP}} = s_{t-1}^{A} + v_t + w_t^{H,\text{ASP}}, \tag{14e}$$

where $w_t^{\text{CDS}} = N_{\text{CDS}}^{-1} \sum_{i=1}^{N_{\text{CDS}}} w_{i,t}^{\text{CDS}}$, $w_t^{\text{ASP}} = N_{\text{ASP}}^{-1} \sum_{j=1}^{N_{\text{ASP}}} w_{j,t}^{\text{ASP}}$, $w_t^{B,\text{CDS}} = N_{\text{BOTH}}^{-1} \sum_{k=1}^{N_{\text{BOTH}}} w_{k,t}^{B,\text{CDS}}$, $w_t^{B,\text{ASP}} = N_{\text{BOTH}}^{-1} \sum_{k=1}^{N_{\text{BOTH}}} w_{k,t}^{B,\text{ASP}}$ and $w_t^{H,\text{ASP}} = N_H^{-1} \sum_{h=1}^{N_H} w_{h,t}^{H,\text{ASP}}$. We substitute the expressions (14) into the Equations (10) and (11) and obtain the following equation (see Appendix 1):

$$\begin{pmatrix} \Delta s_t^A \\ \Delta \bar{s}_t \end{pmatrix} = \frac{H}{B} \begin{bmatrix} -(N_{\text{BOTH}} + N_{\text{CDS}}) \\ (N_{\text{BOTH}} + N_{\text{ASP}}) \end{bmatrix} (1, -\beta_2, -\beta_3) \begin{pmatrix} s_{t-1}^A \\ \bar{s}_{t-1} \\ 1 \end{pmatrix} + \begin{pmatrix} u_t^{\text{ASP}} \\ u_t^{\text{CDS}} \end{pmatrix}, \tag{15}$$

where $(u_t^{\text{ASP}}, u_t^{\text{CDS}})$ is a vector white noise with $E(u_t) = 0$ and $\text{Var}(u_t) = \Omega > 0$. In u_t, we include both the common components and the participants' noises.[26] The model in Equation (15) can be changed into a vector error correction model (VECM) model by the subtracting vector of prices $(s_t^A, \bar{s}_t)'$ from both sides.

Although GS provides the first step for understanding price discovery, current analyses are based on either Hasbrouck's (1995) or Gonzalo and Granger's (1995) methodologies. Contrary to GS, the last two approaches are based on a VAR with an Error Correction Term model. As in FFG, we pretend to match the GS and GG methodology from the use of a VECM specification. Equation (15) can be extended, with lags of vector $(\Delta s_t^A, \Delta \bar{s}_t)'$, and represented according to a VECM specification:

$$\Delta X_t = \alpha \beta' X_{t-1} + \sum_{i=1}^{p} \Gamma_i X_{t-i} + u_t, \tag{16}$$

where $X_t = (s_t^A, \bar{s}_t)'$ and u_t is a white noise vector. According to expression (15),

$$\alpha' = \left(-\frac{H}{B}(N_{\text{BOTH}} + N_{\text{CDS}}), \frac{H}{B}(N_{\text{BOTH}} + N_{\text{ASP}}) \right) \text{ and } \beta' = (1, -\beta_2).$$

In this paper, we adopt GG's methodology and thus, their PT component decomposition to measure market contribution to price discovery (see Appendix 2). We find that the percentages of price discovery of ASP and CDS markets can be defined from the GG price discovery metrics that we denote as GG_1 and GG_2, respectively:

$$\text{GG}_1 = \frac{\alpha_2}{-\alpha_1 + \alpha_2} \quad \text{and} \quad \text{GG}_2 = \frac{-\alpha_1}{-\alpha_1 + \alpha_2} \tag{17}$$

Or equivalently:

$$\text{GG}_1 = \frac{N_{\text{BOTH}} + N_{\text{ASP}}}{2N_{\text{BOTH}} + N_{\text{ASP}} + N_{\text{CDS}}} \quad \text{and} \quad \text{GG}_2 = \frac{N_{\text{BOTH}} + N_{\text{CDS}}}{2N_{\text{BOTH}} + N_{\text{ASP}} + N_{\text{CDS}}}. \tag{18}$$

Note that the number of hedgers are not relevant to define the price discovery metrics and as a consequence in the price discovery process.[27] Note also that although the theoretical model's liquidity variable is defined as the number of market participants in a given market relative to other market, this metric can be easily related with other commonly employed liquidity measures like the number of contracts or the volume in a given market relative to the other.

2.4 *Hypotheses*

According to the price discovery metric in Equation (18), the interaction between both markets due to the market players that operate jointly in CDS and ASP markets is of crucial importance.

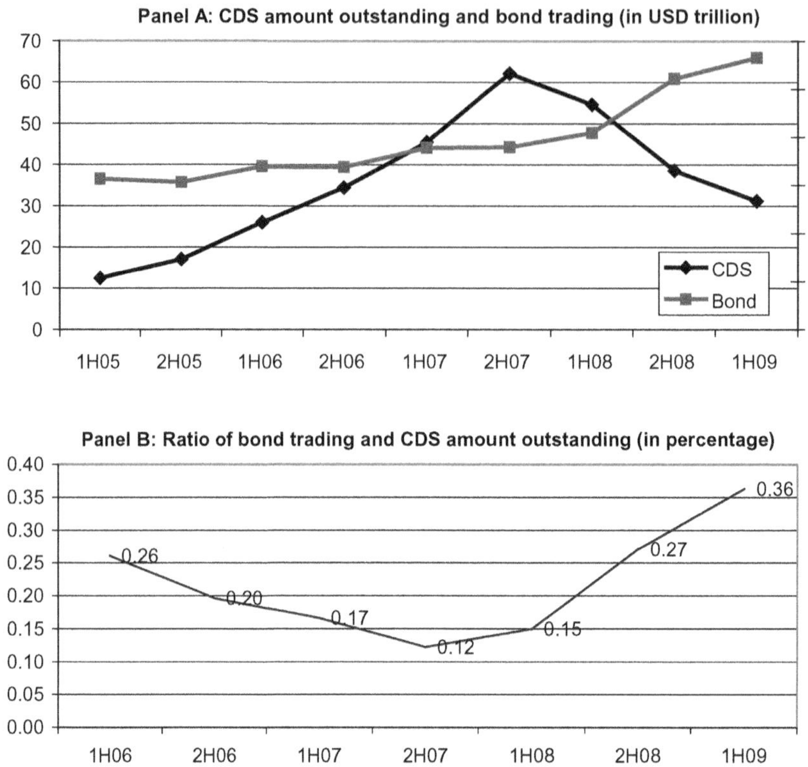

Figure 1. Credit default swap notional amount outstanding and bond trading on exchanges.
Source: CDS Notional Amount Outstanding: International Swaps and Derivatives Association (ISDA) Bond Trading on Exchanges: World Federation of Exchanges.

The subprime crisis has affected liquidity in credit derivatives markets and as a consequence the five types of market players. The subprime crisis leads to a decrease in CDS liquidity. The high counterparty risk in the CDS market jointly with, as Dötz (2007) suggests, the relatively high concentration and the homogeneousness of its often leveraged market players has affected the CDS market severely. According to the International Financial Services London (IFSL) Research (2009a), centralized clearing and voluntary termination of contacts have contributed to a 39% drop in notional amounts outstanding of CDS from $62 trillion at end-2007 to $38 trillion at end-2008, according to the International Swaps and Derivatives Association (ISDA) (see Panel A of Figure 1).[28] However, as the IFSL Research (2009b) states, the fall in liquidity during the subprime crisis has increased the importance of bond markets as a source of finance for companies and governments. The issuance of corporate bonds increased to record levels towards the end of 2008 and the first quarter of 2009, particularly in Europe.[29] With respect to the bond trading activity, IFSL Research (2009b) reports that the trading of bonds on exchanges increased by a quarter in 2008 to over 19$ trillion (see Panel A of Figure 1).

Our first aim is to analyse whether in periods when liquidity is especially low, CDSs maintain their role as the main determinant in the price discovery process. To test this statement, we analyse price discovery for two subperiods which correspond to the periods before and after the subprime crisis such that the break-point is set at July 2007. Given previous published evidence,[30] we expect that before the crisis, CDSs lead the price discovery process or at least, if the role of participants in both markets is highly influential (N_{BOTH} is high), the price discovery measure of Equation (18) should be close to 0.5.[31] According to our model, the leadership of the CDS market can be explained by its higher liquidity (number of participants). The buy-and-hold strategy employed by the ASP or bond investors contrary to the active behaviour of CDS investors, in part due to the leverage associated with a CDSs purchase, could lead to a higher market activity in the CDS market than in the bond market before the subprime crisis.

Hypothesis 1: Under scenarios with high liquidity such as before the subprime crisis, the CDS market should lead the ASP market in the price discovery process.

The reason is that the number of participants (liquidity) in the CDS market is high relative to the number of players in the ASP market ($N_{CDS} > N_{ASP}$). In addition to the previous hypothesis, when the number of individuals who operate in both markets is high (N_{BOTH} is high), the CDS market should reveal information as efficiently as the ASP market.

According to Acharya and Schaefer (2006) and Acharya, Schaefer, and Zhang (2007), in periods with low liquidity one should expect that market makers, who at the same time are price setters in both credit markets, are financially constrained and thus their participation in both markets will decrease. In terms of our model, notation is equivalent to say that $N_{BOTH} \rightarrow 0$ and the new percentages of price discovery would change into a measure similar to the one introduced by GS:

$$\frac{N_{ASP}}{N_{ASP} + N_{CDS}} \quad \text{and} \quad \frac{N_{CDS}}{N_{ASP} + N_{CDS}} \tag{19}$$

According to the IFSL Research (2009a, 2009b) reports, the attraction of bonds, and implicitly ASPs, as an investment has increased since the start of the credit crisis and large institutional, as well as retail, investors increased their holdings due to the losses on equity markets and due to the bonds and ASPs high returns as yields during 2008.[32] On the other hand, there is a drop in both the notional amounts outstanding and the number of participants in the CDS market.[33] Thus, if the crisis has affected activity in the CDS more severely than in the ASP market, we expect the ASPs to reveal information faster and more adequately than before the crisis, up to the point that ASPs could lead the process of price discovery in some cases.[34]

Hypothesis 2: Under scenarios with low liquidity leading to a generalized reduction in market participation in credit derivatives markets, the relative position of the ASP market as an information provider improves with respect to the one observed under high liquid scenarios.

Finally, we analyse the process of price discovery between ASP and bond spreads.

Hypothesis 3: The ASP market always (before and after the subprime crisis) leads the price discovery process with respect to the bond market.

3. Data

Our database contains daily data on Eurobonds and ASPs denominated in Euros and issued by non-financial companies that are collected from Reuters and on CDSs also denominated in Euros and issued by the same non-financial companies that are obtained from GFI.

GFI is a major inter-dealer broker, specializing in the trading of credit derivatives. GFI data contain single-name CDSs market prices for 1, 2, 3, 4 and 5 years maturities. These prices correspond to actual trades, or firm bids and offers where capital is actually committed and so they are not consensus or indications. Thus, these prices are an accurate indication of where the CDS markets have traded and closed for a given day. For some companies and for some maturities, especially 2 and 4 years, the data availability are scarce and in these cases, we employ mid-price quotes from a credit curve also reported by GFI to fill the missing data.[35] GFI data have also been used by Hull, Predescu, and White (2004), Predescu (2006), Saita (2006), Nashikkar and Subrahmanyam (2007), Fulop and Lescourret (2007) or Nashikkar, Subrahmanyam, and Mahanti (2009) among others.

For each bond there is information on both bid and ask prices, the swap spread, the asset swap spread, the sector of the entity and its geographical location, the currency, the seniority, the rating history (Fitch, S&P and Moody's ratings), the issuance date and the amount issued, the coupon and coupon dates and the maturity. We use bonds whose maturity at the investment dates is lower than five years. Several bonds issued by the same company may be used whenever they satisfy all the required criteria. The reason is that although CDS spread quotes refer to the issuer and not to an individual bond, asset swap spreads are quoted for individual bonds. Due to liquidity considerations, bonds with time to maturity equal to or less than 12 months to the date corresponding to their last observation are excluded. Moreover, our sample contains fixed-rate senior unsecured Euro denominated bonds whose issued quantity exceeds 300 million Euros.[36] Other requirements imposed on bonds to be included in the sample are: (i) straight bonds, (ii) neither callable nor convertible, (iii) with rating history available, (iv) with constant coupons and with a fixed frequency, (v) without a sinking fund, (vi) without options, (vii) without an odd frequency of coupon payments, (viii) no government bonds and (ix) no inflation-indexed bonds. We cross-check the data on bonds with the equivalent data obtained from Datastream. Due to liquidity restrictions, investments are restricted to periods where there are 5-year CDS data on either actual trades or bids and offers where capital is committed.

The data spans from 1 November 2005 to 29 June 2009. However, we split the data into two subperiods to take into account the possible effects of the ongoing financial crisis. We estimate the break-points for each series of CDSs by means of the algorithm described in Bai and Perron (2003) for simultaneous estimation of multiple break-points. The ideas behind this implementation are described in Zeileis et al. (2003). The break-point is, on average, the 17 July 2007. For this reason, the first subperiod covers the period from 1 November 2005 to 16 July 2007 while the second one spans from 17 July 2007 to 29 June 2009. The final sample consists of 38 non-financial companies and 50 ASPs and bonds.[37] Panels A and B of Table 1 reports the CDS spread, the asset swap spread, the bond spread and the bases descriptive statistics before and during crisis, respectively.

Table 1. Descriptive statistics.

	CDS spread		ASP spread (ASS)		Bond spread (BS)		Basis ASS − CDS	Basis BS − CDS
Issuer	Mean	SD	Mean	SD	Mean	SD	Mean	Mean
Panel A								
Akzo I	22.99	2.68	16.27	8.36	17.82	8.62	−6.72	−5.17
Akzo II	13.46	3.91	15.31	5.63	16.54	5.28	1.84	3.08
BMW	11.80	4.68	10.57	3.51	12.10	3.63	−1.24	0.30
Bouygues I	20.09	5.67	24.52	6.89	26.00	6.85	4.42	5.90
Bouygues II	18.94	6.02	14.97	5.08	16.03	4.83	−3.96	−2.91
British AM Tob. I	23.77	13.22	19.68	8.84	21.41	8.53	−4.09	−2.36
British AM Tob. II	23.75	6.73	32.26	8.42	34.27	8.57	8.51	10.52
Carrefour I	15.63	4.29	18.72	5.40	20.30	5.45	3.09	4.68
Carrefour II	12.51	3.30	7.48	4.30	8.33	4.26	−5.03	−4.18
Casino I	47.94	8.57	56.73	11.40	59.28	11.28	8.79	11.34
Casino II	47.73	24.70	54.23	26.19	55.86	26.12	6.49	8.13

(Continued)

Table 1. Continued.

	CDS spread		ASP spread (ASS)		Bond spread (BS)		Basis ASS – CDS	Basis BS – CDS
Issuer	Mean	SD	Mean	SD	Mean	SD	Mean	Mean
Compass Group	26.32	18.28	35.19	19.90	36.13	19.37	8.87	9.82
Edison Spa	15.88	3.07	18.67	5.17	19.98	5.31	2.80	4.10
Enel	13.82	3.46	12.65	6.27	14.12	6.39	−1.17	0.29
Energia de Portugal I	11.01	4.78	10.85	4.00	11.77	3.75	−0.16	0.75
Energia de Portugal II	13.68	4.85	16.25	3.58	17.03	3.18	2.57	3.36
E.ON	10.46	2.76	9.32	3.91	10.55	3.77	−1.15	0.09
France Telecom	20.42	8.34	19.67	7.97	20.06	7.34	−0.75	−0.36
Iberdrola I	16.49	5.07	17.55	5.34	19.11	5.21	1.06	2.62
Iberdrola II	11.29	3.16	10.25	3.44	11.69	3.36	−1.05	0.40
Kingfisher	47.86	8.68	48.81	9.50	51.10	9.35	0.95	3.24
Koninklijke KPN	47.32	10.42	53.02	12.48	55.78	12.65	5.70	8.45
Louis Vuitton I	19.34	5.38	23.77	7.71	25.31	7.78	4.42	5.96
Louis Vuitton II	18.63	6.41	22.04	6.89	23.29	6.67	3.40	4.65
PPR	43.62	6.20	49.93	7.14	51.16	7.00	6.31	7.54
Renault	16.03	6.64	21.45	8.72	22.33	8.58	5.41	6.30
Repsol YPF	21.07	6.80	27.16	7.37	27.81	6.92	6.09	6.74
Reuters	19.04	5.66	25.79	5.63	27.20	5.53	6.76	8.16
Saint Gobain I	17.95	4.37	17.75	5.00	19.18	5.08	−0.19	1.23
Saint Gobain II	26.14	5.95	31.77	8.04	33.90	8.16	5.63	7.77
Saint Gobain III	21.64	6.22	26.83	7.74	28.14	7.60	5.19	6.50
Scania	24.83	8.49	24.59	7.06	26.80	7.34	−0.23	1.97
Siemens	12.21	1.59	10.25	1.75	11.19	1.65	−1.96	−1.02
Sodexho	10.17	4.97	19.38	5.60	20.63	5.18	9.22	10.47
Stora Enso	36.02	11.22	37.94	11.12	41.21	11.66	1.92	5.19
Technip	24.41	3.47	33.08	5.14	34.86	5.14	8.67	10.45
Telecom Italia I	45.57	10.80	47.86	12.81	50.22	12.81	2.29	4.65
Telecom Italia II	46.73	11.68	45.54	11.04	44.69	9.91	−1.19	−2.04
Telefonica	34.22	9.86	37.60	9.87	40.36	10.07	3.38	6.14
Telekom Austria	27.04	14.98	27.56	10.47	30.09	10.92	0.52	3.05
Tesco I	9.35	4.93	11.85	4.81	13.12	4.81	2.51	3.78
Tesco II	10.15	4.47	14.47	5.93	16.08	6.14	4.32	5.93
Thales	13.62	3.03	18.66	4.64	20.21	4.71	5.04	6.60
Thyssenkrupp	38.83	12.98	41.02	18.66	42.67	18.70	2.19	3.84
Union Fenosa	20.10	8.35	24.49	6.98	25.61	6.72	4.39	5.51
Vinci	22.62	6.89	22.48	5.72	23.40	5.56	−0.14	0.77
Vivendi	37.86	8.46	42.65	10.12	45.21	9.35	4.79	7.36
Vodafone	15.93	3.80	13.33	7.18	15.03	7.32	−2.60	−0.90
Volkswagen	21.66	5.81	24.25	7.61	26.16	7.83	2.59	4.50
Volvo	20.32	6.88	21.69	7.73	22.80	7.59	1.37	2.48
Average	23.37	7.06	25.76	7.88	27.28	7.80	2.40	3.91
Panel B								
Akzo I	22.91	13.77	15.77	13.08	15.23	13.39	−7.14	−7.67
Akzo II	65.35	43.04	71.75	70.25	73.09	73.10	6.39	7.73
BMW	143.30	145.26	97.84	103.52	100.27	106.85	−45.46	−43.03
Bouygues I	102.37	67.46	101.73	65.78	99.32	64.96	−0.63	−3.05
Bouygues II	46.74	20.56	28.48	13.32	26.13	13.78	−18.26	−20.61
British AM Tob. I	21.75	13.04	27.88	13.73	26.59	15.03	6.13	4.84
British AM Tob. II	59.05	28.23	107.48	61.30	109.66	62.00	48.43	50.61

(Continued)

Table 1. Continued.

	CDS spread		ASP spread (ASS)		Bond spread (BS)		Basis ASS – CDS	Basis BS – CDS
Issuer	Mean	SD	Mean	SD	Mean	SD	Mean	Mean
Carrefour I	49.78	28.57	52.85	43.52	50.35	42.18	3.07	0.57
Carrefour II	47.36	31.76	30.36	19.34	28.90	26.65	−17.00	−18.46
Casino I	142.42	76.61	172.68	96.59	177.36	100.39	30.26	34.94
Casino II	129.82	82.17	111.39	62.01	127.01	86.35	−18.43	−2.81
Compass Group	28.22	11.57	28.99	14.97	26.73	15.02	0.76	−1.49
Edison Spa	64.67	53.41	81.73	63.20	80.56	60.52	17.06	15.89
Enel	181.47	169.90	53.62	40.81	53.68	40.98	−127.85	−127.79
Energia de Portugal I	63.18	31.30	50.25	33.62	70.44	84.02	−12.92	7.26
Energia de Portugal II	72.19	34.54	101.37	66.28	99.56	66.46	29.18	27.37
E.ON	29.97	15.03	23.24	11.17	20.90	10.61	−6.73	−9.07
France Telecom	41.24	20.63	36.15	14.59	33.65	13.16	−5.09	−7.59
Iberdrola I	91.91	58.70	75.33	57.46	73.77	56.47	−16.57	−18.13
Iberdrola II	56.21	17.04	22.62	8.08	21.11	7.63	−33.59	−35.09
Kingfisher	191.71	101.87	218.77	109.45	232.37	119.06	27.06	40.66
Koninklijke KPN	72.67	28.30	113.49	55.43	118.28	59.64	40.82	45.61
Louis Vuitton I	71.18	51.35	70.48	48.09	69.81	47.89	−0.70	−1.37
Louis Vuitton II	65.82	54.71	62.18	49.64	60.81	48.82	−3.63	−5.00
PPR	251.15	200.92	200.10	145.78	206.13	153.20	−51.05	−45.02
Renault	58.74	40.11	34.95	13.50	32.73	13.39	−23.79	−26.02
Repsol YPF	115.08	112.21	107.03	87.49	106.07	89.01	−8.06	−9.02
Reuters	25.21	5.80	31.72	14.25	32.18	14.14	6.51	6.97
Saint Gobain I	71.05	44.75	36.41	13.34	35.05	13.62	−34.64	−36.00
Saint Gobain II	157.12	105.03	158.11	112.11	162.77	116.51	0.99	5.64
Saint Gobain III	142.68	102.03	110.63	72.43	117.04	86.39	−32.06	−25.64
Scania	53.84	22.69	52.89	17.10	55.32	17.84	−0.96	1.47
Siemens	75.68	56.84	62.26	47.49	61.29	46.75	−13.42	−14.39
Sodexho	20.22	11.43	37.02	15.13	34.54	16.24	16.81	14.33
Stora Enso	151.65	99.48	130.83	53.31	138.58	56.83	−20.82	−13.06
Technip	98.15	80.35	109.03	83.60	113.56	89.44	10.88	15.41
Telecom Italia I	183.94	140.76	157.81	96.93	171.91	120.12	−26.14	−12.03
Telecom Italia II	185.40	138.37	216.94	150.62	215.83	152.30	31.54	30.44
Telefonica	97.65	55.63	103.07	56.78	104.85	56.91	5.42	7.21
Telekom Austria	58.36	30.30	94.18	63.32	99.73	66.06	35.82	41.36
Tesco I	58.86	52.31	63.37	62.18	36.48	60.87	4.51	−22.37
Tesco II	63.58	49.52	67.35	54.03	66.59	53.57	3.77	3.01
Thales	78.65	61.84	72.49	67.95	76.33	79.17	−6.16	−2.32
Thyssenkrupp	173.81	157.73	104.64	96.12	112.44	105.46	−69.17	−61.37
Union Fenosa	72.71	69.03	87.48	65.76	85.18	63.58	14.77	12.47
Vinci	51.93	29.75	41.63	17.90	39.68	18.21	−10.30	−12.25
Vivendi	62.87	27.14	80.13	38.10	82.10	39.92	17.26	19.24
Vodafone	39.41	14.36	25.67	11.42	23.75	11.67	−13.74	−15.65
Volkswagen	131.18	91.80	118.90	95.54	122.20	97.98	−12.28	−8.98
Volvo	215.51	235.82	244.23	269.96	254.70	290.16	28.72	39.19
Average	91.11	64.70	86.11	59.15	87.65	63.29	−5.01	−3.46

Notes: This table reports the descriptive statistics (mean and standard deviation) for the CDS spread; the ASP spread; the bond spread; and the bases, which are obtained as the difference between the ASP and the CDS spreads and as the difference between the bond and the CDS spreads, all of them defined in basis points. Panel A reports the descriptive statistics for the period before the crisis (November 2005 to July 2007) and Panel B for the crisis period (July 2007 to June 2009).

4. Price discovery results

We analyse the price discovery process in two different contexts. On the one hand, before July 2007 there exists a scenario of high liquidity where the number of market participants is higher than in the second period, which represents the illiquid scenario.

The process of price discovery is analysed from an equilibrium model based on an Error Correction Model and the long-run equilibrium condition is based on the existence of cointegration between credit spreads. Econometric details on the model estimation of the VECM defined in Equation (16) can be found in Juselius (2006).

Before the price discovery analysis, we firstly verify the series stationarity by means of a Ng-Perron unit root test. Table 2 shows that credit spreads are I(1) for the two periods considered in 46 of the total 50 cases which correspond to 50 different ASPs and bonds.

In Table 3, we report the Johansen (1991) cointegration test results for each reference entity whenever the CDS and ASP spreads are I(1) in the two periods. In 32 of the total 46 cases, we find cointegration between ASP and CDS spreads. We find cointegration between bond and CDS spreads in the same 32 cases.[38] The number of cointegration relationships that we find is similar to one obtained in previous analyses. Norden and Weber (2004), Blanco, Brennan, and Marsh (2005) and Zhu (2006) find cointegration relationships between CDS and bond spreads in 36 of 58 cases, in 26 of 33 cases and in 15 of 24 cases, respectively. De Wit (2006) finds cointegration relationships between CDS and ASP spreads in 88 of 144 cases. With respect to ASP and bond spreads, we find evidence of cointegration between them for all the 46 cases.[39] We then test why there is no cointegration between the ASP and CDS market. To achieve this, we run a Probit regression with heteroskedasticity robust standard errors for the total 92 cases studied in both subperiods, using as dependent variable a dummy variable that equals 1 if there is cointegration and 0 otherwise. In order to control and test the effect of the crisis, we create a dummy variable equal to one if a given case corresponds to the crisis period. The cointegration seems to be more frequent in bonds/ASPs with a high coupon rate and with a long time to maturity. The results suggest that the riskier the underlying bond or the longer the time to maturity, the more similar are the credit spreads in the long run. The first result is consistent with the increase in correlation across financial markets as the risk increases. The second result suggests that the deviations among credit spreads are higher close to the bond maturity. We use other explanatory variables such as the rating; the basis, which is defined as the difference between the ASP and CDS spreads; and the crisis dummy but none of them have a significant effect on cointegration.[40]

The analysis of price discovery is based on the VECM specification presented in Equations (15) and (16) and it is applied to the 32 cases, where we find a long-run equilibrium behaviour of the credit spreads series. The vector in Equation (16) represents the coefficients that determine the market contribution to price discovery. We conclude that a given market leads the process of price discovery whenever its corresponding price discovery metric (GG_i for $i = 1, 2$) is higher than 0.5. Both markets reveal information in an equally efficient way whenever the price discovery metrics are close to 0.5 for both markets ($0.45 < GG_i < 0.55$ for $i = 1, 2$). The GG_i price discovery metric is defined such that it has a lower bound of 0 and an upper bound of 1 in order to be consistent with the definition in Equation (18) and the meaning of this metric.

4.1 *The leadership of the CDS market before the crisis*

Panel A of Table 4 shows that during the period before the crisis, Hypothesis 1 is confirmed and the CDSs appear clearly as the more efficient market in 87.5% of the cases (28 cases). According

Table 2. Unit root test for credit spreads.

	CDS		ASP		Bond	
Issuer	First period	Second period	First period	Second period	First period	Second period
Akzo I	I(1)	I(1)	I(1)	I(1)	I(1)	I(1)
Akzo II	I(1)	I(1)	I(1)	I(1)	I(1)	I(1)
BMW	I(1)	I(1)	I(1)	I(1)	I(1)	I(1)
Bouygues I	I(1)	I(1)	I(1)	I(1)	I(1)	I(1)
Bouygues II	I(1)	I(1)	I(1)	I(1)	I(1)	I(1)
British AM Tob. I	I(1)	I(1)	I(1)	I(1)	I(1)	I(1)
British AM Tob. II	I(1)	I(1)	I(1)	I(1)	I(1)	I(1)
Carrefour I	I(1)	I(1)	I(1)	I(1)	I(1)	I(1)
Carrefour II	I(1)	I(1)	I(1)	I(1)	I(1)	I(1)
Casino I	I(1)	I(1)	I(1)	I(1)	I(1)	I(1)
Casino II	I(1)	I(1)	I(1)	I(1)	I(1)	I(1)
Compass Group	I(1)	I(1)	I(1)	I(1)	I(1)	I(1)
Edison Spa	I(1)	I(1)	I(1)	I(1)	I(1)	I(1)
Enel	I(1)	I(1)	I(1)	I(1)	I(1)	I(1)
Energia de Portugal I	I(1)	I(1)	I(1)	I(1)	I(1)	I(1)
Energia de Portugal II	I(1)	I(1)	I(1)	I(1)	I(1)	I(1)
E.ON	I(1)	I(1)	I(1)	I(1)	I(1)	I(1)
France Telecom	I(1)	I(1)	I(1)	I(1)	I(1)	I(1)
Iberdrola I	I(1)	I(1)	I(1)	I(1)	I(1)	I(1)
Iberdrola II	**I(1)**	**I(1)**	**I(1)**	**I(0)**	**I(1)**	**I(0)**
Kingfisher	I(1)	I(1)	I(1)	I(1)	I(1)	I(1)
Koninklijke KPN	I(1)	I(1)	I(1)	I(1)	I(1)	I(1)
Louis Vuitton I	I(1)	I(1)	I(1)	I(1)	I(1)	I(1)
Louis Vuitton II	I(1)	I(1)	I(1)	I(1)	I(1)	I(1)
PPR	I(1)	I(1)	I(1)	I(1)	I(1)	I(1)
Renault	I(1)	I(1)	I(1)	I(1)	I(1)	I(1)
Repsol YPF	I(1)	I(1)	I(1)	I(1)	I(1)	I(1)
Reuters	**I(0)**	**I(1)**	**I(1)**	**I(1)**	**I(1)**	**I(1)**
Saint Gobain I	I(1)	I(1)	I(1)	I(1)	I(1)	I(1)
Saint Gobain II	I(1)	I(1)	I(1)	I(1)	I(1)	I(1)
Saint Gobain III	I(1)	I(1)	I(1)	I(1)	I(1)	I(1)
Scania	I(1)	I(1)	I(1)	I(1)	I(1)	I(1)
Siemens	**I(0)**	**I(1)**	**I(0)**	**I(1)**	**I(0)**	**I(1)**
Sodexho	I(1)	I(1)	I(1)	I(1)	I(1)	I(1)
Stora Enso	I(1)	I(1)	I(1)	I(1)	I(1)	I(1)
Technip	I(1)	I(1)	I(1)	I(1)	I(1)	I(1)
Telecom Italia I	I(1)	I(1)	I(1)	I(1)	I(1)	I(1)
Telecom Italia II	I(1)	I(1)	I(1)	I(1)	I(1)	I(1)
Telefonica	I(1)	I(1)	I(1)	I(1)	I(1)	I(1)
Telekom Austria	I(1)	I(1)	I(1)	I(1)	I(1)	I(1)
Tesco I	I(1)	I(1)	I(1)	I(1)	I(1)	I(1)
Tesco II	I(1)	I(1)	I(1)	I(1)	I(1)	I(1)
Thales	**I(0)**	**I(1)**	**I(0)**	**I(1)**	**I(0)**	**I(1)**
Thyssenkrupp	I(1)	I(1)	I(1)	I(1)	I(1)	I(1)
Union Fenosa	I(1)	I(1)	I(1)	I(1)	I(1)	I(1)
Vinci	I(1)	I(1)	I(1)	I(1)	I(1)	I(1)
Vivendi	I(1)	I(1)	I(1)	I(1)	I(1)	I(1)
Vodafone	I(1)	I(1)	I(1)	I(1)	I(1)	I(1)
Volkswagen	I(1)	I(1)	I(1)	I(1)	I(1)	I(1)
Volvo	I(1)	I(1)	I(1)	I(1)	I(1)	I(1)

Notes: This table reports the unit root tests for CDS, ASP and bond spreads in two different periods. The first column is divided in two sub-columns that present the order of integration of the CDS premium for the period before the crisis (November 2005 to July 2007) and the crisis (July 2007 to June 2009), respectively. The second column is divided into other two columns that present the order of integration for the ASP spreads for the same two periods. The last column reports the order of integration for the bond spreads for the same periods. The cases where all the credit spreads are not integrated of order one in the two periods are in bold.

Table 3. Cointegration tests based on CDS and ASP spreads.

	November 2005 to July 2007		July 2007 to June 2009	
Issuer	None	At most 1	None	At most 1
Akzo I	13.93**	0.36	16.81**	1.99
Akzo II	20.42***	3.98	13.02**	3.24
BMW	14.88**	3.75	28.87***	3.01
Bouygues I	13.74**	2.77	18.07**	2.04
Bouygues II	19.98**	4.47	20.01**	5.89
British AM Tob. I	**21.14****	**2.30**	**6.40**	**2.38**
British AM Tob. II	**21.84****	**8.10**	**7.46**	**2.72**
Carrefour I	13.70**	0.11	13.58**	0.58
Carrefour II	20.05**	6.12	13.03**	0.48
Casino I	26.90***	4.00	22.29**	1.86
Casino II	20.18**	2.41	24.92***	3.34
Compass Group	49.43***	5.41	17.13**	3.03
Edison Spa	13.21**	3.56	20.75**	2.38
Enel	**21.83****	**1.64**	**10.79**	**1.97**
Energia de Portugal I	**22.80****	**8.42**	**6.88**	**2.70**
Energia de Portugal II	17.44***	3.23	12.60**	0.00
E.ON	15.36**	1.67	24.11**	2.18
France Telecom	**16.40**	**3.82**	**8.17**	**2.13**
Iberdrola I	14.19**	2.90	22.41**	2.55
Kingfisher	42.19***	6.21	21.78**	3.11
Koninklijke KPN	13.22**	3.57	23.32**	4.13
Louis Vuitton I	17.30**	0.60	21.26**	2.36
Louis Vuitton II	15.16**	2.43	32.78***	2.79
PPR	17.85**	1.34	21.80**	2.03
Renault	15.57**	0.93	15.46**	1.97
Repsol YPF	13.74**	1.70	26.70***	2.38
Saint Gobain I	**21.67****	**6.45**	**9.67**	**2.24**
Saint Gobain II	12.67**	3.04	16.47**	1.59
Saint Gobain III	20.77**	4.78	20.77***	0.01
Scania	**7.33**	**2.82**	**20.302****	**2.41**
Sodexho	17.36**	3.50	13.06**	0.01
Stora Enso	**15.60**	**4.20**	**11.69**	**4.50**
Technip	**12.01**	**1.60**	**21.47****	**2.93**
Telecom Italia I	23.71**	1.69	25.43***	2.62
Telecom Italia II	12.98**	0.60	20.10**	2.32
Telefonica	16.41**	1.75	20.10**	2.78
Telekom Austria	**19.99****	**9.14**	**12.43**	**3.65**
Tesco I	**11.42**	**3.41**	**24.48****	**2.70**
Tesco II	27.13***	3.65	21.25**	2.33
Thyssenkrupp	19.18**	1.82	16.93**	0.16
Union Fenosa	19.67**	6.01	13.23**	0.10
Vinci	**14.26****	**2.62**	**5.70**	**0.53**
Vivendi	**12.58**	**1.15**	**7.76**	**3.26**
Vodafone	21.00**	3.56	17.95***	0.21
Volkswagen	**10.31**	**3.27**	**22.94****	**2.78**
Volvo	17.17**	3.76	12.54**	0.06

Notes: This table reports the results obtained in the cointegration analyses applied to the CDS and the ASP spreads. The first two columns of Table 3 report Johansen trace test statistics for the number of cointegrating relations between the CDS and the ASP spreads for the period before the subprime crisis (November 2005 to July 2007). The last two columns of Table 3 report the same statistics for the crisis period (July 2007 to June 2009). A constant is included in the long-run relation if it is significantly different from zero. The number of lags in the vector autoregression is optimized using the AIC and attending to the autocorrelation LM residual test such that there is no autocorrelation at an adequate lag order. The cases where we do not find evidence of cointegration between credit spreads for the two periods are given in bold.

*Rejection of null at 10% level.

**Rejection of null at 5% level.

***Rejection of null at 1% level.

Table 4. Contributions to price discovery (CDS *vs.* ASP).

Issuer	α_1	t-Stat	α_2	t-Stat	β_3	β_2	PD_1	PD_2	GG_1
Panel A: Contributions to price discovery (CDS *vs.* ASP) before the crisis									
Akzo I	−0.037	−2.607	−0.005	−0.619	0.000	0.580	−0.146	1.085	0.000
Akzo II	−0.075	−3.786	0.004	0.600	0.000	1.152	0.050	0.942	0.050
BMW	−0.085	−3.023	−0.015	−1.547	0.000	0.771	−0.198	1.153	0.000
Bouygues I	−0.015	−1.340	0.016	2.964	0.000	1.382	0.425	0.413	0.507
Bouygues II	−0.034	−1.169	0.041	3.410	0.133	0.864	0.594	0.487	0.550
Carrefour I	−0.058	−2.4462	−0.015	−1.079	0.000	1.128	−0.374	1.422	0.000
Carrefour II	−0.101	−3.418	0.008	0.527	−10.492	1.461	0.069	0.899	0.072
Casino I	−0.089	−4.310	−0.034	−1.354	1.837	1.213	−0.709	1.859	0.000
Casino II	−0.050	−2.634	0.013	0.662	3.205	1.048	0.200	0.791	0.202
Compass Group	−0.094	−5.141	0.008	0.561	29.194	0.631	0.084	0.947	0.081
Edison Spa	−0.018	−1.145	0.022	2.688	0.000	1.543	0.422	0.350	0.547
Energia de Portugal II	−0.021	−1.159	0.023	3.616	0.000	1.316	0.448	0.410	0.522
E.ON	−0.092	−3.307	0.011	1.255	0.000	0.920	0.109	0.900	0.108
Iberdrola I	−0.054	−2.661	0.019	2.171	0.000	1.096	0.250	0.726	0.256
Kingfisher	−0.163	−6.045	0.006	0.184	−3.706	1.077	0.033	0.964	0.033
Koninklijke KPN	−0.074	−1.858	0.073	2.351	0.000	1.129	0.468	0.472	0.498
Louis Vuitton I	−0.116	−3.405	0.032	2.032	−2.542	1.357	0.201	0.728	0.216
Louis Vuitton II	−0.094	−3.535	0.007	0.501	0.000	1.107	0.071	0.921	0.072
PPR	−0.036	−3.495	0.024	2.017	−13.492	1.658	0.318	0.473	0.402
Renault	−0.112	−2.707	0.075	3.864	0.000	1.353	0.352	0.524	0.402
Repsol YPF	−0.064	−3.438	0.002	0.153	0.000	1.229	0.023	0.971	0.023
Saint Gobain II	−0.078	−2.914	0.013	0.734	0.000	1.189	0.142	0.831	0.146
Saint Gobain III	−0.045	−2.9105	0.019	2.039	−7.708	1.614	0.255	0.588	0.303
Sodexho	−0.038	−1.372	0.033	2.668	6.973	1.257	0.413	0.481	0.462
Telecom Italia I	−0.103	−3.296	0.062	2.386	−7.878	1.221	0.346	0.577	0.375
Telecom Italia II	−0.056	−2.323	0.055	2.297	0.000	0.972	0.503	0.511	0.496
Telefonica	−0.063	−2.287	0.055	2.526	1.246	1.063	0.454	0.518	0.467
Tesco II	−0.056	−2.987	−0.031	−3.259	4.779	0.906	−1.095	1.992	0.000
Thyssenkrupp	−0.071	−3.099	0.054	2.260	−14.014	1.465	0.360	0.473	0.432
Union Fenosa	−0.073	−2.780	0.003	0.248	5.833	0.942	0.037	0.965	0.037
Vodafone	−0.056	−2.301	−0.010	−1.238	−9.632	1.443	−0.241	1.348	0.000
Volvo	−0.070	−3.369	−0.003	−0.306	−7.900	1.460	−0.042	1.062	0.000
Average	−0.068	−2.883	0.018	1.104	−0.755	1.173	0.119	0.837	0.227
95% conf. interval LL	−0.080		0.008		−3.457	1.077			0.151
UL	−0.057		0.028		1.947	1.270			0.302
Panel B: Contributions to price discovery (CDS *vs.* ASP) during the crisis									
Akzo I	−0.068	−2.878	0.021	2.063	−33.021	1.616	0.204	0.670	0.233
Akzo II	−0.011	−0.374	0.020	2.009	0.000	0.785	0.757	0.406	0.651
BMW	−0.045	−1.527	0.069	4.390	0.000	0.667	0.757	0.495	0.605
Bouygues I	−0.011	−0.369	0.065	3.346	−3.965	1.029	0.831	0.145	0.852
Bouygues II	−0.030	−1.267	0.058	2.893	3.483	0.513	0.964	0.506	0.656
Carrefour I	−0.018	−0.8861	0.034	2.832	0.000	1.169	0.585	0.316	0.649
Carrefour II	−0.036	−1.258	0.061	3.089	0.000	0.562	0.867	0.512	0.629
Casino I	−0.022	−1.401	0.068	3.717	−20.117	1.354	0.595	0.194	0.754
Casino II	−0.048	−3.912	0.002	0.154	24.198	0.755	0.041	0.969	0.041
Compass Group	−0.102	−2.142	0.029	2.072	−0.647	1.043	0.220	0.770	0.222
Edison Spa	−0.027	−1.264	0.049	3.454	6.619	1.112	0.603	0.330	0.646
Energia de Portugal II	−0.080	−3.072	0.016	1.219	0.000	1.508	0.153	0.769	0.166
E.ON	−0.015	−0.604	0.025	2.340	5.165	0.586	0.840	0.507	0.623

(Continued)

Table 4. Continued.

Issuer	α_1	t-Stat	α_2	t-Stat	β_3	β_2	PD_1	PD_2	GG_1
Iberdrola I	−0.037	−1.364	0.101	4.096	−19.347	1.010	0.726	0.267	0.732
Kingfisher	−0.126	−3.339	0.068	1.682	45.657	1.029	0.348	0.642	0.351
Koninklijke KPN	−0.066	−2.676	0.014	1.340	−31.071	1.643	0.153	0.749	0.169
Louis Vuitton I	−0.046	−2.065	0.078	3.466	2.706	0.949	0.647	0.386	0.626
Louis Vuitton II	−0.054	−2.055	0.082	4.315	4.995	0.857	0.658	0.437	0.601
PPR	−0.059	−2.339	0.127	2.980	16.282	0.718	0.844	0.394	0.682
Renault	−0.062	−1.110	0.132	3.068	10.265	0.594	0.938	0.443	0.679
Repsol YPF	−0.010	−0.384	0.126	4.919	13.871	0.800	1.142	0.087	0.929
Saint Gobain II	−0.027	−1.841	0.039	2.576	−17.603	1.109	0.558	0.381	0.594
Saint Gobain III	−0.115	−4.3677	0.021	1.001	0.000	0.764	0.160	0.878	0.154
Sodexho	−0.017	−0.592	0.053	3.527	0.000	2.239	0.392	0.123	0.761
Telecom Italia I	−0.115	−4.569	0.001	0.021	45.865	0.636	0.005	0.997	0.005
Telecom Italia II	−0.071	−1.702	0.088	2.562	13.265	1.104	0.522	0.424	0.552
Telefonica	−0.030	−0.898	0.082	2.975	−4.623	1.073	0.692	0.257	0.729
Tesco II	−0.004	−0.159	0.087	4.140	−5.743	1.073	0.892	0.043	0.954
Thyssenkrupp	−0.030	−1.571	0.043	2.156	2.880	0.527	0.823	0.567	0.592
Union Fenosa	−0.007	−0.478	0.077	3.583	0.000	1.025	0.894	0.083	0.915
Vodafone	−0.031	−0.8451	0.043	2.118	0.000	0.672	0.723	0.516	0.584
Volvo	−0.068	−1.898	0.045	2.581	0.000	1.229	0.364	0.552	0.397
Average	−0.047	−1.725	0.057	2.709	1.847	0.992	0.591	0.463	0.554
95% conf. interval LL	−0.059		0.044		−4.209	0.855			0.461
UL	−0.035		0.070		7.903	1.129			0.647

Notes: This table reports the price discovery analysis results. Panel A reports the contributions to price discovery of CDS and ASP spreads (s_t^A and $\bar{s}_{t-j}$) during the period before the subprime crisis. Panel B presents the contribution of the previous spreads during the crisis. The measures of price discovery are based on the following system of two equations:

$$\Delta s_t^A = \alpha_1(s_{t-1}^A - \beta_3 - \beta_2\bar{s}_{t-1}) + \sum_{j-1}^{p}\delta_{1,j}\Delta s_{t-j}^A + \sum_{j-1}^{p}\eta_{1,j}\Delta\bar{s}_{t-j} + u_{1,t}$$

$$\Delta\bar{s}_t = \alpha_2(s_{t-1}^A - \beta_3 - \beta_2\bar{s}_{t-1}) + \sum_{j=1}^{p}\delta_{2,j}\Delta s_{t-j}^A + \sum_{j=1}^{p}\eta_{2,j}\Delta\bar{s}_{t-j} + u_{2,t}.$$

The values of coefficients α_1, α_2, β_1 and β_2^a and the *t-statistics* of coefficients α_s are reported in Panels A and B. The columns are named by the coefficients themselves. The last three columns in Panels A and B report the price discovery measure attributed to the ASP (PD_1), the price discovery measure attributed to the CDS (PD_2) and the percentage of price discovery attributed to the ASP market (GG_1) which is equivalent to the Gonzalo and Granger price discovery metric attributed to the ASP market for a parameter β_2 equal to 1. The ASP market leads the process of price discovery whenever GG_1 is higher than 0.5. However, when GG_1 is below a value of 0.5, the CDS market leads the process of price discovery. The last rows in Panels A and B show the average coefficient or metric and the corresponding lower limit (LL) and upper limit (UL) for their 95% confidence interval.

[a]The parameters β_2 and β_3 which are reported in Panels A and B of Table 4 are significant at 5% level in all the cases.

to our model, the role of price discovery leadership comes from the relative number of market participants in the CDS with respect to the ASP market. An implication of the above results is that the market activity in Euro-denominated corporate bonds and ASPs is more limited than in CDS markets. A possible explanation is that the former are often held by investors until maturity which affects in a negative sense during periods of high liquidity their role as information providers. The ASP market reflects credit risk more efficiently in the remaining four cases. In eight cases, we observe that the CDS market reveals information as efficiently as the ASP market (GG_1 is between 0.45 and 0.55). According to Equation (18), the last eight cases where both markets reveal information in an equally efficient way could be explained by a higher market participation of the agents who operate in both markets (N_{BOTH} is high). On average, we find that the CDS market leads the ASP market during the period before the crisis as the value of 0.227 for the corresponding GG average metric in the ASP market reveals. The 95% confidence interval for the average GG metric is 0.151–0.302, where even the upper limit implies that the CDS market leads the ASP market. The minimum GG metric is 0, which means that the CDS market reveals all the information, while the maximum is 0.55.

4.2 *The leadership of the ASP and bond markets during the crisis*

Panel B of Table 4 reports the results for the subprime crisis period. Comparing Panels A and B of Table 4, we observe that during the crisis, ASP spreads reveal more efficiently credit risk than before. This result is consistent with Hypothesis 2 up to the point that in 71.88% of the cases (23 cases), ASP spreads lead CDS spreads in the price discovery process. The CDS market reflects credit risk more efficiently in the remaining nine cases. Thus, ASPs' predominant position as information providers during the crisis is in line with the evidence reported in the IFSL Research (2009a, 2009b) about CDS and bond notional amounts outstanding and trading activity. Dötz (2007) states that the turbulence in the credit markets in spring 2005 was apparently handled much better by the bond market than by the CDS market. The role of ASP as information providers improves with respect to the one observed before the crisis in 84.4% of the cases (27 cases). This role only worsens in five cases which could be explained by a drop in the ASPs' liquidity that even exceeds the drop in CDS liquidity. On average, we find that the ASP market leads the CDS market during the crisis as the value of 0.554 for the corresponding GG average metric reveals. The 95% confidence interval for the average GG metric is 0.461 to 0.647. The minimum GG metric is 0.005, which means that the CDS market reveals almost all the information, while the maximum is 0.954, which means that the ASP market reveals almost all the information. The range for this metric is wider than in the period before crisis which may be related to a decrease in the presence of the agents that operate in both markets. This idea is reinforced because in Panel B of Table 4, we do not find any GG metric close to 0.5 ($0.45 < GG < 0.55$). Comparing results before and during the crisis, the ASP spreads reveal credit risk more efficiently during than before the crisis given that the average GG measure during the crisis (0.554 with a standard deviation of 0.258) is almost 2.5 times the one observed before the crisis (0.227 with a standard deviation of 0.209). We then test whether pre and during-crisis GG measures are different. The average difference (0.327) is significantly greater than zero with asymptotic *t-statistic* equal to 5.3 (p-value ≈ 0). Also, using a test of means, we obtain that the average GG measure during the crisis is higher than the average GG measure before the crisis with asymptotic *t-statistic* equal to 2.7 (p-value ≈ 0.005). Panels A and B of Figure 1 help to understand these results given that there is one main determinant of price discovery that we are considering in this paper: liquidity. We realize that there is no generally held definition of liquidity. Many other measures have been suggested in the literature. In fact there is a close relationship between many of the measures and actual transactions costs, and the assumption that liquidity proxies measure liquidity seems to be granted, see Goyenko, Holden and Trzcinka (2009). The analysis of price discovery is extended to the case where the informational efficiency of CDS spreads are compared with bond spreads. Results are similar to the ones presented for CDS and ASP spreads and Hypotheses 1 and 2 also hold.[41]

Other factors that may influence the price discovery process across markets are the CTD option embedded in the CDS, a potential illiquidity premium and the existence of a high counterparty

Table 5. Bootstrap estimation of the significance level of the price discovery metrics.

Issuer	GG(CDS)	*t*-Stat	*p*-Val	GG(ASP)	*t*-Stat	*p*-Val
Akzo I	1.000	369.499	0.000	0.233	−29.107	1.000
Akzo II	0.950	29.214	0.000	0.651	12.216	0.000
BMW	1.000	62.696	0.000	0.605	6.407	0.000
Bouygues I	0.493	−0.689	0.755	0.852	17.237	0.000
Bouygues II	0.450	−4.255	1.000	0.656	7.960	0.000
Carrefour I	1.000	158.322	0.000	0.649	24.527	0.000
Carrefour II	0.928	63.718	0.000	0.629	16.713	0.000
Casino I	1.000	159.017	0.000	0.754	14.534	0.000
Casino II	0.798	27.359	0.000	0.041	−67.913	1.000
Compass Group	0.919	51.098	0.000	0.222	−41.068	1.000
Edison Spa	0.453	−4.647	1.000	0.646	10.407	0.000
Energia de Portugal II	0.478	−2.390	0.991	0.166	−27.630	1.000
E.ON	0.892	198.328	0.000	0.623	8.809	0.000
Iberdrola I	0.744	29.706	0.000	0.732	12.883	0.000
Kingfisher	0.967	47.427	0.000	0.351	−13.782	1.000
Koninklijke KPN	0.502	0.080	0.468	0.169	−41.129	1.000
Louis Vuitton I	0.784	61.625	0.000	0.626	6.382	0.000
Louis Vuitton II	0.928	44.549	0.000	0.601	7.035	0.000
PPR	0.598	17.425	0.000	0.682	15.184	0.000
Renault	0.598	12.688	0.000	0.679	10.335	0.000
Repsol YPF	0.977	42.715	0.000	0.929	29.679	0.000
Saint Gobain II	0.854	21.746	0.000	0.594	2.104	0.018
Saint Gobain III	0.697	23.907	0.000	0.154	−42.130	1.000
Sodexho	0.538	4.207	0.000	0.761	27.442	0.000
Telecom Italia I	0.625	16.017	0.000	0.005	−52.782	1.000
Telecom Italia II	0.504	0.727	0.234	0.552	0.078	0.469
Telefonica	0.533	2.817	0.002	0.729	17.927	0.000
Tesco II	1.000	119.058	0.000	0.954	33.782	0.000
Thyssenkrupp	0.568	9.903	0.000	0.592	6.755	0.000
Union Fenosa	0.963	32.525	0.000	0.915	24.949	0.000
Vodafone	1.000	89.653	0.000	0.584	6.705	0.000
Volvo	1.000	93.904	0.000	0.397	10.677	1.000

Notes: In this table we present the estimates of the *t*-statistics which are employed to test whether a given GG metric is significantly higher than 0.5 before and during the crisis for the CDS and the ASP markets, respectively. These hypotheses are tested by means of *t*-statistics which are constructed using the bootstrapped standard errors. Columns 2 and 3 report the results obtained when we test if the GG metrics for the CDS market, column 1, are higher than 0.5 before the crisis. Columns 5 and 6 report the results obtained when we test if the GG metrics for the ASP market, column 4, are higher metrics for the ASP market, column 4, are higher than 0.5 during the crisis. Columns 1 and 4 are extracted from Panels A and B of Table 4.

risk in the CDS. Regarding the first two factors, Ammer and Cai (2007) find that the main reason supporting the price leadership of bond spreads with respect to CDS premiums is the existence of a higher CTD option and the illiquidity. Actually, these two factors as well as the counterparty risk are assumed to be more influential during the current subprime crisis and it is precisely in this period when we find that both ASP and bond markets reflect the information more efficiently that the CDS market.

For the cases in which the credit spreads are I(1) but the existence of cointegration is rejected, the VECM representation is not valid. For these cases, we use a price discovery analysis on the basis of a Granger causality test for a VAR in first differences and for the three same periods.[42] According to the *p*-value of the *chi-square* statistics of the Granger causality test and the sum of the coefficients on lagged spreads which are significantly different from zero, we conclude that in the first subperiod, CDS prices Granger-cause ASP spreads for 5 of the 14 cases, we find causation in the opposite direction in two cases, bidirectional causation in one case and no causation in the remaining six cases. In the second subperiod, we find that ASP spreads Granger-cause CDS prices in three of the fourteen cases, we find causation in the opposite direction in one case, bidirectional causation in five cases and no causation in the remaining five cases. The sum of the significant coefficients on lagged CDS and ASP spreads confirm the results of the Granger causality test.

Table 6. Contributions to price discovery (bond *vs.* ASP).

	November 2005 to July 2007	July 2007 to June 2009
Issuer	GG_1 metric	GG_1 metric
Akzo I	0.696	1.000
Akzo II	0.640	0.801
BMW	0.705	1.000
Bouygues I	0.634	1.000
Bouygues II	1.000	0.683
British AM Tob. I	1.000	1.000
British AM Tob. II	1.000	1.000
Carrefour I	0.607	0.856
Carrefour II	0.346	1.000
Casino I	0.732	1.000
Casino II	1.000	0.787
Compass Group	0.800	0.653
Edison Spa	1.000	1.000
Enel	0.701	0.619
Energia de Portugal I	0.985	0.967
Energia de Portugal II	1.000	0.694
E.ON	0.622	1.000
France Telecom	0.670	1.000
Iberdrola I	0.635	1.000
Kingfisher	0.842	1.000
Koninklijke KPN	0.730	0.737
Louis Vuitton I	0.864	0.980
Louis Vuitton II	1.000	0.869
PPR	1.000	1.000
Renault	0.614	0.254
Repsol YPF	1.000	1.000
Saint Gobain I	0.874	0.427
Saint Gobain II	1.000	1.000
Saint Gobain III	0.653	0.839
Scania	0.712	1.000
Sodexho	0.843	1.000
Stora Enso	0.603	1.000
Technip	1.000	0.825
Telecom Italia I	0.556	0.832
Telecom Italia II	0.844	1.000
Telefonica	0.745	1.000
Telekom Austria	0.708	1.000
Tesco II	0.556	0.949

(Continued)

Table 6. Continued.

	November 2005 to July 2007	July 2007 to June 2009
Issuer	GG_1 metric	GG_1 metric
Thyssenkrupp	0.723	0.915
Union Fenosa	0.565	1.000
Vinci	0.750	1.000
Vivendi	0.883	1.000
Vodafone	0.488	0.525
Volkswagen	0.983	1.000
Volvo	0.622	1.000
Average	0.781	0.893
95% confidence interval LL	0.729	0.841
UL	0.833	0.945

Notes: This table reports the contributions to price discovery of bond and ASP spreads (bs_t and s_t^A). The first column presents the contribution of ASP spreads with respect to bond spreads during the period before the crisis. A value equal to or higher to 0.5 indicates that ASP markets lead bond markets in the process of price discovery while a value equal to or higher than 1 indicates that negligible information about credit risk is reported by bond spreads relative to the one reported by ASP spreads. The second column reports the same information for the crisis period. As in Table 4, the measures of price discovery are based on the following system of two equations:

$$\Delta s_t^A = \alpha_1(s_{t-1}^A - \beta_3 - \beta_2 bs_{t-1}) + \sum_{j=1}^{p} \delta_{1,j}\Delta s_{t-j}^A + \sum_{j=1}^{p} \eta_{1,j}\Delta bs_{t-j} + u_{1,t}$$

$$\Delta bs_t = \alpha_2(s_{t-1}^A - \beta_3 - \beta_2 bs_{t-1}) + \sum_{j=1}^{p} \delta_{2,j}\Delta s_{t-j}^A + \sum_{j=1}^{p} \eta_{2,j}\Delta bs_{t-j} + u_{2,t}.$$

We directly report the Gonzalo and Granger metric (GG_1) that is obtained as the ratio between the price discovery measure attributed to the ASP (PD_1) and the sum of PD_1 and PD_2, where PD_2 is the price discovery measure attributed to the bond. This ratio indicates the percentage of price discovery attributed to the ASP.

As a robustness test and to overcome the shortcoming that the precision of our estimates cannot be assessed analytically, we use the bootstrap method for cointegrated systems developed by Li and Maddala (1997). We choose to bootstrap from the estimated residuals of the VECM in order not to distort the dynamic structure of our model. Using estimated parameters and initial values, we create a new set of system variables (with the same number of observations as in the original data) by drawing observations randomly with replacement from the innovations. Based upon the generated data, the common trend relationship and the subsequent price discovery measures are re-estimated. This process is then repeated 1000 times and the standard errors are calculated from the empirical distribution. Finally, we test whether the corresponding GG metric is significantly higher than 0.5 before and during the crisis for both markets. To test these hypotheses, we construct a t-statistic using the bootstrapped standard errors. Results are reported in Table 5. Before the crisis, the CDS spreads lead, in most cases, the price discovery process with respect to the ASP spreads. During the crisis, the roles are reversed being the ASP spreads lead CDS spreads in the price discovery process.[43]

4.3 *Comparing the informational efficiency of the ASP and bond spreads*

In Table 6, we show that Hypothesis 3, which states that the ASP market reflects credit risk more efficiently than the bond market, is consistent with the empirical evidence for the two periods of time analysed. This result confirms empirically for the first time, at least to our knowledge, that the ASP spread is a better measure for credit risk than bond spreads are. Only in two of a total of 46 cases in the first subperiod, do bond spreads lead ASP spreads. This occurs in two cases in the second subperiod. The reason that explains these results may be a higher relative liquidity in the ASP market, which means that the number of market participants in the ASP market (liquidity) is greater than the number of players in the bond market.

5. Conclusions

We find that liquidity does affect the price discovery process in credit derivatives markets. We make three contributions to the literature. Firstly, we offer a theoretical model for testing price discovery in credit derivatives markets that allows for simultaneous agent participation in different markets. Secondly, we analyse the price discovery process between ASPs and CDSs and find that the leadership, in terms of price discovery, between ASPs and CDSs is very sensitive to the appearance of the subprime crisis. Before the crisis, the CDS market leads the ASP market but during the crisis the ASP market leads the CDS market. Thirdly, to our knowledge, this is the first price discovery analysis based on the ASP and bond markets. We find, according to GS terms, that the bond market is a 'pure satellite' of the asset swap market. Thus, the ASP spread is a more accurate measure of credit risk than the bond spread. For this reason, it seems more appropriate to use the ASP spread as an alternative or as a complement to the CDS rather than the bond spread.

Finally, we highlight the four main policy implications that emerge from our study and which could be of special interest for investors and regulators alike. First, we find that during the crisis, the ASP market reveals credit risk more efficiently that the CDS market. Reasons explaining this finding include the CTD option embedded in the CDS spread, the liquidity premium and the counterparty risk in CDSs.[44] The key implication of this result is that inferences on the creditworthiness of a given firm based solely in CDS spreads in periods of high market turbulence and low liquidity are bound to be misleading. Second, we find that the ASP spread leads the price discovery process of credit risk more efficiently than the bond spread, before and during the crisis. For this reason, it is more appropriate to use the ASP spread as an alternative or as a complement to the CDS spread as a measure of credit risk rather than the bond spread. However, most of the existing literature has focused primarily on the bond and CDS spreads ignoring the role of the ASP spread as a credit risk indicator. Third, our theoretical model and empirical results highlight the importance of the agents that operate in both markets (N_{BOTH}) in order to provide stability to the credit markets. The arbitrageurs also play a special role in these markets given that their demands are defined in terms of a long-run equivalence or adjustment which could reduce deviations from the equilibrium prices. Fourth, the debt hedgers do not play any apparent role in the price discovery process if they are fully hedged. However, when they only hedge a given proportion of the total investment in ASPs or bonds, they also contribute to the price discovery process.

Acknowledgements

We are grateful to the Editors of this special issue: John Wilson, Barbara Casu, and David McMillan for their useful comments. We owe thanks to two anonymous referees for many astute comments that considerably improved the study. We also thank Isabel Figuerola-Ferretti, Javier Gil, Carlos González-Aguado, Jesús Gonzalo, Neil Kellard, María Rodríguez, Pedro Serrano, Javier Suárez and seminar participants at the XVII Foro de Finanzas and at the Emerging Scholars in Banking and Finance Conference at Cass Business School for all their comments and suggestions. Sergio Mayordomo and

Juan Ignacio Peña acknowledge financial support from MICINN Grant Ref: ECO2009-12551. Juan Romo acknowledges financial support from MICINN Grant Ref: ECO2008-05080. The usual disclaimer applies.

Notes

1. Acharya and Schaefer (2006) posit that the liquidity risk can be defined as unpredictable changes in transaction costs and in liquidity. These adverse liquidity shocks, systematic or idiosyncratic, are mainly due to high and negative changes in financial products' returns and reduce the amount of capital available to financial intermediaries which lowers the ability of their trading desk to provide liquidity.
2. The value of CDSs outstanding at the end of 2004, 2005 and 2006 was \$8.42, \$17.1 and \$34.4 trillion, respectively. The CDS market exploded over the past decade to more than \$45 trillion in mid-2007 and more than \$62 trillion in the second half of the same year, according to the ISDA. The size of the CDS market in mid-2007 is roughly twice the size of the US stock market (which is valued at about \$22 trillion) and far exceeds the \$7.1 trillion mortgage market and \$4.4 trillion US treasuries market. However, the notional amount outstanding decreased to \$38.6 trillion at the end of 2008.
3. The main reason is the existence of a higher CTD option due to the higher risk of borrowers and also to liquidity reasons given that the higher the number of bonds issued, which they use as a liquidity measure, the more difficult is that the CDS market leads price discovery.
4. According to Dötz (2007), the relatively large contribution of the CDS market to price discovery is not necessarily tantamount to general and lasting improvement in the processing of information; the turbulence in the credit markets in the spring of 2005 was apparently handled much better by the bond market than by the CDS market. The weaknesses of the CDSs are likely to consist in the relatively high concentration and homogeneousness of its market players, whose herding behaviour, particularly in times of crisis, can strain liquidity, amplify market volatility and hamper price discovery.
5. Chan-Lau and Kim (2004) relate the same three financial instruments but for emerging market sovereign issuers. In most countries, they do not find any equilibrium price relationship between equity and bond markets and in terms of price discovery, it is difficult to conclude that one particular market dominates the price discovery process.
6. As far as we know, the relationship between ASP and CDS has only been treated in De Wit (2006). However, the perspective adopted in De Wit (2006) is based on the long-run equilibrium that should exist, and which the author finds, between ASP and CDS, ignoring the price discovery process.
7. Although we develop the case of CDS and ASP prices, the model can also be applied to study the interaction between CDS and bond spreads or between ASP and bond spreads.
8. A popular arbitrage strategy employed by hedge funds in credit derivatives markets defines the correct price from a long-term equilibrium price based on the cointegration methodology. The arbitrageur is betting only that the spread between the two cointegrated assets will narrow, which can be understood as a permanent adjustment process towards an economic equilibrium.
9. As Dötz (2007) state, the market for synthetic CDO products, which as opposed to cash CDS products are not backed by bonds or loans but by CDSs, presents some advantages such as the better availability of CDSs relative to bonds or loans and the heavy demand among investors for unfunded supersenior tranches.
10. We may also find protection sellers who hedge their positions, again, in the CDS market or individuals that participate in the CDS market in order to hedge their exposures to other institutions that are not due to debt positions.
11. We include this type of agents in order to make the model more comprehensive, given that the nature of CDSs is to provide insurance. In fact, CDSs are usually used to manage the credit risk.
12. As CDSs are over-the-counter (OTC) instruments, it is possible to buy a CDS contract whose maturity coincides with the bond's maturity and whose premium payments timing is agreed by the parties. As the bond's maturity date approaches, the use of CDSs with a 5-year constant maturity would lead to overhedging, given that the maturity dates of CDSs and asset swaps do not coincide. The consequence is that the investor will pay a CDS spread above the one needed to be fully hedged. Thus, we take advantage of the range of CDSs maturities to fit a CDS curve using a Piecewise Cubic Hermite Interpolating Polynomial algorithm that allows us to match asset swap and CDS maturities. This method is also used in Levin, Perli, and Zakrajšek (2005).
13. In order to proceed in this way, we assume that the investor can borrow money at Euribor flat.
14. If $s_t^A - \bar{s}_t > 0$, then a profitable arbitrage opportunity exists. The investor should take long positions in both CDS and ASP and borrow the required quantity of money in order to finance the investment at 3 months Euribor. If $s_t^A - \bar{s}_t < 0$, the inverse strategy will lead to an arbitrage opportunity.

15. A combination of short positions on both the CDS and ASP leads to a net payment for the investor equal to the difference between CDS and ASP spreads, $\bar{s}_t - s_t^A$.
16. The net payoff is also zero at coupon payment dates while at the bond's maturity, as in every quarterly payment, the net payoff is equal to the basis.
17. Assumption A1 is necessary to reach a two-sided bound on the CDS rate and to guarantee that the equivalence relationship holds.
18. An example of a statistical arbitrage analysis in credit derivatives markets according to the technique and concept introduced Hogan et al. (2004) can be found in Mayordomo, Peña, and Romo (2009).
19. Cossin and Lu (2005) state that the liquidity premium, the CTD option and the market segmentation explain the pricing differences between bonds and CDS. The effect of the CTD option is more important as default risk increases.
20. If the two markets price credit risk equally in the long run, then their prices should be cointegrated with cointegrating vector [1,-1,c], suggesting a stationary basis.
21. Shorting a corporate bond or an ASP with a required maturity, even years, is not an easy task. The short sale of bonds or ASPs could be done via a repurchase agreement (repo) but as Blanco, Brennan, and Marsh (2005) explain, it is impossible to borrow a bond via a repo. The reason is that repo market for corporate bonds is illiquid and even if it is possible to short a bond via a repo, the tenor of the agreement would be short. Schonbucher (2003) states that this limitation could be solved by issuing credit-linked notes linked to the corresponding bond and selling them to the investors in the asset swap market. This alternative presents other limitations given that the issuance of credit-linked notes takes time and implies high fixed cost. This fact implies that deviations in the equivalence relationship might not imply arbitrage opportunities whenever an asset swap short sale is needed. Thus, in some cases traders are not able to exploit price differentials when the CDS premium is higher than the asset swap spread and as Blanco, Brennan, and Marsh (2005) suggest, this asymmetry may affect significantly the dynamic adjustment of credit spreads. The restrictions on short-sales could be even more severe in periods of financial distress.
22. These individual interpret that $R_{i,t}^{\text{CDS}}$ is the CDS price, given its probability of default. As the market price $\bar{s}_t$ is above the reservation price, the investor is interested in selling protection in exchange of $\bar{s}_t$.
23. Note that the total endowments can increase exogenously from period t to period $t + 1$, for instance, by means of CDS or bond issuances.
24. The idea is that under the assumptions employed when defining the arbitrageurs demand, the fact that the ASP spread is a good indicator, although not perfect, of the CDS spread and given that both spreads are prices of the credit risk of a given firm, it seems reasonable to assume that the elasticities are similar.
25. The objective of this paper is not related with the literature of credit risk pricing and so, Equations (10) and (11) are not pricing equations of credit risk, such as the ones defined from the probability of default and recovery rates, but simply the ASP and CDS prices that clear both markets.
26. We do not report the whole expression of u_t in order to save space and also, because of the assumptions on residuals they are not going to appear in our analysis.
27. Although hedgers are not important in the price discovery process, they must be included in the model because these individuals really participate in credit markets and we need them in order to make the model more comprehensive.
28. This decline in trading during the second half of 2008 reflects a combination of significantly reduced risk appetite, expectations of stable low interest rates in major markets and lower hedge fund activity. Exchange rate movements may also have affected to this decline. Most institutions report their positions in US dollars and the euro and the pound sterling depreciated by 30% and 12%, respectively, against the US dollar between June and December 2008.
29. During the first quarter of 2009, issuance of investment grade corporate bonds in Europe totalled a record €140bn, well above quarterly levels of less than €50bn seen in recent years. It is motivated, among other reasons, by the use of bond markets for funding and the government guarantees to aid to the bond issuance. IFSL Research (2009b) reports that the amounts outstanding on the global bond market, which includes bonds, notes and money market instruments, increased 6% in 2008 to $83 trillion.
30. See for instance Norden and Weber (2004), Blanco, Brennan, and Marsh (2005), Zhu (2006), Baba and Inada (2007), Dötz (2007), Forte and Peña (2009) and Coudert and Gex (2010).
31. In a limit case, if N_{BOTH} tends to infinity, the price discovery is equal to 0.5.
32. Allocation to bonds from high-net-worth individuals increased from 27% to 29% during 2008 with equities seeing the largest decline in their share of portfolio allocation.
33. The nominal of CDSs with respect to ASP contracts serves to show how in periods of financial distress it is much more difficult to participate in CDS than in ASP markets. The standard bond's faced value is €1000 while the CDS typical notional amount is €10–20 million for investment grade credits and €2–5 million for high yield credits.
34. Ammer and Cai (2007) state that the main reason to support that bond spreads lead CDS premiums is the existence of a higher CTD option and for liquidity reasons. In particular they employ as a liquidity measure the number of

bonds outstanding by a given firm and find that the higher the number of bonds the less likely it is that CDSs will lead price discovery. Under illiquid scenarios, the CTD option embedded in CDS becomes more valuable and the liquidity premium to bear liquidity risk increases.

35. The GFI FENICS® Credit curve gives preference to real trades and quoted mid- points where available, and in their absence, it is based on the calculation of a running point level using the John Hull and Alan White methodology to ensure a credit curve always exists for each reference entity. This curve is a good approximation for CDSs at any maturity as several error analyses reveal. The median of the absolute difference in basis points between five years CDS premiums as defined from credit curve and the actual quotes or transaction prices for the period between April 2001 and May 2002, is equal to 1.16, 2.01 and 3.82 basis points for AAA/AA, A and BBB ratings for a total of 2659, 9585 and 8170 companies, respectively. Moreover, market CDS spread could be different from what we are assuming to be the true CDS spread by as much as 3.725 bps. on average.
36. This limit is set in order to avoid the selection of bonds with a small volume which could require higher transaction costs due to their reduced liquidity.
37. Our initial sample was 285 corporate bond issuers. We found a total of 116€ denominated bonds that mature before February 2012 but only 67 of them include information on 5-year bid/ask CDS spreads, asset swap spreads and Fenics Curve for at least 90 trading days. Of these, two bonds have been discarded because the issued amount does not exceed 300 millions of Euros, another four bonds were discarded because they were not investment grade bonds throughout the whole sample period. Another four bonds were discarded because their asset swap spreads were persistently negative and, finally, seven bonds were discarded because prices were too far from par.
38. We do not report these results because they are similar to the ones presented in Table 3. However, these results are available upon request.
39. Cointegration test detailed results for ASP and bond spreads are available upon request.
40. The detailed results are available upon request.
41. Results of this analysis are available upon request.
42. These results are available upon request.
43. The t-statistics presented in Table 5 are obtained using the GG metrics reported in Table 4. Moreover, we employ the average GG metric obtained across the 1000 bootstrap repetitions and obtain similar results.
44. Amato and Remolona (2003) state that when it turns out to be very costly to undertake transactions in a given instrument, the investors must be compensated for it. This compensation is reinforced in the presence of uncertainty about the liquidity (or illiquidity) of an ASP, bond or CDS at a given time, and thus the investors could require a premium to bear this risk. This liquidity premium has been proved to exist both in CDS and bond markets. Longstaff, Mithal and Neis (2005) and Tang and Yan (2007) among others support the presence of a liquidity premium in CDS spreads. Collin-Dufresne, Goldstein, and Martin (2001), Perraudin and Taylor (2003), Elton et al. (2001), Delianedis and Geske (2001) and Chen, Lesmond, and Wei (2007) among others find that liquidity is an additional factor to credit risk which is present in bond spreads.
45. We do not report the whole expression of u_t in order to save space and also, because of the assumptions on residuals they are not going to appear in our analysis.

References

Acharya, V., and S. Schaefer. 2006. Liquidity risk and correlation risk: Implications for risk management. Working Paper, London Business School.

Acharya, V., S. Schaefer, and Y. Zhang. 2007. Liquidity risk and correlation risk: A clinical study of the General Motors and Ford Downgrade of May 2005. Working Paper, SSRN.

Amato, J., and E. Remolona. 2003. The credit spread puzzle. *BIS Quarterly Review*, December: 51–63.

Ammer, J., and F. Cai. 2007. Sovereign CDS and bond pricing dynamics in emerging markets: Does the cheapest-to-deliver option matter? International Finance Discussion Papers Number 912, Board of Governors of the Federal Reserve System.

Baba, N., and M. Inada. 2007. Price discovery of credit spreads for Japanese mega-banks: Subordinated bond and CDS. Duscussion Paper 2007-E-6, Institute for Monetary and Economic Studies, Bank of Japan.

Bai, J., and P. Perron. 2003. Computation and analysis of multiple structural change models. *Journal of Applied Econometrics* 18: 1–22.

Blanco, F., S. Brennan, and I.W. Marsh. 2005. An empirical analysis of the dynamic relation between investment grade bonds and credit default swaps. *Journal of Finance* 60, no. 5: 2255–81.

Chan-Lau, J.A., and Y.S. Kim. 2004. Equity prices, credit default swaps, and bond spreads in emerging markets. Working Paper, IMF.

Chen, L., D.A. Lesmond, and J. Wei. 2007. Corporate yield spreads and bond liquidity. *The Journal of Finance* 62, no. 1: 119–49.

Collin-Dufresne, P., R. Goldstein, and S. Martin. 2001. The determinants of credit spread changes. *Journal of Finance* 56, no. 6: 2177–207.

Cossin, D., and H. Lu. 2005. Are European corporate bonds and default swap markets segmented? Working Paper 153, FAME.

Coudert, V., and M. Gex. 2010. Contagion inside the credit default swaps market: The case of the GM and Ford crisis in 2005. *Journal of International Financial Markets, Institutions and Money* 20, no. 2: 109–34.

De Jong, F., and J. Driessen. 2006. Liquidity risk premia in corporate bond markets. Working Paper, University of Amsterdam.

De Wit, J. 2006. Exploring the CDS-bond basis. Working Paper, National Bank of Belgium.

Delianedis, G., and R. Geske. 2001. The components of corporate credit spreads: Default, recovery, tax, jumps, liquidity, and market factors. Working Paper, University of California.

Dötz, N. 2007. Time-varying contributions by the corporate bond and CDS markets to credit risk price discovery. Discussion Paper Series 2: Banking and Financial Studies No 08, Deutsche Bundesbank.

Elton, E., D. Gruber, D. Agrawal, and C. Mann. 2001. Explaining the rate spread on corporate bonds. *Journal of Finance* 56, no. 1: 247–77.

Engle, R., and C.W.J. Granger. 1987. Co-integration and error correction: Representation, estimation, and testing. *Econometrica* 55, no. 2: 251–76.

Felsenheimer, J. 2004. *CDS: Mechanism, pricing and application*. HVB Global Markets Research, 2 June.

Figuerola-Ferretti, I., and J. Gonzalo. 2010. Modelling and measuring price discovery in commodity markets. *Journal of Econometrics* 158, no. 1: 95–107.

Forte, S., and J.I. Peña. 2009. Credit spreads: An empirical analysis on the informational content of stocks, bonds and CDS. *Journal of Banking and Finance* 33, no. 11: 2013–25.

Francis, C., A. Kakodkar, and B. Martin. 2003. *Credit derivative handbook 2003*. Merrill Lynch Global Securities Research and Economics Group.

Fulop, A., and L. Lescourret. 2007. An analysis of intra-daily patterns on the CDS market. Working Paper, ESSEC Business School.

Garbade, K.D., and W.L. Silver. 1983. Price movements and price discovery in commodity markets. *Review of Economics and Statistics* 65, no. 2: 289–97.

Gonzalo, J., and C.W.J. Granger. 1995. Estimation of common long-memory components in cointegrated systems. *Journal of Business and Economics Statistics* 13, no. 1: 27–35.

Goyenko, R.Y., C.W. Holden, and C.A. Trzcinka. 2009. Do liquidity measures measure liquidity? *Journal of Financial Economics* 92, no. 2: 153–81.

Hasbrouck, J. 1995. One security, many markets: Determining the contributions to price discovery. *Journal of Finance* 50, no. 4: 1175–99.

Hogan, S., R.A. Jarrow, M. Teo, and M. Warachka. 2004. Testing market efficiency using statistical arbitrage with applications to momentum and value strategies. *Journal of Financial Economics* 73, no. 3: 525–65.

Hull, J., M. Predescu, and A. White. 2004. The relationship between credit default swap spreads, bond yields, and credit rating announcements. *Journal of Banking and Finance* 28: 2789–811.

International Financial Services London (IFSL) Research. 2009a. *Derivatives 2009*.

International Financial Services London (IFSL) Research. 2009b. *Bond Markets 2009*.

Johansen, S. 1991. Estimation and hypothesis testing of co-integration vectors in gaussian vector autoregressive models. *Econometrica* 59, no. 6: 1551–80.

Juselius, K. 2006. *The cointegrated VAR model: Methodology and applications*. Oxford: Oxford University Press.

Levin, A., R. Perli, and E. Zakrajšek. 2005. The determinants of market frictions in the corporate market. Working Paper, Federal Reserve Board, Washington.

Li, H., and G.S. Maddala. 1997. Bootstrapping cointegrating regressions. *Journal of Econometrics* 80, no. 2: 297–313.

Longstaff, F.A., S. Mithal, and E. Neis. 2005. Corporate yield spreads: Default risk or liquidity? New evidence from the credit default swap market. *Journal of Finance* 60, no. 5: 2213–53.

Mayordomo, S., J.I. Peña, and J. Romo. 2009. Are there arbitrage opportunities in credit derivatives markets? A new test and an application to the case of CDS and ASPs. Working Paper, Universidad Carlos III de Madrid.

Nashikkar, A.J., and M.G. Subrahmanyam. 2007. Latent liquidity and corporate bond yield spreads. NYU Working Paper No. FIN-07-013.

Nashikkar, A.J., M.G. Subrahmanyam, and S. Mahanti. 2009. Limited arbitrage and liquidity in the market for credit risk. NYU Working Paper No. FIN-08-011.

Norden, L., and M. Weber. 2004. Informational efficiency of credit default swap and stock markets: The impact of credit ratings announcements. *Journal of Banking and Finance* 28, no. 11: 2813–43.

Perraudin, W., and A. Taylor. 2003. Liquidity and bond market spreads. Working Paper, Bank of England.

Predescu, M. 2006. The performance of structural models of default for firms with liquid CDS spreads. Working Paper, Rotman School of Management, University of Toronto.

Saita, L. 2006. The puzzling price of corporate default risk. Working Paper, Standford Graduate School of Business.

Schonbucher, P.J. 2003. *Credit derivatives pricing models: Models, pricing, implementation.* Wiley Finance.

Stein, J.L. 1961. The simultaneous determination of spot and future prices. *The American Economic Review* 51, no. 5: 1012–25.

Tang, D.Y., and H. Yan. 2007. Liquidity and credit default swap spreads. Working Paper, Kennesaw State University.

Working, H. 1948. Theory of the inverse carrying charge in futures markets. *Journal of Farm Economics* 30, no. 1: 1–28.

Yan, B., and E. Zivot. 2007. The dynamics of price discovery. Working Paper Series, University of Washington.

Zeileis, A., C. Kleiber, W. Krämer, and K. Hornik. 2003. Testing and dating of structural changes in practice. *Computational Statistics and Data Analysis* 44, nos. 1–2: 109–23.

Zhu, H. 2006. An empirical comparison of credit spreads between the bond market and the credit default swap market. *Journal of Financial Services Research* 29, no. 3: 211–35.

Appendix 1

In order to obtain an expression for the credit spreads we substitute the expressions (14) into the Equations (10) and (11) and obtain the following equation:

$$\begin{pmatrix} s_t^A \\ \bar{s}_t \end{pmatrix} = \frac{H\beta_3}{B}\begin{bmatrix} (N_{\mathrm{BOTH}} + N_{\mathrm{CDS}}) \\ -(N_{\mathrm{BOTH}} + N_{\mathrm{ASP}}) \end{bmatrix} + Q\begin{pmatrix} s_{t-1}^A \\ \bar{s}_{t-1} \end{pmatrix} + \begin{pmatrix} u_t^{\mathrm{ASP}} \\ u_t^{\mathrm{CDS}} \end{pmatrix}, \tag{A1}$$

where $(u_t^{\mathrm{ASP}}, u_t^{\mathrm{CDS}})$ is a vector white noise with $E(u_t) = 0$ and $\mathrm{Var}(u_t) = \Omega > 0$. In u_t we include both the common components and the participants' noises.[45] The model in Equation (15) can be changed into a VECM model by subtracting vector of prices $((s_t^A, \bar{s}_t)'$ from both sides:

$$\begin{pmatrix} \Delta s_t^A \\ \Delta \bar{s}_t \end{pmatrix} = \frac{H\beta_3}{B}\begin{bmatrix} (N_{\mathrm{BOTH}} + N_{\mathrm{CDS}}) \\ -(N_{\mathrm{BOTH}} + N_{\mathrm{ASP}}) \end{bmatrix} + (Q - I)\begin{pmatrix} s_{t-1}^A \\ \bar{s}_{t-1} \end{pmatrix} + \begin{pmatrix} u_t^{\mathrm{ASP}} \\ u_t^{\mathrm{CDS}} \end{pmatrix} \tag{A2}$$

with

$$Q - I = \frac{1}{B}\begin{bmatrix} -H(N_{\mathrm{BOTH}} + N_{\mathrm{CDS}}) & H\beta_2(N_{\mathrm{BOTH}} + N_{\mathrm{CDS}}) \\ H(N_{\mathrm{BOTH}} + N_{\mathrm{ASP}}) & -H\beta_2(N_{\mathrm{BOTH}} + N_{\mathrm{ASP}}) \end{bmatrix}. \tag{A3}$$

The previous expression can be transformed into the following final expression (Equation (15)):

$$\begin{pmatrix} \Delta s_t^A \\ \Delta \bar{s}_t \end{pmatrix} = \frac{H}{B}\begin{bmatrix} -(N_{\mathrm{BOTH}} + N_{\mathrm{CDS}}) \\ (N_{\mathrm{BOTH}} + N_{\mathrm{ASP}}) \end{bmatrix}(1, -\beta_2, -\beta_3)\begin{pmatrix} s_{t-1}^A \\ \bar{s}_{t-1} \\ 1 \end{pmatrix} + \begin{pmatrix} u_t^{\mathrm{ASP}} \\ u_t^{\mathrm{CDS}} \end{pmatrix}. \tag{A4}$$

Appendix 2

In this paper, we adopt GG's methodology and thus, their PT component decomposition to measure market contribution to price discovery. GG PT decomposition has the following form:

$$X_t = A_1 f_t + A_2 z_t, \tag{A5}$$

where f_t is the permanent component, z_t is the transitory component, and A_1 and A_2 are loading matrices. The components f_t and z_t are linear combinations of X_t such that $f_t \sim I(1)$, $z_t \sim I(0)$, z_t does not Granger cause f_t in the long run and:

$$f_t = \gamma' X_t \tag{A6a}$$

$$A_1 = \beta_\perp(\alpha'_\perp \beta_\perp)^{-1} \quad \text{and} \quad \gamma = (\alpha'_\perp \beta_\perp)^{-1}\alpha'_\perp, \tag{A6b}$$

where $\alpha_\perp$ and $\beta_\perp$ are 2×1 vectors such that $\alpha'_\perp \alpha_\perp = 0$ and $\beta'_\perp \beta_\perp = 0$ or equivalently:

$$\alpha_{1,\perp} = \frac{H}{B}(N_{\mathrm{BOTH}} + N_{\mathrm{ASP}}) \tag{A7a}$$

$$\alpha_{2,\perp} = \frac{H}{B}(N_{\mathrm{BOTH}} + N_{\mathrm{CDS}}), \tag{A7b}$$

while $\beta_\perp = (\beta_2, 1)$. Taking all these things together we have that:

$$\gamma' = \left[\frac{(N_{\mathrm{BOTH}} + N_{\mathrm{ASP}})}{\beta_2(N_{\mathrm{BOTH}} + N_{\mathrm{ASP}}) + (N_{\mathrm{BOTH}} + N_{\mathrm{CDS}})}, \frac{(N_{\mathrm{BOTH}} + N_{\mathrm{CDS}})}{\beta_2(N_{\mathrm{BOTH}} + N_{\mathrm{ASP}}) + (N_{\mathrm{BOTH}} + N_{\mathrm{CDS}})} \right] \tag{A8}$$

and the permanent component f_t is defined as:

$$\frac{(N_{\mathrm{BOTH}} + N_{\mathrm{ASP}})}{\beta_2(N_{\mathrm{BOTH}} + N_{\mathrm{ASP}}) + (N_{\mathrm{BOTH}} + N_{\mathrm{CDS}})} s_t^A + \frac{(N_{\mathrm{BOTH}} + N_{\mathrm{CDS}})}{\beta_2(N_{\mathrm{BOTH}} + N_{\mathrm{ASP}}) + (N_{\mathrm{BOTH}} + N_{\mathrm{CDS}})} \bar{s}_t, \tag{A9}$$

where the factor that multiplies s_t^A represents the price discovery measure attributed to the ASP (PD_1) and the factor that multiplies $\bar{s}_t$ represents the price discovery measure attributed to the CDS (PD_2). The ratio γ in Equation (A8) that is obtained from the orthogonal vector to α, which is denoted as $\alpha_\perp$ (see Equations (A7a) and (A7b)), can be understood as the relative number of market participants in a given market with respect to the other.

The percentage of price discovery attributable to ASP and CDS markets can also be defined as:

$$\frac{\mathrm{PD}_1}{\mathrm{PD}_1 + \mathrm{PD}_2} = \mathrm{GG}_1 \quad \text{and} \quad \frac{\mathrm{PD}_2}{\mathrm{PD}_1 + \mathrm{PD}_2} = \mathrm{GG}_2, \tag{A10}$$

where GG_1 and GG_2 represent the GG price discovery metrics for the ASP and the CDS markets, respectively.

These metrics can be defined equivalently as:

$$\mathrm{GG}_1 = \frac{\alpha_2}{-\alpha_1 + \alpha_2} \quad \text{and} \quad \mathrm{GG}_2 = \frac{-\alpha_1}{-\alpha_1 + \alpha_2}. \tag{A11}$$

After substituting we obtain:

$$\mathrm{GG}_1 = \frac{N_{\mathrm{BOTH}} + N_{\mathrm{ASP}}}{2N_{\mathrm{BOTH}} + N_{\mathrm{ASP}} + N_{\mathrm{CDS}}} \quad \text{and} \quad \mathrm{GG}_2 = \frac{N_{\mathrm{BOTH}} + N_{\mathrm{CDS}}}{2N_{\mathrm{BOTH}} + N_{\mathrm{ASP}} + N_{\mathrm{CDS}}}. \tag{A12}$$

In order to be consistent with our model we investigate price discovery based on the metrics that when transformed into relative terms are equivalent to the GG approach's metrics of Equation (A10). A cointegrating vector between credit spreads different from $(1, -1)$ can be theoretically supported by our price discovery model given that the standard requirement that $\beta_2 = 1$ may be very restrictive.

Return reversals and the compass rose: insights from high frequency options data

Thanos Verousis[a] and Owain ap Gwilym[b]

[a] *School of Business and Economics, Swansea University, Singleton Park, Swansea SA2 8PP, UK;* [b] *Bangor Business School, Bangor University, Bangor LL57 2DG, UK*

We study the occurrence and visibility of the compass rose pattern in high frequency data from individual equity options contracts. We show that the compass rose pattern in options contracts is more complex than portrayed in prior work with other asset classes. We find that the tick/volatility ratio proposed in prior studies gives inconclusive results on the pattern's visibility. A major contribution arises from linking the compass rose pattern with return reversals, which gives new insights into the pattern's predictability. We show that return reversals are revealed as an element of the compass rose pattern and are particularly evident at higher sampling frequencies. We study the determinants of these reversals and report that return reversals are primarily associated with high transaction frequency and decrease with the presence of additional market makers. Also, the hypothesis that there is a reaction to overnight events which is reflected in prices at the market open is not supported. Reversals are less prevalent for larger firms and when trade sizes are larger.

1. Introduction

Researchers and practitioners are increasingly focused on analysis and trading at a high frequency (intraday) level. This is one of the main growth areas in financial market research in recent years. New insights into market practice and price behaviour are revealed by research on this type of data. This paper focuses on option markets, where the leverage effect magnifies the potential profit from any trading opportunities identified. This is the first study to link the compass rose pattern with intraday return reversals. This feature could significantly influence the predictability arising from the pattern. We also present a regression model which identifies many important influences on the presence of return reversals. Reversals are more evident when transaction frequency is high and when prices are high. They are less prevalent when more market makers are present, for larger firms and when trade sizes are larger.

In the market microstructure literature, the compass rose pattern dates back to Crack and Ledoit (1996). The pattern appears when plotting present and lagged returns, whereby symmetrical lines that radiate from the origin are produced. As prices must be multiples of the minimum tick size, the number of lines radiating from the zero return is restricted and lines are more prevalent at the more popular ticks. The issue of seeking predictability from the compass rose can be linked to other strands of literature, e.g. on serial correlation or the random walk (dating back as far as Kendall (1953) and Roberts (1959)). Return reversals are an additional layer to the analysis in this paper. Return reversals are embedded in the compass rose pattern but are more evident at higher sampling frequencies.

Some prior studies have concentrated on the predictive powers of the pattern (Chen 1997; Lee, Mathur, and Gleason 2005); however, no direct relationship between the compass rose and forecasted returns has been documented. Lee, Mathur, and Gleason (2005) suggest that the compass rose pattern increases returns' predictability in an autoregressive conditional heteroskedasticity (ARCH) or generalized ARCH (GARCH) model when the return from the compass rose contains (marginally) more information than the forecasted returns from the model. Szpiro (1998) argues that the discrete nature of prices is the only condition that causes the compass rose pattern to emerge. Previous evidence for the existence of the pattern has been presented for equity and foreign exchange markets (e.g. Cai, Hudson, and Keasey 2003; Lee, Mathur, and Gleason 2005). The calculation of returns for at-the-money options involves changing strike prices over time, which can lead to more complex dynamics in the compass rose pattern. We also show that the tick/volatility ratio is not supported as a consistent indicator of the visibility of the compass rose in individual equity options. We report that the effectiveness of the ratio deteriorates as the data frequency increases. Hence, at an ultra-high frequency (UHF) level, the tick/volatility ratio cannot be used as a basis for implementing trading strategies.

The remainder of this paper is organized as follows. Section 2 discusses the literature on the compass rose pattern, and Section 3 outlines the data sample and methods. Section 4 analyses the compass rose pattern in individual equity options, and Section 5 presents the empirical evidence. Section 6 concludes the paper.

2. Literature review

Crack and Ledoit (1996) show that the plot of daily stock returns against their lagged values (also known as a phase portrait) reveals a structure that resembles a compass rose. The plot produces symmetrical lines that radiate from the zero return, located at the origin. The number of these lines is restricted by the minimum tick size. Szpiro (1998) demonstrates that when prices do not vary, a grid pattern emerges, whereas when prices are allowed to float, a smeared pattern (in addition to being grid) becomes apparent.[1] Extreme volatility of prices causes the pattern to disappear as the plot becomes smudged. Crack and Ledoit (1996) suggest three conditions for the pattern to appear: price discreteness, the fact that price changes are relatively small (especially over intraday intervals), and that the price level of the asset varies over a relatively wide range. However, Szpiro (1998) identifies that the 'sole necessary and sufficient condition' for the pattern to emerge is that trading is in discrete prices.

The underlying motivation for the study of the compass rose pattern lies in its potential predictive power and its implications for statistical tests. It is reported that the existence of the pattern in intraday and daily returns affects the Jarque–Bera and the Lilliefors tests for normality (Annaert, Claes, and De Ceuster 2004) and alters the statistical properties of the Brock–Dechert–Scheinkmann (BDS) chaos test (Kramer and Runde 1997). Fang (2002) shows that for tick-by-tick data with a high tick/volatility ratio, the compass rose pattern distorts the asymptotic theory for random walk test statistics. Amilon (2003) notes that the compass rose pattern affects the parameter estimates in ARCH and GARCH models. Finally, embedded non-linearities in the pattern may increase return predictability (Chen 1997; Antoniou and Vorlow 2005; Batten and Hamada 2008).

Previous research has studied daily or intraday versions of the compass rose pattern in equity markets (Wang, Hudson, and Keasey 2000; Fang 2002; Amilon 2003; Cai, Hudson, and Keasey 2003), the foreign exchange market (Szpiro 1998; Lee, Mathur, and Gleason 2005), and futures markets (Lee, Gleason, and Mathur 1999). Wang and Wang (2002) show that the compass rose pattern may be visible in returns on equally weighted portfolios. Chen (1997) and Lee, Gleason, and Mathur (1999) note that the existence of daily price limits influences the appearance of the pattern.

Gleason, Lee, and Mathur (2000) demonstrate that the ratio of the tick size to returns' volatility (measured as the standard deviation of returns) determines the threshold value above which the pattern is visible (see also McKenzie and Frino 2003; Lee, Mathur, and Gleason 2005). Wang, Hudson, and Keasey (2000) show that the pattern might not be visible for thinly traded stocks as too few observations fall into each radiant. Cai, Hudson, and Keasey (2003) show that there is an optimal frequency of observations that produce the clearest compass rose. Although a quantifiable measure of the pattern's visibility is proposed by Wang and Wang (2002), the large amount of zero returns in the context of high frequency data tends to lead to inconsistent results on the application of this measure (Mitchell and McKenzie 2006).

3. Data and methodology

The data include all trades and quotes for individual equity option contracts traded at the NYSE-Euronext London International Financial Futures Exchange (Euronext-LIFFE) during 2005. In order to avoid stale pricing problems while capturing a sufficient number of contracts, we select equity options that report at least one trade per day for the data period. The total number of observations for the 28 firms included in the sample is 133,375,200.[2]

To calculate the returns on individual equity options, we follow the procedure introduced by Sheikh and Ronn (1994). Returns are calculated only for the at-the-money, nearest to mature contracts. Using the midpoint quote, even for the highly traded options, may lead to the use of stale prices, and hence only ask prices are used in the returns calculation (Bollerslev and Melvin 1994; ap Gwilym, Buckle, and Thomas 1997). At each time interval, the first ask price is obtained. For the closing return calculation, the last ask price of the day is obtained. The closing ask price and the first ask quote of the next day are used for the computation of the opening returns. Different strike prices can meet the at-the-money criteria for a given asset in consecutive intervals. The procedure adopted is the following: at every interval[3] t, the first ask price for the at-the-money nearest maturity contract is obtained. Then, at the next time interval $t + 1$, the ask price with the same strike price is obtained. The logarithmic return is calculated from these two prices. If, however, there is no ask with the same strike price in the next interval $t + 1$, we search for the last available ask price in interval t which satisfies the criteria. When the return for the interval t to $t + 1$ is calculated, the same procedure is repeated for the next interval $t + 2$.

Previous studies have focused solely on trade data to generate the pattern, whereas, for options, calculating returns on trades is not recommended because of the thin trading in options with specific exercise price and maturity combinations. In order to demonstrate the effect of thin trading on the visibility of the pattern, we also compute returns using trade data only. For comparison purposes, we also calculate returns using UHF quotes data (i.e. all observations).

A further section of the analysis is dedicated to the linkage between return reversals and the compass rose pattern. A regression model is applied to test several hypotheses. We expect that return reversals are less common for high-priced securities since these securities tend to be followed by more analysts, and hence they should be more efficiently priced on an intraday basis (Gosnell 1995). TS is the average trade size per interval and controls for differences in the traded size per interval. Similarly, in order to control for the trading frequency effect, Liq is defined as the average number of observations per interval. It is expected that a low proportion of reversals will be observed at the market open associated with a reaction to overnight events and a higher proportion of reversals observed at the close associated with less information arrival (Buckle et al. 1998). We expect that the designated market maker scheme[4] increases the dissemination of information, such that a lower proportion of reversals is expected for options contracts included within this scheme. Also, we hypothesize that options approaching the maturity date will exhibit a higher proportion of reversals as a result of the increased certainty about option value (assuming the absence of other major news events). Finally, higher valued firms will tend to have greater liquidity and hence a lower proportion of reversals.

The model studied is the following:

$$\mathrm{RR}_{i,t} = \alpha_1 + \alpha_2\,\mathrm{Pr}_{i,t} + \alpha_3\,\mathrm{TS}_{i,t} + \alpha_4\,\mathrm{Liq}_{i,t} + \alpha_5\,\mathrm{OD}_t + \alpha_6\,\mathrm{CD}_t + \alpha_7\,\mathrm{DMM}_i + \alpha_8\,\mathrm{TTM}_{i,t} + \alpha_9\,\mathrm{FV}_{i,t} + \varepsilon_{i,t}, \tag{1}$$

where RR is the percentage of return reversals per asset i and at each hourly time interval t. Pr is the natural log of the average trade price at each time interval per contract. TS is the natural log of the average trade size at each time interval per contract. Liq denotes the average number of observations at each time interval per contract. OD and CD are the open and close dummies, respectively. DMM is the designated market maker dummy. TTM is the average time to maturity at each time interval. FV denotes the firm size as the natural log of market capitalization per day for each contract.

4. Analysis of the compass rose pattern in options contracts

Let R_t be the simple arithmetic return for the period $t-1$ to t, P_t the price at the close of the interval t, n_t the price change in ticks h at interval t, and S_i the strike price, $i \in T$, where T is the time series of prices for a single contract. When the strike price, S, is uniform across all contracts (or not applicable, for example, in other asset classes), the ratio of R_{t+1} over R_t gives the following:

$$\frac{R_{t+1}}{R_t} = \frac{n_{t+1}}{n_t}, \text{ when } P_t \approx P_{t-1} \text{ (Crack and Ledoit 1996)} \tag{2}$$

or

$$\frac{R_{t+1}}{R_t} = \frac{n_{t+1}}{n_t}\left(1 - \frac{n_t h}{P_t}\right), \text{ when } P_t \neq P_{t-1} \text{ (Szpiro 1998).} \tag{3}$$

In options markets, the assumption that prices are continuously distributed cannot be achieved, as the appropriate computation of intraday returns is not contract-specific but depends on the relevant (at-the-money) strike prices at each consecutive interval. This makes it unlikely that $P_t = P_{t-1}$, and differences between P_t and P_{t-1} can be relatively large. Also, Equation (3) is true only for a uniform S. Hence, Equation (3) is not universal; sub-formulas arise because of the restrictions applied for the strike price S. When we expand these restrictions, the ratio of R_{t+1} over R_t gives the following:

$$\frac{R_{t+1}}{R_t} = \frac{(P_{t+1,k+1} - P_{t,k})/P_{t,k}}{(P_{t,i} - P_{t-1,i-1})/P_{t-1,i-1}}, \forall S_k = S_{k+1}, S_i = S_{i-1}, \tag{4}$$

where $\{k, k+1, i, i-1\} \in S$ and $t \in T$. It follows that the assumption of a uniform S for all T, namely $k = i$, cannot be inferred.[5] Since $n_t \equiv (P_t - P_{t-1})/h$ and h is constant, Equation (4) becomes:

$$\frac{R_{t+1}}{R_t} = \frac{n_{t+1,k+1}/P_{t,k}}{n_{t,i}h/(P_{t,i} - n_{t,i}h)} = \frac{n_{t+1,k+1}}{n_{t,i}} \left(\frac{P_{t,i} - n_{t,i}h}{P_{t,k}} \right) \quad (5)$$

Even though the use of nearest-to-mature, at-the-money contracts significantly reduces the variability of strike prices included in the final returns' sample, we cannot preclude the use of different strike prices for consecutive returns; hence, the following functions are true for R_t and R_{t+1}:

$$R_t = f(n_t h, P_t, S_i) \text{ and } R_{t+1} = g(n_t h, P_t, S_k). \quad (6)$$

The latter implies that the compass rose pattern in options contracts is more complex than that portrayed in Szpiro (1998) for other asset classes.

5. Empirical evidence on the compass rose pattern in high frequency options data

5.1 *The tick/volatility ratio as a determinant of the compass rose pattern*

Gleason, Lee, and Mathur (2000) and Lee, Mathur, and Gleason (2005) demonstrate the potential importance of the tick/volatility ratio as an indicator of the quality of the compass rose pattern. Wang and Wang's (2002) Q measure for the pattern's visibility is not reliable for assets with a tick/volatility ratio greater than 0.5 (Mitchell and McKenzie 2006). Following from these studies, this section analyses the tick/volatility ratio in order to achieve further insights into its applicability in high frequency data and in options contracts. We propose that the visual inspection of the pattern is ultimately necessary because the existing attempts to propose quantitative measures are not adequate for options contracts or for any application based on UHF data (for any asset class).

Table 1 presents the tick/volatility ratio for all 28 firms (only calls are presented) for different time intervals. Panel A is based on employing the UHF (full, quotes) dataset. Panels B and C present the results for tick/volatility ratios and visual quality at 15 and 30 min intervals, respectively. Panel D results are based on actual trades. Panels A and D (UHF and trades) demonstrate the importance of time in the appearance of the pattern, which will be discussed later. The other important category of information documented in Table 1 is the percentage of observations that fall on the horizontal and vertical axes.

Based on Panels B and C of Table 1, it is easily asserted that the quality of the pattern is not only determined by the tick/volatility ratio, as this would mean that the quality would actually improve for decreasing volatility levels (taking into account tick size changes, i.e. intra-tick levels). In particular, Table 1 shows that the quality of the pattern is not an increasing function of the tick/volatility ratio. As an example, Figure 1(a) and (b) shows two option contracts (OAZA and OCPG) that exhibit contrasting results on the appearance of the pattern when sampled at 15 min intervals. It is clear that the pattern is more (less) visible for OCPG (OAZA), which contrasts with the tick/volatility ratio supposition of Lee, Mathur, and Gleason (2005), as OCPG has the lower ratio.

At relatively high tick/volatility ratios (within a given tick size), the pattern is clearly visible at higher sampling frequencies. For lower sampling frequencies, there are not enough data points to make the pattern appear. The latter is demonstrated in Figure 2 for OBBL, in which the pattern starts to emerge at the higher sampling frequency (Figure 2b in contrast to Figure 2a). Table 1 shows that when a higher frequency of data is studied, the quality of the pattern consistently increases.

Table 1. Price level, tick/volatility ratios, and visual inspection of the compass rose pattern for all contracts.

			Panel A: UHF quotes			Panel B: 15 min			Panel C: 30 min			Panel D: Trades		
Name	Tick size	Average price level	Tick/vol.	% on axes	Visual quality	Tick/vol.	% on axes	Visual quality	Tick/vol.	% on axes	Visual quality	Tick/vol.	% on axes	Visual quality
OAWS	0.25	13.85	7.26	30.80	Good	11.06	38.24	Fair	9.91	31.07	Poor	15.65	72.73	Bad
OBBL	0.25	16.36	1.05	33.51	Good	10.35	34.32	Fair	9.47	29.29	Bad	13.37	66.19	Bad
OBTG	0.25	7.04	1.22	44.21	Excellent	13.01	67.40	Fair	11.32	62.23	Poor	16.73	80.92	Bad
OSAN	0.25	10.86	1.52	33.76	Good	10.80	44.89	Fair	9.67	38.08	Poor	16.22	78.26	Bad
OTCO	0.25	11.36	6.02	43.13	Excellent	11.36	46.48	Good	9.89	40.55	Fair	11.60	60.68	Bad
OVOD	0.25	3.67	1.01	52.40	Excellent	17.69	88.05	Fair	14.74	82.32	Poor	20.53	92.26	Bad
OAAM	0.5	60.15	18.98	37.45	Fair	21.99	27.65	Poor	19.31	20.75	Bad	23.07	41.84	Bad
OAZA	0.5	72.89	1.99	25.16	Fair	21.39	21.83	Bad	19.11	16.07	Bad	24.95	52.30	Bad
OBLT	0.5	31.91	16.55	39.23	Good	22.30	36.83	Fair	19.65	29.02	Fair	22.79	50.63	Bad
OBOT	0.5	22.82	11.98	36.74	Excellent	21.79	40.71	Good	19.55	34.66	Fair	24.88	65.10	Bad
OBP	0.5	32.06	2.16	36.90	Good	21.90	42.69	Good	19.65	37.79	Bad	27.59	67.96	Bad
OBSK	0.5	18.87	2.01	37.67	Excellent	22.74	53.77	Good	19.67	44.25	Fair	31.51	77.72	Bad
OCPG	0.5	18.35	9.44	9.99	Excellent	18.23	26.85	Good	18.66	33.62	Good	25.85	73.61	Bad
OCUA	0.5	18.60	2.18	38.08	Excellent	21.30	46.57	Fair	20.03	44.68	Poor	22.48	64.29	Bad
OEMG	0.5	55.97	23.42	13.80	Fair	22.48	24.13	Poor	19.41	18.13	Bad	28.15	63.91	Bad
OGNS	0.5	19.55	1.97	39.38	Good	21.72	52.19	Fair	20.43	48.07	Poor	34.34	78.25	Bad
OGXO	0.5	38.02	2.15	33.99	Fair	21.08	31.97	Poor	18.84	23.77	Bad	23.97	58.92	Bad
OHSB	0.5	21.43	2.21	39.23	Good	23.41	50.09	Good	20.83	41.71	Fair	32.43	81.07	Bad
OKGF	0.5	20.32	11.98	27.93	Excellent	20.08	39.59	Good	19.07	36.08	Fair	34.34	81.25	Bad
OLS	0.5	42.68	14.60	21.15	Fair	21.52	26.05	Fair	18.88	22.92	Bad	26.33	54.44	Bad
OPRU	0.5	28.86	3.29	36.48	Fair	21.39	38.74	Poor	19.73	37.21	Bad	24.34	65.78	Bad
ORBS	0.5	43.39	1.96	26.57	Fair	21.02	29.02	Poor	19.30	23.68	Bad	26.04	63.88	Bad
ORTZ	0.5	70.97	2.04	21.85	Fair	22.08	23.92	Poor	18.72	17.26	Bad	24.69	43.68	Bad
ORUT	0.5	29.59	16.29	36.81	Good	22.42	35.85	Fair	20.29	31.34	Poor	24.13	60.16	Bad
OSCB	0.5	38.22	16.75	46.00	Fair	21.77	31.11	Poor	19.43	24.27	Bad	26.55	59.70	Bad
OSPW	0.5	14.93	8.91	24.88	Excellent	21.20	52.24	Good	20.45	53.16	Fair	30.10	80.50	Bad
OTAB	0.5	33.30	2.18	26.26	Good	20.89	33.58	Poor	19.39	27.75	Bad	30.51	71.17	Bad
OTSB	0.5	24.08	2.05	38.59	Good	21.82	46.83	Fair	20.03	40.68	Poor	24.38	65.00	Bad

The table presents the tick/volatility ratio for all 28 contracts (call only) for different time intervals. Panel A uses the UHF (full, quotes) dataset, and Panel D is created using trades. Panels B and C show tick/volatility ratios and visual quality at 15 and 30 min intervals, respectively. The visual quality of the pattern is ranked as follows: bad, poor, fair, good, excellent (Wang and Wang 2002).

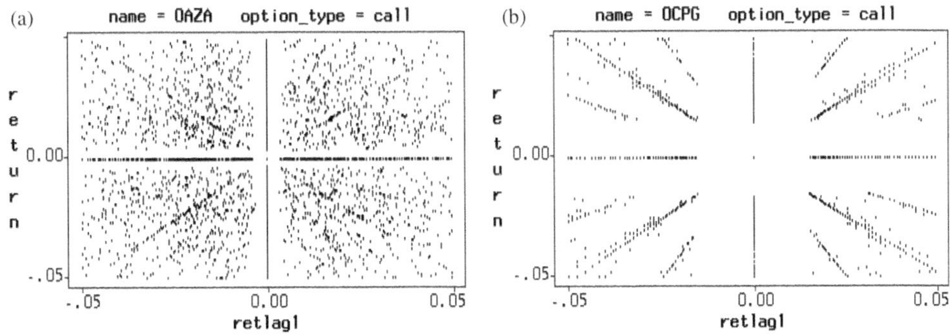

Figure 1. (a and b) 15 min time interval plots for OAZA (21.39) and OCPG (18.23), respectively. Tick/volatility ratios in parentheses.

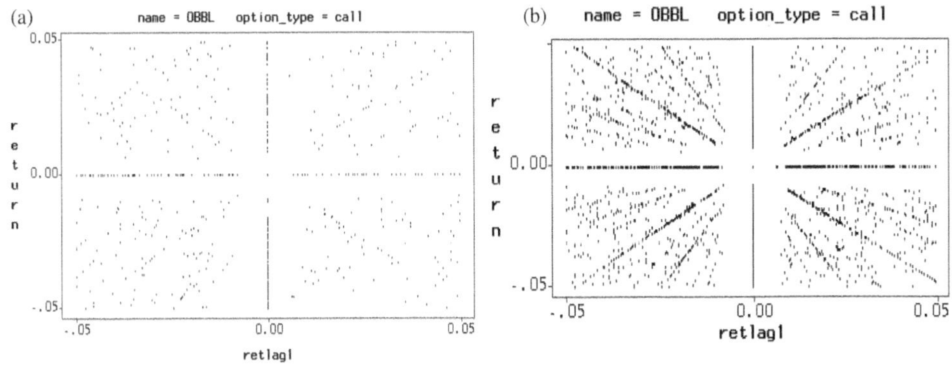

Figure 2. (a) 30 min and (b) 15 min interval plots for OBBL.

The above analysis implies that the tick/volatility ratio alone gives inconclusive results on the strength of the pattern. The analysis of Cai, Hudson, and Keasey (2003) captures the fact that trading frequency, and especially the percentage of observations that lie on the axes, plays an important role in the quality of the pattern. The latter partially explains why contracts with similar tick/volatility ratios do not produce similar quality patterns. The second explanation of the above is associated with differences in the price level of securities, which is embedded in the calculation of returns and is discussed in previous research (Gleason, Lee, and Mathur 2000; McKenzie and Frino 2003; Lee, Mathur, and Gleason 2005).

We argue that prior studies have failed to grasp the full extent of the trading process by imposing artificial restrictions (clock time) on the trading process. That is, by using data collected at 1 and 5 min intervals and at lower frequencies, a substantial amount of information is lost when observations are discarded. Panel A of Table 1 confirms that the compass rose pattern is easily visible at the UHF level. Figure 3(a) shows that even for very low tick/volatility ratios, the compass rose pattern is easily discernible. For the UHF level, Table 1 indicates that there is no close link between tick/volatility ratios and the pattern's visual quality. This result is very much affected by the fact that as the number of observations increases, the price and volatility levels remain relatively stable. Even at the UHF level, when prices vary sufficiently, the compass rose pattern becomes 'smudged' and 'smeared' (as expected by Szpiro 1998). This means that some rays

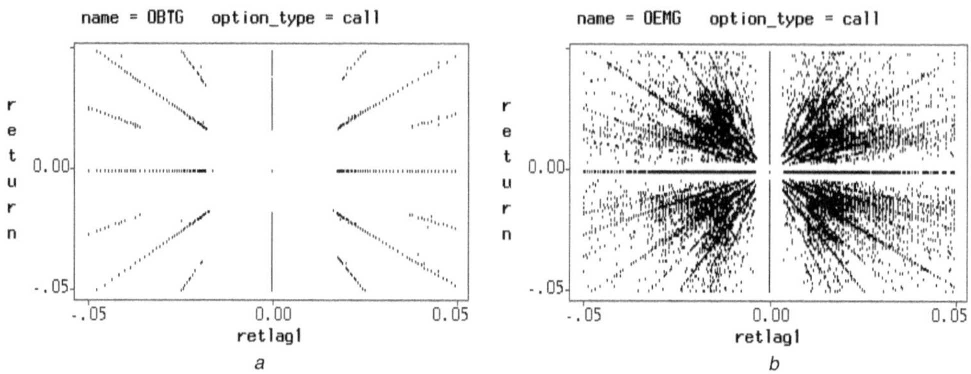

Figure 3. (a and b) UHF plots for OBTG (1.22/44.21%) and OEMG (23.42/13.80%), respectively. Tick/volatility ratios and the percentage of observations on the axes are in parentheses.

overlap and cause the pattern to disappear, which is demonstrated to some extent in Figure 3(b). Finally, Panel D of Table 1 shows that the appearance of the pattern deteriorates when trade data are used. Hence, the tick/volatility ratio, when used for trade data, gives no indication on the strength of the pattern. The high proportion of observations on the axes is at least partially one of the reasons for the low visibility of the compass rose pattern in trade data (Cai, Hudson, and Keasey 2003).

5.2 *The compass rose pattern and return reversals*

An issue that has not been previously documented in the literature is the relationship of the compass rose pattern with return reversals. A price reversal is defined as 'a price change in the opposite direction to the previous price change' (Gosnell 1995, 226). Similarly, a return reversal occurs when a positive (negative) return follows a negative (positive) return.

Evidence of intraday price reversals is previously documented (Buckle et al. 1998; Grant, Wolf, and Yu 2005). The frequency of reversals is closely linked to the rate of information arrival to the market and the correction of previous mispricings (Cox and Peterson 1994). That is, when a price change (return) is followed by another price change (return) in the same direction, it is assumed that new information is being incorporated into prices. If a return reversal occurs, there is no new information. Gosnell (1995) identifies that controlling for price reversals is important for testing market efficiency. Also, Grant, Wolf, and Yu (2005) note that price continuations at the market open may lead to an overreaction and any jump in prices at the market open will often be followed by a correction, which means that price reversals will appear. While the latter suggests that a contrarian strategy may potentially exploit this overreaction, Grant, Wolf, and Yu (2005) report that positive returns generated by this strategy are eroded by transaction costs.

In a compass rose plot, price reversals are found in the north-west (NW) and south-east (SE) quadrants. These are cases in which negative returns are followed by positive (NW) and positive returns are followed by negative (SE). Zero lagged returns and/or zero returns fall on the axes and, hence, are neither reversals nor continuations. The existing literature on the compass rose pattern has shown no clear indications of a prevalence of return reversals.

Figure 4(a) reveals that when UHF returns are plotted, a parabolic line that declines from the NW to the SE through the origin can emerge.[6] Before we investigate the properties of the pattern, we discuss some explanations found in the literature. Firstly, the non-linearity of the pattern

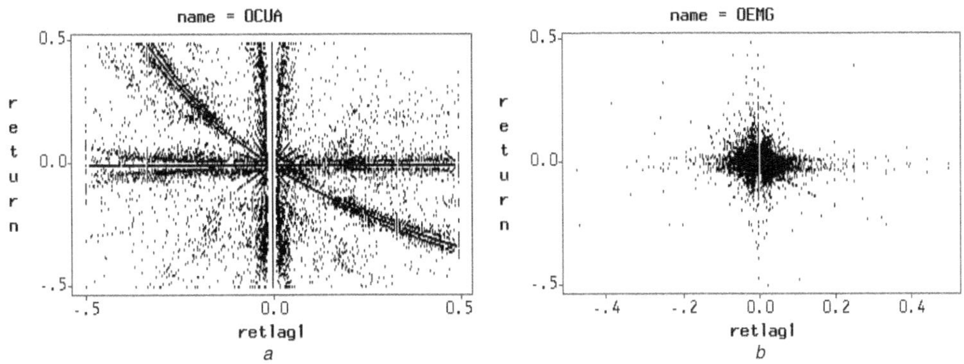

Figure 4. (a and b) UHF plot of OCUA and OEMG, respectively.

arises from the arithmetic computation of returns. The use of logarithmic returns would replace the parabolic line with a straight line. Secondly, Park (1995) shows that bid–ask bounce, i.e. successive quotes or trades where ask and bid prices follow each other, generates price reversals. However, in the context of the findings presented in Figure 4, bid–ask bounce explanations of the pattern are not feasible because these options returns series are created using only ask prices.

A question remains as to why the magnitude of this pattern varies and in some cases is not noticeable (e.g. Figure 4b). Figure 5 presents the average duration observed between two consecutive returns for all option contracts in the UHF sample. The horizontal axis denotes duration in seconds, and the vertical axis denotes the percentage of observations reported during the particular time interval. The columns are observations-weighted so that transaction frequency differences across firms do not affect the results. We hypothesize that if trading differences exist between the four quadrants, these will be exploited by traders, and duration will reveal the speed of adjustment in ways similar to that found in Christie and Schultz (1994), where it is reported that traders react differently in assets with clustered prices. The hypothesis is also closely linked to the fact that volume is evenly distributed across the four quadrants.

Figure 5 shows that at a duration of 1 s, positive momentum is the most common observation and as the plot is observations-weighted, duration differences across the four quadrants disappear. However, the results also reveal that there is a greater tendency for return reversals at durations

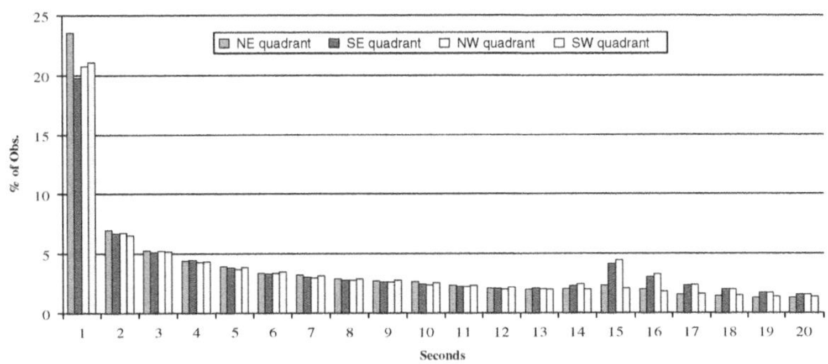

Figure 5. Average duration estimates.

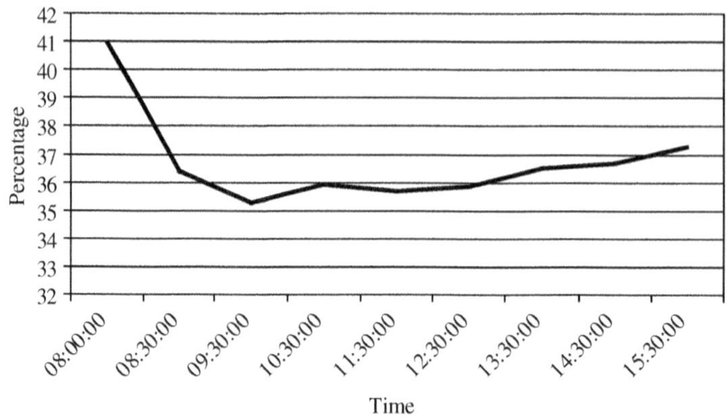

Figure 6. Intraday distribution of reversals.

of 15 s or more. The latter is documented across all options contracts, and it might be partially explained by strategic quote behaviour.

Buckle et al. (1998) show for the Short Sterling and FTSE100 futures contracts that price reversals are relatively low at the market open and high at the market close. The findings on the market open and close imply information arrival at the open and the implementation of trading strategies by day traders at the market close. Also, the authors suggest that there is a strong link with scheduled macroeconomic announcements, and thus, the intraday proportion of reversals reaches its lowest point at the time of these announcements. Similarly, Gosnell (1995) shows that price reversals for NYSE stocks are low at the market open and relatively stable during the trading day and near the market close.

Figure 6 shows that a clear intraday pattern of return reversals emerges from our dataset. In particular, reversals are most prevalent at the market open and the market close, whereas during the middle of the trading day, they are less common. This does not support the hypothesis that overnight news is disseminated at the market open. In contrast, Figure 6 suggests that information arrival is maximized 2 h after the market open (10:00 a.m.). This coincides with the release time of the scheduled macroeconomic announcements from the Bank of England and the Office of National Statistics.[7]

Table 2 presents the results for the regression model of return reversals.[8] Hypotheses for the signs of the coefficients were discussed in Section 3. We anticipate that higher-priced securities exhibit fewer return reversals due to being more efficiently priced. However, the results show that there is a strong positive association between the price level and the percentage of return reversals. This finding is in contrast with Gosnell (1995). Hence, return reversals are more common for high-priced options. As hypothesized, larger trade size is associated with a lower proportion of return reversals. In line with the price level variable, we hypothesize that the more liquid firms will exhibit less return reversals (Gosnell 1995). The liquidity variable shows that higher trading frequency is associated with more return reversals which may reflect strategic trading or quotation.

The opening and close dummies are both highly significant and positive, confirming the U-shaped pattern of Figure 6. The result for OD is not consistent with Buckle et al. (1998), but supports the hypothesis that liquidity traders operate at the market open (Cox and Peterson 1994). The CD dummy is consistent with a lack of information arrival at the market close.

Table 2. OLS regressions.

Variable	Expected sign	Call	Put
Intercept		53.67[a]	56.83[a]
		42.56	45.37
Pr	−	4.96[a]	4.55[a]
		29.70	26.72
TS	−	−3.00[a]	−2.70[a]
		−15.98	−14.57
Liq	−	0.02[a]	0.01[b]
		5.86	2.06
OD	−	5.46[a]	6.05[a]
		14.62	16.67
CD	+	1.10[a]	1.07[a]
		3.18	3.18
DMM	−	−3.79[a]	−3.44[a]
		−13.57	−12.65
TTM	+	−0.02[c]	−0.01
		−1.80	−0.73
FV	−	−2.10[a]	−2.42[a]
		−13.11	15.89
R^2		0.10	0.09
No. of obs.		54,235	54,410

Note:

$$\mathrm{RR}_{it} = \alpha_1 + a_2 \mathop{\mathrm{Pr}}_{it} + a_3\mathrm{TS}_{it} + a_4\mathrm{Liq}_{it} + a_5\mathrm{OD}_t + a_6\mathrm{CD}_t$$

$$+ a_7\mathrm{DMM}_i + a_8\mathrm{TTM}_{it} + a_9\mathrm{FV}_{it} + \varepsilon_{it},$$

where RR is the percentage of return reversals per time interval; Pr the natural log of the average trade price at each time interval per contract; TS the natural log of the average trade size at each time interval per contract; Liq the average number of observations at each time interval per contract; OD and CD the open and close dummies, respectively; DMM the designated market maker dummy; TTM the average time to maturity at each time interval; and FV the firm size as the natural log of market capitalization per day for each contract. T-statistics are reported.

[a]Significant at the 1% level.

[b]Significant at the 5% level.

[c]Significant at the 10% level.

The DMM dummy is highly significant and positive which reflects the Euronext-designated market makers' obligation to offer continuous prices at each price level (hence, a lower proportion of reversals). The time-to-maturity variable is significant for calls only. The findings suggest that return reversals marginally increase close to expiration dates. Finally, the firm value variable is negative and highly significant, which is consistent with the hypothesis of Gosnell (1995) that assets of larger firms are more liquid.

Table 2 indicates that return reversals in individual equity options are more common at higher price levels and when liquidity levels are higher. Liquidity seems more important than information at the market open. The designated market maker scheme enhances the dissemination of information, and thus more market makers lead to fewer reversals. Finally, options that are closer to the expiration date tend to exhibit more frequent return reversals.

6. Conclusions

The paper studies the occurrence and visibility of the compass rose pattern in high frequency individual equity options data. We show that the compass rose pattern in options contracts is more complex than that for other asset classes (e.g. Szpiro 1998) because the at-the-money strike price can change over time. The tick/volatility ratio is not a reliable indicator for the strength of the compass rose pattern, and its effectiveness decreases at higher data frequencies. This point is very important because it is widely claimed that the compass rose pattern is an inherent feature of discrete asset prices, and thus identifying a measure of its visibility is of great significance.

Lee, Mathur, and Gleason (2005) suggest that the visibility of the compass rose pattern may give rise to increased returns' predictability. Such indications have particular significance for options contracts because their relatively low price levels enhance the implications of discreteness (Amilon 2003), while the leverage effect in options magnifies potential profits from any market inefficiencies. The manifestation of return reversals in the compass rose pattern may indicate an increase in returns' predictability in some situations, arising from serial correlation. High frequency traders are well placed to capitalize on any such predictability. The paper contributes new evidence that the pervasiveness of the compass rose pattern is strongly associated with trading frequency. However, our findings do not indicate clear trading strategies based on any metric for the visibility of the pattern.

A major element of the paper's contribution arises from linking return reversals with the compass rose pattern. We show that return reversals are captured within the compass rose pattern, especially at higher sampling frequencies. The parabolic diagonal line that can distort the compass rose pattern when UHF data are used is caused by an increased presence of return reversals. Duration estimates show that strategic trading may be associated with the timing of reversals. In contrast with Gosnell (1995), return reversals are found to increase with the price level and with the frequency of price observations. However, reversals are inversely related to trade size, as hypothesized. Hence, the evidence on the relationship between return reversals and liquidity proxies is mixed. This is a potential avenue for future research.

The hypothesis that there is a reaction to overnight events which is reflected in prices at the market open is not supported. Return reversals could remain prevalent at this time due to heterogeneous expectations among market participants. However, intraday news arrival does have an impact by reducing the percentage of reversals observed in a given interval. Finally, a lower proportion of return reversals is associated with assets which have designated market makers, implying an increase in the information content of quotes in these cases.

Acknowledgements

The authors are very grateful for the comments and suggestions received from two anonymous referees. We also thank David McMillan for his comments as discussant at the conference.

Notes

1. These patterns refer to simulated scenarios. For a detailed illustration, see Szpiro (1998).
2. Six (22) firms have a tick size of 0.25 (0.50). No tick size changes are reported during the sample period.
3. The regression variables are calculated on an hourly basis. In order to show the effect of sampling frequency on the visibility and properties of the compass rose pattern, we also compute returns using 15 and 30 min intervals (following the same procedure).
4. Designated market makers are assigned by NYSE-Euronext to increase liquidity in specific individual equity options. Out of 28 firms in this sample, 16 are covered by DMMs.

5. As the returns' calculation formula is for the nearest-to-mature contracts only, the formulae discussed refer only to different strike prices. If maturity was also allowed to float, the complexity of the formulae would increase.
6. A similar effect is observed in electricity prices (Batten and Hamada 2008). Lee, Mathur, and Gleason (2005) note that the same feature can emerge using a Monte Carlo simulation.
7. The release time for the scheduled macroeconomic announcements is 09.30 GMT, and the figure uses hourly data.
8. Estimation is by OLS. No autocorrelation or heteroskedasticity is detected.

References

Amilon, H. 2003. GARCH estimation and discrete stock prices: An application to low-priced Australian stocks. *Economics Letters* 81, no. 2: 215–22.

Annaert, J., A.G.P. Claes, and M.J.K. De Ceuster. 2004. Does the compass rose pattern matter for testing normality? In *Kwantitatief bekeken: liber amicorum prof. dr. Robert Van Straelen*, ed. Kesenne Stefan, 207–18. Antwerpen: Garant.

Antoniou, A., and C. Vorlow. 2005. Price clustering and discreteness: Is there chaos behind the noise? *Physica A* 348: 389–403.

ap Gwilym, O., M. Buckle, and S. Thomas. 1997. The intraday behaviour of bid–ask spread, returns, and volatility for FTSE-100 stock index options. *Journal of Derivatives* 4, no. 4: 20–32.

Batten, J.A., and M. Hamada. 2008. The compass rose in electricity prices. *Chaos* 19, no. 4: 043106 (15 pages).

Bollerslev, T., and M. Melvin. 1994. Bid–ask spread and volatility in the foreign exchange market: An empirical analysis. *Journal of International Economics* 36, no. 3–4: 355–72.

Buckle, M., O. ap Gwilym, S.H. Thomas, and M.S. Woodhams. 1998. Intraday empirical regularities in interest rate and equity index futures markets, and the effect of macroeconomic announcements. *Journal of Business, Finance and Accounting* 25, no. 7: 921–44.

Cai, C., R. Hudson, and K. Keasey. 2003. Trading frequency and the compass rose. *Applied Economics Letters* 10, no. 8: 511–7.

Chen, A. 1997. The square compass rose: Evidence from Taiwan. *Journal of Multinational Financial Management* 7, no. 2: 127–44.

Christie, W., and P. Schultz. 1994. Why do NASDAQ market makers avoid odd-eighth quotes? *Journal of Finance* 49, no. 5: 1813–40.

Cox, R.D., and D.R. Peterson. 1994. Stock returns following large one-day declines: Evidence on short-term reversals and longer-term performance. *Journal of Finance* 49, no. 1: 255–67.

Crack, F.T., and O. Ledoit. 1996. Robust structure without predictability: The compass rose pattern of the stock market. *Journal of Finance* 51, no. 2: 751–62.

Fang, Y. 2002. The compass rose and random walk tests. *Computational Statistics and Data Analysis* 39, no. 3: 299–310.

Gleason, K.C., C.I. Lee, and I. Mathur. 2000. An explanation for the compass rose pattern. *Economics Letters* 68, no. 2: 127–33.

Gosnell, T.F. 1995. The distribution of reversals and continuations and tests for intraday market efficiency. *Journal of Business Finance and Accounting* 22, no. 2: 225–43.

Grant, J.L., A. Wolf, and S. Yu. 2005. Intraday price reversals in the US stock index futures market: A 15-year study. *Journal of Banking and Finance* 29, no. 5: 1311–27.

Kendall, M.G. 1953. The analysis of economic time series – Part 1: Prices. *Journal of the Royal Statistical Society* 116, no. 1: 11–34.

Kramer, W., and R. Runde. 1997. Chaos and the compass rose. *Economics Letters* 54, no. 2: 113–8.

Lee, C.I., K.C. Gleason, and I. Mathur. 1999. A comprehensive examination of the compass rose pattern in futures markets. *Journal of Futures Markets* 19, no. 5: 541–64.

Lee, C.I., I. Mathur, and K.C. Gleason. 2005. The tick/volatility ratio as a determinant of the compass rose pattern. *The European Journal of Finance* 11, no. 2: 93–109.

McKenzie, M.D., and A. Frino. 2003. The tick/volatility ratio as a determinant of the compass rose: Empirical evidence from decimalisation on the NYSE. *Accounting and Finance* 43, no. 2: 331–44.

Mitchell, H., and M.D. McKenzie. 2006. A note on the Wang and Wang measure of the quality of the compass rose. *Journal of Banking and Finance* 30, no. 12: 3519–24.

Park, J. 1995. A market microstructure explanation for predictable variations in stock returns following large price changes. *Journal of Financial and Quantitative Analysis* 30, no. 2: 241–56.

Roberts, H. 1959. Stock-market patterns and financial analysis: Methodological suggestions. *Journal of Finance* 14, no. 1: 1–10.

Sheikh, A.M. and I.E. Ronn. 1994. A characterization of the daily and intraday behaviour of returns on options. *Journal of Finance* 49, no. 2: 557–79.

Szpiro, G.G. 1998. Tick size, the compass rose and market nanostructure. *Journal of Banking and Finance* 22, no. 12: 1559–69.

Wang, E., R. Hudson, and K. Keasey. 2000. Tick size and the compass rose: Further insights. *Economics Letters* 68, no. 2: 119–25.

Wang, H.Q. and C. Wang. 2002. Visibility of the compass rose in financial asset returns: A quantitative study. *Journal of Banking and Finance* 26, no. 6: 1099–111.

Index

Note: Page numbers in **bold** type refer to **figures**
Page numbers in *italic* type refer to *tables*
Page number followed by 'n' refer to notes

For Product Safety Concerns and Information please contact our EU
representative GPSR@taylorandfrancis.com Taylor & Francis Verlag GmbH,
Kaufingerstraße 24, 80331 München, Germany

Batch number: 10732714

Printed by Printforce, the Netherlands